HARVARD EAST ASIAN MONOGRAPHS

75

THE HOME BASE OF AMERICAN CHINA MISSIONS,
1880–1920

THE HOME BASE OF AMERICAN CHINA MISSIONS,
1880–1920

by

Valentin H. Rabe

Published by
Council on East Asian Studies
Harvard University

Distributed by
Harvard University Press
Cambridge, Massachusetts
and
London, England
1978

The Council on East Asian Studies at Harvard University publishes
a monograph series and, through the Fairbank Center for East
Asian Research, administers research projects designed to further
scholarly understanding of China, Japan, Korea, Vietnam, Inner
Asia, and adjacent areas.

Library of Congress Cataloging in Publication Data

Rabe, Valentin H., 1930–
  The home base of American missions, 1880–1920.

  (Harvard East Asian monographs ; 75)
  Bibliography: p.
  Includes index.
  1. Missions—China—Societies, etc. 2. Protestant
churches—Missions—Societies, etc. 3. Missions, American.
I. Harvard University. Council on East Asian Studies. II. Title.
III. Series.
  BV3410.R3   266'.00951   78–13635
  ISBN 0–674–40581–1

For Michael and Margarete Beer Rabe

FOREWORD

This book is a good deal more than it may seem to be at first glance. It deals with the home base of American Protestant missions in general, not of China missions alone. It tells how missions became businesslike institutions while claiming still to be a movement, how their supporters raised the necessary millions every year and recruited the thousands of missionaries, in short, how a great national activity was nurtured over a generation to reach a high point about 1920. This story has long been neglected.

As background to our present age of concern for human rights and welfare abroad, Valentin Rabe's study shows us our grandparents' concern for spreading the Christian faith and the social gospel at the turn of the century. Let no one doubt that this part of our heritage still has vitality, mixed in with our doctrines of defense and our capacity for warfare. In giving us the nuts and bolts of the business of missions as well as the doctrinal sanctions for its promotion, Dr. Rabe describes a major aspect of America's chosen role in the world. This self-image still colors our relations with the new China.

This is a mature work of scholarship which began as a Ph.D. dissertation at Harvard in 1964, a manuscript of 900 pages amassed from many thousands of documents, and shrank like a star to its present size only by a notable increase of density, such that every paragraph presents carefully winnowed evidence, mature reflection, and critical judgment. During half my time of teaching at Harvard, in fact, Dr. Rabe has kept at this task while finding a post, securing tenure, and rising to chair the Department of History at the State University of New York at Geneseo. It is a satisfaction to both of us, I am sure, to see the results available now. Like many books that break new ground, this will be a standard work until it stimulates a future generation to supplant it with a whole industry of research topics and studies.

John K. Fairbank
July 1978

CONTENTS

ACKNOWLEDGMENTS

A contemporary Dutch scholar has warned that the history of missions viewed from a human standpoint leads one down "a path of endless confusion, despair, error, degeneration, and discouragement."* If I have not succumbed to all these perils, it was initially due to the guidance of Frank Freidel of Harvard University, who supervised an earlier version of this study and provided support whenever I threatened to falter. John King Fairbank's contributions, both direct and by example, were incalculable. Without him, this study would simply never have become a book.

Even a reasonable sampling of the literature produced by over one hundred American Protestant mission societies and a score of interdenominational auxiliaries would have been impossible without the exceptional courtesy and sympathetic interest of more librarians and archival custodians than can be mentioned here. Two, however, gave so much that they must be thanked by name. Mary Walker, librarian by profession, historian in fact and spirit, led a novice through a mass of material in the American Board Library, provided invaluable guidance, and shared her thorough knowledge of this country's oldest foreign mission board. Laura Person introduced me to the resources of the Missionary Research Library in New York, and uncovered the invaluable papers of the Laymen's Missionary Movement after much expert opinion had determined that these no longer existed.

Dorothy Borg and M. Searle Bates read parts of the original study, and provided encouragement and suggestions. I benefited from the critical reading of other chapters by Gunther Barth, Van L. Perkins, and Richard G. Townsend. A grant-in-aid by the American Council of Learned Societies, and a fellowship from the Research Foundation of the State University of New York during

---

*J. H. Bavinck, *An Introduction to the Science of Missions* (Philadelphia, 1960), p. 282.

the summers of 1967 and 1968, freed me from other obligations and resulted in the completion of a substantial segment of this manuscript.

My greatest debt I owe to Susan Schulenberg Rabe, whose contribution is a combination of most of those already acknowledged.

Geneseo, New York   V. H. R.
August 1978

INTRODUCTION

What the average American knew as the foreign mission movement a decade after the Civil War consisted of about two dozen societies and boards, most of them attached to the major Protestant denominations.[1] They varied widely in influence and resources, supporting staffs in the field ranging from less than ten to several hundred. No coordinating body united these disparate agencies in their work; no spokesmen could represent what contemporaries nevertheless treated as a single movement in American religious life.

It was a movement that had taken organized form with the establishment of the American Board of Commissioners for Foreign Missions in 1810, in response to a petition presented by a delegation of young seminarians who were members of a secret fraternity dedicated to sending American missionaries abroad for the first time. Additional support organizations were established in subsequent decades, most of them voluntary societies directed by dedicated laymen and clergymen rather than official denominational agencies. They were led and supported by individual Protestants dedicated to the cause, because there was no clearcut theological or doctrinal imperative to look beyond domestic church extension or religious philanthropy.[2]

Although the efforts of these early societies were modest in scope, they established the basis for later expansion in every continent. They also directed a substantial proportion of their activity toward the American Indian before he became the concern of home mission societies.[3] By mid-century, divisions over the issues leading to the Civil War accelerated a spirit of sectarianism which resulted in the closer identification of foreign mission agencies with distinct denominations.[4] The end of the first stage of the movement's development, then, was marked less by the disruptions of the Civil War than by the process in which the enterprise of a minority of foreign mission advocates was generally absorbed by the Protestant churches.

1

Like the home mission, temperance, Bible and tract societies with which the foreign mission agencies shared similar origins and support, their future seemed uncertain in the aftermath of a disruptive war that had submerged or eliminated many traditional objectives and divided the Protestant churches. The more rapid pace of industrialization and urbanization posed unfamiliar challenges and seemed to be producing an increasingly materialistic society apathetic when not hostile to traditional evangelical enterprises. Old values wavered under attack from skepticism and scientific thought, while the population changed character with the arrival of a growing tide of immigrants unsympathetic to Protestant leadership and precepts.

These retrospective rationalizations were not available to the denominational leaders and mission society spokesmen who publicly bewailed the retarded growth of their enterprise after the Civil War. Their perceptions were probably as much the product of unrealized hopes, or of the temporary setbacks caused by a series of economic recessions, as of objective analysis. Progress before the war had been rapid and, with the Union restored, the black man free, and the Indian soon to be domesticated and legally assimilated, there was reason to hope for the redirection of wartime idealism and resources into remaining areas of evangelical concern. "Now that God has smitten slavery unto death," Edward Beecher wrote hopefully, "he has opened the way for the redemption and sanctification of our whole social system, which was before impossible."[5]

Many proponents of foreign missions expected success in the effort to rekindle the enthusiasm of the prewar decades' aborted crusade to create a Christian commonwealth. It seemed logical that the missionary cause would benefit also from a remobilization of evangelical reformers, but perplexingly few showed interest in extending activities overseas. The challenge of evangelizing the world had been no match for abolitionism before the war. Afterwards those who had not exhausted their moral fervor in the crusade against slavery had plenty to occupy them at home. Concern with the problems of this world obscured the plight of unevangelized pagans with no access to the next one.

The signs of arrested growth in the postwar decades worried the representatives of both old and new mission societies. "The earnest supporters of modern missions are almost as few as ever," a secretary of the half-century-old American Board reported in 1865.[6] Although the board's publications were filled with pleas for funds with which to seize new opportunities, only once between the end of the war and 1880 did the ABCFM's receipts reach even the 1865 level.[7] Meanwhile personnel losses in the field suffered during the hiatus of the Civil War were only slowly rectified in the face of "an increasing reluctance to engage in this service" perceived by mission societies on both sides of the Atlantic.[8] By 1881, despite an unprecedented $1,000,000 bequest and the end of the economic depression, the now largely Congregational constituency of the American Board was warned that "with all our enlarged opportunities, with all our growth in numbers and in power as churches of Christ in this country, it is a painful fact that distinctively missionary effort has not kept pace with other religious activities."[9]

Similar feelings were expressed shortly after the formation of a distinct Foreign Christian Missionary Society by the Disciples of Christ in 1875. "With the brotherhood numbering 500,000, sharing largely with other religious societies the wealth and intelligence of the country," lamented one of the new officers after two years of effort, "we stand before the world today with three foreign missionaries as evidence of our faith in the great plea we make."[10] There was at least circumstantial evidence, in other words, to support the message of a Presbyterian minister's emotionally written volume published in 1886 "to impress the great fact that we have reached the most critical point in mission history." "We do not say the crisis of missions *is* coming,—it *has come,*" warned the Reverend Arthur Pierson, "and it is even now upon us."[11]

Arthur Pierson was not a board officer, nor destined to be acknowledged one of the new missionary statesmen of the first rank. His unbending theological orthodoxy and sometimes visionary zeal alienated allies and handicapped him in becoming a spokesman for the still fragmented mission movement during the last quarter of the nineteenth century. But Pierson's polemic did speed up the collective if not coordinated effort to take stock in the mission movement. Others bewailed the decades during which " 'Retrench!' became the keynote of missions."[12] The unprecedented opportunities created by imperialism's opening of new mission fields, made accessible by modern transportation, clearly required a reassessment of objectives. Methods by which to acquire the necessary resources had to be reconsidered in a period in which the burgeoning industrial economy produced more wealth than ever before, the evangelical churches claimed a larger membership, and yet the proportionate support of missions lagged.[13]

In his analysis, Pierson took his motives and theology from the past, but proposed adopting the techniques of modern industrialized America. He combined the evangelical view of American history, which identified a spiritual crisis in the midst of rapid change, with the mission advocate's singleminded dedication to his particular cause and approach to this crisis. The condition of the foreign mission movement was symptomatic of "the low ebb of spiritual life" and "the practical insensibility and indifference of the church as a whole." For its own sake, American Protestantism needed a spiritual revival to combat the unprecedented "worldliness and wickedness, materialism and naturalism, skepticism and atheism" which marked what was later called the Gilded Age.[14]

But Pierson's practical prescription for achieving this renaissance was less a return to the evangelical revival tradition, than a reflection of the secular developments and values of his day: "Why not, in these days of business schemes that are colossal in capital, magnificent in plan, and world-wide in their extent,—why not undertake the King's business as something that requires haste, and should summon to its prompt prosecution every loyal disciple!"[15]

Contained in that rhetorical question, as well as in his suggestions for practical planning and an international directorate to coordinate the Protestant enterprise for world evangelization, is the predominant theme of the new foreign mission movement: If spontaneous enthusiasm and spiritual dynamism are lacking, then substitute businesslike planning, organization, and promotion to achieve the same objectives. The first tangible response to this suggestion, and one Pierson helped to launch with his inspired preaching at a youth conference, was the Student Volunteer Movement for Foreign Missions, conceived the year *The Crisis of Missions* was published. In the spirit of his didactic jeremiad, the Student Volunteers adopted as their watchword: "The Evangelization of the World in this Generation." Although the watchword was later qualified and explained by older members of the generation, it expressed the characteristic spirit of the age and of missionary resurgence in the last quarter of the century.

The process of combining a businesslike approach with the commitment to getting the job done "in this generation" characterized the second stage of American Protestant foreign missions, and is the subject of this study. Before World War I and the accumulation of complex changes in American Protestantism marked the beginning of a third stage, the impatient generation had achieved impressive results. The barely two dozen mission societies of the 1880s had multiplied to 122 by 1928, and supported ten times as many missionaries abroad.[16] Only eleven American societies had been represented in the China of the 1870s; some 65 were prepared by 1923 to transform what had become the most important single field for American evangelical efforts overseas.[17]

Although the focus of this study is what the movement's supporters referred to as the "home base" of missions, references to the complementary "foreign field" will emphasize the plans and work in China. Since it was impossible to survey equally all sectors of the worldwide foreign field, it seemed appropriate to select the non-Western nation that attracted both a major proportion of the general public's attention, and became by the 1920s the country in which more American missionaries applied a greater proportion of the movement's resources than any other.[18]

In the final decades of the nineteenth century the developing preoccupation with China in mission circles was based largely on the fusing of evangelical hope with fuzzy geopolitical and racial theories.[19] "China is to be the great missionary field of the next half-century," wrote an American Board missionary reflecting this attitude in 1894. "In possibility and prophecy it is the grandest missionary field on this planet."[20]

Without surrendering these assumptions of China's strategic importance, the emphasis shifted after 1900 to the unique opportunity provided by a nation in the throes of revolution—a country also in which the nineteenth-century pioneering efforts had laid the base for far more rapid advance.[21] Thus, despite setbacks suffered during the Boxer uprising, an American Board deputation returned from an inspection tour in 1907 to report that "the opportunity for missionary endeavor in China is surpassed by that of no country in the world."[22] The same year a conference of Baptist missionaries reported home their conviction that "the conditions in this field are such as to make a far-reaching and aggressive movement for the complete evangelization of the people in this generation practicable."[23] And even a missionary stationed in Egypt could ask: "To christianize the national life of China! Would not that, more than any other thing, mean the conquest of the world for Christ?"[24] Particularly after the 1911 revolution, the hope of providing Christian leadership for the accelerated process of modernization led a number of mission spokesmen to identify China with unprecedented opportunity. "China, for the next ten or fifteen years," Vice-President J. E. Williams of Nanking University told a select conference of missionaries and board secretaries in 1912, "will constitute the greatest opportunity that has been offered the Christian Church since the coming of our Lord."[25]

The effort launched in response to these convictions was massive in scope if not in results. In 1898, twenty-three American societies supported a foreign staff of 968 in China.[26] Despite the reverses suffered in the Boxer uprising, the resources and attention diverted to colonial acquisitions after the war with Spain, and the turmoil following the 1911 revolution and outbreak of the World War, more than twice as many American societies supported a foreign staff of 2862 in China by 1916.[27] "China is the leading mission land," concluded a general survey of the American movement in 1924.[28] This missionary generation's preoccupation with

China is reflected in all aspects of home base activity considered in this study, but should not be allowed to obscure the continuation and expansion of American mission work in dozens of other countries.

The definitive account of a movement, in which the activities of single denominations have led to multivolume histories, will never be compiled by one scholar. Even limiting the treatment to a forty-year period, and to the home base and logistics rather than actual missionary work, does not allow for an inclusive description of the scores of sending agencies and auxiliary organizations that made up the foreign mission movement. It was necessary therefore to risk the charge of superficiality in taking a selective approach to the subject matter, while also treating an uncoordinated and fragmented movement as a unit.

For the most part, the smaller sects with their sometimes atypical activities have been ignored in favor of the major denominations. Leaders and spokesmen well known to their generation have been cited instead of mavericks, exponents of individual "faith" missions, or traditionalists opposing the changes that occurred. Because they provide a convenient common denominator, non- or interdenominational agencies are stressed at the expense of equal treatment for all denominational boards. Furthermore, intellectual or theological developments are slighted in favor of a functional and institutional description of the movement.

Contemporaries and participants referred to the agglomeration of denominational agencies involved in overseas evangelization as a movement, a fact that reinforces the practical reasons for describing the home base of foreign missions in a collective fashion. For all the theological and doctrinaire diversity reflected in the need to establish so many societies, both dedication to the missionary task and its conduct helped unify the movement, and provide a basis for meaningful generalizations. The same basic commitment to the spread of Christianity ran afoul of similar problems in the field, and faced comparable conditions in trying to raise support at home. It would nevertheless be illusory to see the foreign mission movement as either a homogeneous or integrated entity, or to consider the distinctive characteristics of the three phases alluded to earlier as rigid rather than evolutionary.

The vigor and ingenuity of the generation which directed the foreign mission enterprise after the 1880s produced unprecedented growth for the movement. The innovations introduced continued to bear fruit for some years after the temporary decrease of activity during World War I, but the spirit of optimism soon waned and was replaced by a period of reassessment during which missions were conducted in a uniquely self-conscious atmosphere. The mission movement of the expansive decades at the turn of the century had not been isolated from the changes affecting the society that supported it, and characteristic accommodations were made in the process of achieving unprecedented success and stature.

Chapter 1

THE MOVEMENT ORGANIZED

*The tendency will be more and more for churches to turn
over their missionary obligations to societies, for societies to
turn it over to boards, for boards to turn it over to executive
committees, and executive committees to secretaries; so that
in the last result, the chief responsibility for the great work
will rest on the shoulders of a dozen men.*

Francis Wayland[1]

At the end of the Civil War, a list of the existing sending
agencies would have provided an inclusive chart of the whole
American foreign mission movement. By 1900, these agencies
formed only part of the movement and were relegated to a largely
functional role. Expanded interest and enthusiasm for the cause
was expressed by other groups. The Student Volunteer Movement
enlisted thousands, while the Missionary Education Movement
spread the message to other thousands who could not go. The
Laymen's Missionary Movement agitated for the necessary funds,
and the Foreign Missions Conference of North America provided a
unified voice for the dozens of sending agencies. A Continuation
Committee of the unprecedented World Missionary Conference in
1910 developed into the World Missionary Council and became an
international sounding board for the movement.

Within the various denominations, the independence of the
mission societies was restricted, and missions were increasingly
treated as an integral part of the churches' everyday concern. Administrative restrictions and the submergence of foreign mission
interests into the general benevolent work of the churches were
acceptable, because its leaders had always insisted that ultimately
the extension of Christianity was the duty of the *ecclesia.* "It is the
business of the whole Church to preach the whole gospel to the
whole world," as a Laymen's Movement publicist restated the traditional objective of American mission leaders.[2] The beginnings of

9

the American movement were in accord with the pietistic emphasis on *ecclesiola in ecclesia,* on select brotherhoods within the churches assuming responsibility for evangelization.[3] Despite the survival of this ideal in Europe, American mission leaders had always hoped for a general assumption of responsibility by the churches, and seen the initiative and indeed existence of their societies and boards as temporary expedients necessitated by Christian apathy and dereliction of duty.[4]

Instead of allowing the temporary organizational structure to wither away as the Protestant denominations gave evidence of accepting their missionary obligations, however, the societies proliferated and the movement expanded. Consolidation and functional reorganization became the dominant trend in the American foreign mission movement during the era that also produced the great industrial trusts. Although both the common name for the general effort and the appellation of the new auxiliary agencies incorporated the word "movement," the designation became increasingly inaccurate.

Movement or Institution?

A religious movement commonly reflects the dissatisfaction of a minority with the constraints and formalization of institutionalized beliefs. Henri Bergson wrote that religion is "the crystallization, brought about by a scientific process of cooling, of what mysticism had poured, while hot, into the soul of man." Consequently, a church or denomination might represent a sincere effort to conserve the insights of revivalistic enthusiasm, or the gains of a revolt against formalism, but the mere act of organization was inherently conservative and a betrayal of the original movement.[5] The pattern of revolt might continue, and occasionally effect a change of direction in the older organization, but the end result was inevitably encrustation or yet another institution.

Although a movement dating back to the first decade of the nineteenth century can hardly lay claim to spontaneity by these standards, there is a legitimate question to ask about the essential nature of the foreign mission upsurge at the end of the century. It

was either a natural reaction to an imperative inadequately expressed by the Protestant churches, which was institutionalized
and absorbed in turn, or it was the artificial creation of new organizations and auxiliaries by ministers and leaders of a long-established
cause. Was the widespread use of the word "movement" in the
names of various new mission auxiliaries descriptive of their origin,
or part of an effort to promote a revival?

While its youthful founders guided the Student Volunteer
Movement, it came closest to meeting the psychological definition
that describes a religious movement as barely institutionalized,
with a minimum of organization, no formal membership, and a
plural leadership dedicated to an ideal.[6] Serious doubt about the
application of this test to the SVM, however, is justified at the end
of the first decade of its organized endeavors. In contrast to the
relatively spontaneous origin of the Student Movement stands a
purposefully created functional agency like the Missionary Education Movement which could lay no claim to that particular appellation. Somewhere between these two examples of new forms in
Protestant foreign missions stands the Laymen's Missionary Movement, which was also the organization most conscious about its
spontaneity and spiritual goals.

The Laymen's Missionary Movement was conceived in a prayer
meeting, and expressed a search for religious experience and values
not met by the churches. "Partly, perhaps, because of the increasing
claims of what we call the humanitarian and the philanthropic,"
wrote Samuel Capen two years before he met with the other founders in New York, "and partly because of the interest given to
theological discussions in the years gone by, we have lost sight of
some of the great fundamental truths, which furnish the very basis
and motive of missions."[7] To rediscover and revivify these truths
was one of the movement's goals. For the LMM was " 'an aspiration,
not an administration,' " wrote its executive secretary. "It is a Movement, rather than an organization."[8] The distinction continued to
be defended, and the label was self-consciously worn. After the
LMM had been successfully launched, Capen indicated that he
hoped to effect a revival by this means, and confessed that he had

always liked the word "movement": "It expresses life, energy, progress. It represents something not necessarily bound to old tradition and certainly something that does not run in ruts. It is a *dynamo* giving added force and power to existing machinery. It is a *promoting agency* to facilitate, if possible, a tremendous energy which shall be felt through all our churches."[9]

The didactic and functional intent of a promoting agency staffed by professionals casts doubt on the spontaneity of the uprising among men. An organized movement to interest church-men in foreign missions and to educate them to do their duty is not the same as a spontaneous movement among American men to become active in the churches and to participate in the evangeliza-tion of the world. Certainly the Laymen's Movement represents less an instinctive clustering around an idea or ideal than some of the political and social movements that developed during the same period. And since the majority of American men were not eligible to join unless they changed their basic religious views, the Laymen's Movement, like the Student Volunteer Movement, was an exclusive rather than a general movement, and could not appeal to the general public for either support or membership. In the form of its national membership, in particular, it was not Gustav Warneck's select brotherhood led by the Holy Spirit as much as a club of moneyed men led and organized by professional secretaries.

Some missionary leaders considered the new emphasis on plans, methods, and organization misplaced because it transferred rather than demanded an individual response to duty. " 'The greatest prob-lem which confronts us for the opening century,' " the Foreign Missions Conference of North America was told in 1906, " 'is that of distributing the missionary responsibility which has become con-gested in official centers.' "[10] The convenience of meeting mission obligations by proxy, in other words, was held responsible for the apathetic support provided by American Protestants. "Piety has now become more nearly, perhaps too nearly, synonymous with action," Horace Bushnell had complained during the heyday of the pre-Civil War evangelical reformers. "As if God would offer to man a mechanical engine for converting the world with the least possible expenditure of piety;" he chided, "or as if types of lead and sheets of paper may be the light of the world."[11]

Despite occasional warnings, and the routine reassertion of spiritual goals by leaders of the Laymen's and Volunteer movements, the construction of a mechanical engine for converting the world received priority during the decades before World War I. If it was not wholly a consciously constructed mechanism, it nevertheless became an impressive structure of societies connected by movements and topped by conventions and councils. A combine replaced individual reapers, and it had a more efficient guidance system and more parts and power than ever before.

The trend in the organization of the movement was toward cooperation, interdenominational bodies, and increasing size in individual agencies. Although the ecumenical hopes of some mission leaders were factors in this trend, the primary pressure toward functional merger and cooperation was practical and originated in contemporary American society. Neither the Protestant churches nor their foreign missions organizations were to escape the tendency toward centralization, and "closer integration of the institutions of control, economic and political," described by such contemporary political scientists as Charles E. Merriam.[12] If Frederick W. Taylor's principles of scientific management could not be directly applied to the mission enterprise, the movement's leaders reflected the same awareness that success depended upon superior methods and organized skills which commended his ideas to industrial executives in the decade after 1900.[13] The gospel of efficiency won converts in educational circles and charitable enterprises, in what Samuel Haber described as "a secular Great Awakening," during which "efficient and good came closer to meaning the same thing . . . than in any other period of American history."[14]

The mission movement's adaptation to this trend was neither simple imitation, nor engaged in solely for reasons of internal efficiency. At least as important a motive was the desire to create an image for their generation which would make the conversion of the world seem practical and feasible, rather than a visionary task to be postponed until the millennium. This message was particularly needed to convince the wealthy businessmen whose support for the final offensive was considered essential, and whose predilections for dealing with efficient philanthropic trusts was made obvious. Thus John D. Rockefeller's unspent millions lent volume to his voice when he advised an end to unscientific giving. Ignoring the petty and individual appeals received by all men of reputed wealth, he wrote, "The prudent and thoughtful giver will, more and more, choose these great and responsible organizations as the medium for his gifts and the distribution of his funds to distant fields." Because of his long experience he had determined to deal only with "an organization which knows all the facts, and can best decide just where the help can be applied to the best advantage."[15]

During the second decade of the twentieth century, mission publicists claimed that their organizations had met such standards, and completed a revision of the traditional imagery associated with the mission movement. "We are in the business of doing good on the widest possible scale," wrote American Board secretary Cornelius Patton, "and in a way which should commend it to business minds." The objective observer must recognize foreign missions as an altruistic enterprise which had reached majestic proportions and become "the Great Business of the Church." Patton was not referring to motives, but to the character and conduct of the work which dictated a new symbolism. "Enough of armies, of strategy, of firing-lines, of trenches, of conquests, of crusades!" wrote the practical secretary in defense of a new vocabulary. "We are living in a business age, the church is made up largely of business men and women, we believe as never before in business efficiency, in business results. It is a working, rather than a fighting Church to which we belong. Both figures are Biblical, and we have the right to take our choice."[16] By the third decade of the twentieth century many mission leaders had chosen the business image to characterize their enterprise, and business methods to conduct its work. The Christian soldier became a salesman, the church martial a specialized organization supporting, supplying, and directing a sales force in new territory.

The Sending Agencies

Despite desultory sniping at the idea of mission boards throughout the nineteenth century, the organized sending agency was the accepted form of conducting America's mission to the world at the turn of the century. Critics condemned the power concentrated in the hands of aristocratic and self-perpetuating committees and boards, but could not stem a tide of organization in which Western Protestantism produced 249 new foreign mission societies during the last three decades of the century, 22 in the single year 1890.[17] Despite this proliferation, the end of the foreign mission enterprise was not in sight at the end of the century, and even some friends of the movement argued that the dissolution of the organizations and a return to New Testament missionary methods seemed a more logical response than further multiplication.[18]

American sending agencies divided into three basic types, of which the most common was the board or society representing a single denomination. Such societies were administrative subdivisions of the general organizational structure of particular churches. Independently organized or chartered societies that nevertheless relied for support largely on one or more denominations constituted a second type. Nondenominational societies drawing their support from the general public formed a third category. They tended to reflect either a distinctive theological approach, or interest in a particular field or type of work. These categories are, of course, not absolutes. The trend by the beginning of the twentieth century was toward a two-part division into agencies controlled by and serving the larger churches, and inter- or nondenominational societies largely supported by the smaller and more recently organized denominations or by splinter groups.

The typical denominational board had experienced a greater degree of independence during its early years than it was likely to have retained by the twentieth century. Since foreign missionary work typically was the concern of a special interest group within a denomination, it was this minority which prevailed on some conference or assembly to provide an outlet for their zeal. Thus the Methodist Mission Society was organized within the New York Annual Conference, and did not become organically related to the national General Conference of the Methodist Episcopal Church for over two decades.[19] Presbyterians made their mission contribution through the American Board until 1837, when the Presbyterian Church incorporated the former Western Foreign Missionary Society and formed its own Board of Foreign Missions. The Baptists varied the pattern, since a special missionary convention was formed before there was any effective denominational organization.[20] By the end of the century, however, each of these churches, and dozens of other denominations helped support agencies devoted exclusively to the foreign mission work of their respective communions.

These boards were supervised in some fashion by denominational committees, but despite a progressive tightening of control managed to retain considerable independence of action for their executive committees or boards of managers.[21] Control was usually exercised through the interlocking membership of denominational and board governing bodies, but if asserted too vigorously was sometimes answered with threats of secession.[22] Unless the boards were guilty of committing major indiscretions in appointments or administration, they could expect a relatively free hand in determining policy and supervising normal operations.

The Foreign Christian Missionary Society and American Board of Commissioners for Foreign Missions were in the category of semi-independent boards, although several Lutheran bodies such as Hauge's Synod China Mission also drew support across existing denominational lines. The Foreign Christian Missionary Society was formed in 1875 in the face of the stubborn resistance of the Disciples of Christ to any organized effort at overseas evangelization through their twenty-six-year-old American Christian Missionary Society. Independent of denominational control, the society nevertheless relied almost exclusively on the support of the Disciples of Christ through the sale of individual memberships and directorships. With its governing board drawn from Disciples who had paid $100 to become life members, the society was criticized for being the toy of a "moneyed aristocracy." In 1919 independence was traded for denominational funding, with the reunion of the two agencies in the United Christian Missionary Society.[23]

The American Board's independence can be traced both to the issuance of its 1812 charter by the Commonwealth of Massachusetts rather than by an ecclesiastical body, and to its willingness to function as a channel for Presbyterian and Reformed Church foreign mission efforts in addition to serving the Congregational churches.[24] When the board lost its last non-Congregational affiliate in 1870, it received only a recommendation of church support from the National Council of Congregational Churches.[25] Totally dependent upon voluntary support, and vulnerable to theological partisans and politicians in such matters as the Andover Controversy, "The Board had fallen upon a time when the organization had lost the reason for its undenominational character, and yet had not assumed the safeguards of denominational control."[26] The safeguards or shackles were firmly applied in 1913, when National Council and board membership became largely identical. A Commission on Missions appointed by the National Council supervised the work of all Congregational boards, and the proud old pioneer of foreign missions became a denominational agency.[27]

Like similar self-perpetuating corporations, the American Board was theoretically governed through annual meetings of officers and corporate members.[28] These sparsely attended assemblies, however, tended to be edifying reunions for old supporters, friends, and ministers, rather than working business sessions. The actual direction of the Board's affairs was in the hands of a plural executive termed the Prudential Committee, elected by the corporate members.[29] A select minority, not hundreds of members or even the denominational supervisory committee, thus guided the affairs of the oldest nondenominational foreign mission board, which, like most agencies of its type, eventually chose security over independence.[30]

The third category of mission societies consisted of the wholly independent or nondenominational agencies, which usually subscribed to traditional evangelical or fundamentalist principles. Characteristically evangelical zeal led to splinter churches which either began as mission groups and hardened into sects, or began their organized existence dominated by missionary fervor. Thus the Reverend Albert Simpson's perfectionism and missionary interest took him out of the Presbyterian Church in the 1880s to carry on evangelistic work among the unchurched. To provide avenues for evangelical activism, he organized a Christian Alliance and the International Missionary Alliance, without requiring the members to sever their connections with established churches or denominations. Even after the two societies that had been established for home and foreign work were merged in 1897 into the present Christian and Missionary Alliance, Simpson continued to describe the Alliance as a non-denominational union of like-minded evangelicals.[31]

Smaller sects originating in missionary enthusiasm have survived for more than half a century, maintaining their identity not on the basis of theological distinctions but because of their abiding dedication to evangelization.[32] Others, formed around the personal drive of a single leader, or incorporating socially unacceptable idiosyncracies such as communism, survived only a few decades.[33] The evangelical enthusiasm that produced such groups was similar to the motivation of hundreds of faith missionaries who went to the field, and only later developed supporting agencies at home. Such men and women have been a constant if minor part of the foreign mission effort. Their numbers increased as transportation became easier and remote non-Christian nations were opened to the unsponsored traveler. They disdained the restrictions, conditions, and security of the established mission boards, but eventually found it necessary to establish channels for regular support.

The career of Charles E. Cowman, a barely educated Illinois farmer's son whose lack of credentials to complement his evangelical enthusiasm prevented him from receiving a regular appointment from the Methodist Missionary Society, illustrates the successful outcome of this individualistic pattern. When he was thirty-three, he quit his telegrapher's job in Chicago and sold his home and possessions, determined that he and his wife would answer their call to missionary service. He preached and taught for some weeks at an Ohio Bible school until contributions from converts and his former co-workers in the Western Union office sufficed to pay the Cowmans' fare to Japan. "This seemed to Charles Cowman to be the Apostolic plan," wrote his wife, "to go forward at God's call, letting Him supply the need. He plunged gladly into a life of trusting the Lord alone, and he found that the resources of God are promised to those who undertake the program of God." Before his death in 1924, Cowman disposed of some $1,500,000, building Bible schools in China, Korea, and Japan, and setting up over 300 mission stations connected with his Oriental Missionary Society.[34]

A similar spirit lay behind Henry Frost's formation of the North American Branch of the China Inland Mission. While Cowman and Simpson initially had no geographical preferences for their field, Frost's evangelical zeal was concentrated on China's millions. When he was rejected as a candidate by the China Inland Mission because of family obligations, Frost sailed to Britain in 1887 to urge the formation of an American branch of the society. Although the officers of the British society dissuaded Frost, Hudson Taylor agreed to stop in the United States on his next trip to China. The funds collected for North American CIM candidates during Taylor's 1888 tour finally led him to see God's will for a North American Branch.[35]

Henry W. Frost directed the new agency through its lean first decades with a skeleton staff and no regular promotional machinery. The CIM drew its candidates and funds from all American denominations. It attracted those who shared its orthodox evangelical views and preoccupation with China's unreached millions as well as sympathizers who admired the mission's courageous concentration on inaccessible virgin territory. The CIM claimed it neither competed with nor detracted from the support of any existing board. But the hundreds of missionaries sent forth, and the millions of dollars collected to support them, did not come from the apathetic church members who neglected their own boards.[36]

Finally there was a type of independent agency based not on

theological or geographical preferences, but on the accident of sex. Through delayed marriages and direct casualties, the Civil War seems to have created an unusually large class of unmarried, educated, middle-class women living in eastern and middle western cities and towns with little opportunity to employ their talents. It would be surprising if the existence of these widows and women with restricted opportunities for marriage did not partly account for the fact that the women's boards were almost all formed in the immediate postwar period.[37]

The nondenominational ancestor of these boards was the Woman's Union Missionary Society of America. For a few years after its formation in 1861, it was content to support women appointed by other agencies. But after 1868, it both commissioned its own missionaries and established educational and medical facilities in various parts of the world.[38] All facets of administration and promotion were handled by unsalaried women volunteers from most evangelical denominations. The Woman's Union Missionary Society continued its independent existence into the twentieth century; its most lasting contribution was probably the example set for denominational emulation.[39] By 1890, 34 American women's societies were supporting 926 missionaries in various fields. They far surpassed their British cousins in these activities.[40] As women were given a voice on some regular boards after 1900, and the male directors overcame their reluctance to send unmarried ladies overseas, the women's boards were absorbed into the general denominational agencies.

The standards of business efficiency maintained by all types of sending agencies were high despite the increased promotional costs of the modern mission movement. The denominational agencies were particularly subject to questioning concerning their administrative expenses, as when the Methodist General Conference demanded a detailed accounting from its boards in 1880.[41] A Foreign Mission Conference study in 1902, found the cost of collection and administration for the general mission establishment to "vary from four to six and a half per cent on the dollar," reflecting in the words of the compiler, "economy and care such as few other enterprises report."[42]

Although inflation and unexpected expenses could temporarily increase board "overhead," Cornelius Patton maintained in 1924 that "the percentage of income used for administration varies from seven to twelve per cent in average years."[43] He added that from one-third to one-half of even this expenditure could be saved if the churches were alive to their missionary obligations, and did not require constant prodding to contribute. Evidence over a long period of time thus indicates remarkably economic administration of the funds entrusted to the foreign mission boards.

One other area of the sending agencies' operations bears mention because of the light it sheds on the mission movement's ability to serve external interests. The American Board's reluctant participation in the Andover Controversy of the 1870s provides an early example of the effort to enlist a semi-independent and large benevolent agency on the side of a particular doctrinal faction in a denomination. The contention between fundamentalists and modernists in most of the major denominations during the 1920s also involved efforts to seize control of at least foreign mission personnel policies. Despite scrupulous efforts to remain neutral, board officers were maligned and attacked for their reluctance to choose sides. Because of the sending agencies' relative immunity to control, few of these efforts succeeded. But all foreign mission societies suffered wounds and often a loss of support, while some watched as rival agencies were established. Arthur Judson Brown, after four decades of service to the Presbyterian Board, recalled the fundamentalist attacks as the most troublesome and damaging problems he had to contend with.[44]

In terms of the foreign mission boards' influence on American foreign policy, or of their relation to economic imperialism, two things should be noted about these incidents. The boards successfully survived various attacks on their independence in matters of policy, and all of the attacks involved either questions of denominational control or of religious doctrine. Foreign mission boards consistently avoided taking a concrete stand on political issues, largely because they could not afford to antagonize part of their constituency. Even on the denominational or doctrinal issues that they could not evade, they could be influenced only by a diffuse and generally ineffective exercise of the power of the purse. In matters of operations and policy, the executives of the boards probably had greater freedom than the average American college president has from the strictures of his alumni or board of trustees.

From mission committees representing a minority in the local churches, through apathetic or hostile ministers, to amateur trustees and councillors meeting only at long intervals, the chain of command was atomistic and confused. And even if the professional directors had not found it expedient to avoid controversial issues, they would have faced formidable obstacles in trying to effect their policies in distant mission fields. Mission board governance was astonishingly inefficient for any purpose but sending men and women to foreign countries. The societies were not designed to effect a policy, but to collect generally like-minded and religiously motivated people, and to maintain their logistic support for extended periods in distant lands. Once sent, their individualism and distance from home made them relatively immune to control as well until they had finished a seven or ten-year tour of duty. Had a theoretical corporation president desired a certain policy to be carried out in China by a board to which he had made substantial contributions, he would have had a hellish time getting it transmitted through the secretaries, and no guarantees at all that it would be observed by the missionary staff in the field. Direct correspondence with individual missionaries might have been more effective, but resorting to his own company employees on the scene would have been the most productive and logical procedure of all.

America's Protestant missionaries took their secular outlook and national biases with them to the field, and inevitably this included both subconscious and open expansionist and racist views. When examples of this are found, however, it is reflective of contemporary American thought, not the product of mission boards who had neither the desire nor the constitutional capacity to affect the individual missionary's outlook on matters other than doctrine.

Auxiliary and Interdenominational Organizations

The primary area of expansion, and the source of much of the dynamism of the foreign mission movement at the turn of the century, were the religious organizations that supplemented the traditional sending agencies. One broad category of these auxiliaries of the mission boards consisted of existing religious and benevolent organizations that were infiltrated or otherwise induced to include the foreign mission cause in their work. Another category consisted of interdenominational organizations which were the offspring of the foreign mission movement itself. Thus the Missionary Education Movement, the Student Volunteers, and the Laymen's Missionary Movement arose in response to specific needs of the sending agencies. They had no prior existence or broader objectives as was the case, for example, with the Bible or Christian Endeavor societies which began to cooperate with the mission boards.

Because this trend reflects an interest in expanding missionary activity beyond the accomplishments of the regular sending agencies, its appearance at least in part represents unprecedented support for the foreign mission cause. It also reflects the growing influence of laymen and of the new type of denominational functionary who was anxious to transcend traditional bounds, and to transform the fragmented movement into an efficient organization. For the most part the initiative for this coordination envisioned by laymen and carried out by nonclerical professionals, did not originate with the existing sending agencies.

John Mott, the ablest and most versatile of the new interdenominational career men, concluded an inventory of foreign mission achievements and prospects in 1906 with a practical prescription: "It is going to take a larger combination organized on the best modern business lines, and flooded with the spirit of God," he told the Haystack Centennial assembly, "to meet the present situation."[45] While the interdependence of both factors is not denied, Mott had given business efficiency precedence over the functional efficacy of the spirit of God.

Several years earlier, the businessman-president of the American Board had called upon men of every faith in the English-speaking world "to combine, in something larger than a billion-dollar steel trust." "No more rivalry, no more overlapping," asked Samuel Capen. "With economy and efficiency at every point, let us finish the work that has been so gloriously begun."[46] In collaboration with Mott and others he pursued this objective until he could quote his own prescription in 1910, and then declare that "through the Laymen's Missionary Movement that world-wide trust has been formed."[47]

The promoters of the foreign missions trust allocated responsibility in clear and simple fashion. Personnel recruitment would be handled by a more efficiently organized Student Volunteer Movement, directed now by salaried professionals instead of idealistic college youths. Although its executive committee continued to be drawn from the Inter-Seminary Missionary Alliance and the Student Young Men's and Women's Christian Associations, the secretarial staff of these organizations provided the members. The majority of the SVM secretaries were volunteers on temporary duty before leaving for the foreign field, but a number of senior officers grew old in harness despite Mott's warnings that the movement was in danger of losing contact with the enthusiasm of youth.

The abiding problem faced by the Student Volunteer Movement, however, was to provide continuity to an organization composed of hundreds of loosely affiliated campus Volunteer Bands despite the frequent turnover of student leadership. The quadrennial convention, supplemented by more frequent regional meetings and summer training courses, were only partially successful in binding each succeeding student generation to the common cause. The New York administrative committee and the executive officers who produced the literature, arranged the convention agendas and dispatched the traveling secretaries, were thus crucial factors in the movement's continued existence.

Although there was occasional criticism of the SVM's tendency to make inflated claims, and of its officers' readiness to gloss over complex administrative problems, the sending agencies valued the movement's contributions and maintained effective liaison with its headquarters. The Student Volunteer Movement received early representation at the annual conferences of mission society secretaries and officers, and an official advisory committee of board representatives served the movement on a permanent basis.[48]

The Student Volunteers and the International Committee of the YMCAs had combined in 1902 to create the Young People's Missionary Movement, a new agency designed both to serve a broad propaganda function and to reach a larger number of prospective missionaries.[49] Changing its name to the Missionary Education Movement in 1911, it became less a recruiting service than a general propaganda and educational agency. Through pamphlets, mission course outlines and texts, slides, films, and conventions, it served the fifteen denominational boards that had helped to found the body. It was a movement neither directed by its constituency, nor including them as members, but acting as a clearing house or federation of young people's and Sunday school officials.[50] A majority of its board of managers had to be secretaries of home and foreign mission boards, and it had a standing agreement to consult regularly with the SVM, Women's Home Mission Council, and Committee on the United Study of Missions, the latter representing the major women's foreign societies. It worked out a similar arrangement with the Laymen's Movement, abandoning its Laymen's Department after the new movement was formed.[51]

Unlike the Student Volunteer Movement, the Missionary Education Movement was largely a creature of the mission agencies designed to bring their message to nearly 20,000,000 Sunday school scholars and members of young people's societies, and eventually to include and train mission leaders for local congregations as well.[52] "The Missionary Education Movement is the powerhouse of the missionary propaganda of the world, the 'central' of its spiritual wireless; the clearing house of its ideals and plans and methods," explained the *Missionary Review* in 1919. "Every mission board regards its continued existence and expansion as vitally necessary to every denominational enterprise."[53]

The Laymen's Missionary Movement

Even more vital to the emerging mission trust, and the most significant new development during the pre-World War I period, was the Laymen's Missionary Movement. It was unique because there were precedents for organized student and women's groups in support of foreign missions, but this was the first men's body dedicated to the cause in the hundred-year history of the American movement. Thus its organization in 1907 was interpreted as an omen of a new day, a revolutionary development that alone could convert the ambitious Student Volunteer watchword into a practical and realizable goal. Officials of the Episcopal and Southern Presbyterian churches "declared their conviction that this movement is the most epoch-making that has occurred in the Christian world since the Protestant Reformation in the sixteenth century."[54] Similarly Commission VI of the World Missionary Conference found that "the possibilities for the church and the cause of missions that already begins to appear in this Movement are beyond estimation."[55]

Although the significance of the Laymen's Movement to American missions cannot be doubted, its precise nature is more difficult to define, and its status as a mighty national movement is scarcely tenable. Coterminous with the progressive era, it constituted at best a ripple in that movement, and one that probably ran counter to the prevailing tide. Concerned only with professed evangelical Protestants, among its leaders in particular, it seemed to provide an outlet for conservative enthusiasm which was reluctant to deal with domestic social and political reform. The records of the movement reveal that almost everyone approached for service on its governing board had already established a reputation as "a leading layman of his denomination," or "a regular and generous contributor" to some phase of the church's work. A campaign to interest successful Protestant business and professional men who were already faithful church members in the cause of foreign missions, cannot claim the status of a major movement on the American scene in the pre-World War I decade.

The Laymen's Movement developed a tightly centralized

organization directed from the tallest office building in New York, largely supported by eastern members able to attend committee meetings regularly. The rank and file membership was neither solicited for ideas, nor allowed to participate in policy making.[56] Instead it constituted a semi-captive audience to receive the promotional literature devised at No. 1 Madison Avenue. Formal ties to the movement were never strong, for if it was easy to sign the declaration of purpose along with one's friends after an enthusiastic convention presentation, it was equally simple to forget the new affiliation after returning home.

As a Boston storeowner serving as president of the American Board at the same time, Samuel Capen's direction of the movement as chairman of the Executive Committee was delegated to a General Secretary who was officially designated the executive officer of the organization.[57] Both he and his subordinates had to be laymen, but this term did not mean that ordinary business or professional men served in these capacities. The dynamic first general secretary, J. Campbell White, who had helped found the movement, had long experience in religious organization with the International Committee of the YMCAs and the United Presbyterian Church. His successors and assistants had similar backgrounds and were professionals in the field.[58]

Shortly after its formal organization, the LMM sent William Jay Schieffelin to Great Britain to promote a sister movement, or in the words of John Jay's great-great-grandson, "to negotiate a treaty of Alliance of the English speaking world in the great campaign for the spread of the Kingdom of Heaven."[59] Schieffelin, a chemist and member of an old New York mercantile family, was representative of the majority of the movement's founders and committee members: belonging to an old eastern family, moderately wealthy from an established business, politically conservative, and active in many religious and benevolent associations. Together with a few professional religious leaders such as John R. Mott and Robert E. Speer, these men constituted the Executive Committee which sought broader geographical and social representation in the General Committee. They were men still actuated by a sense of noblesse oblige, and did not consider it necessary to emphasize the fact that they represented a natural and traditional elite. Their concern for foreign missions was based on religion.[60]

The secretarial staff meanwhile gave the lie to the regular protestations that the Laymen's Movement was not an organization by extending staff and offices outside New York. As a result of inadequacies observed during a national campaign, the Executive Committee authorized the establishment of regional offices in seven major cities in 1911. Most had an ephemeral existence between national drives, but several became flourishing branches with their own staffs and committee structure.[61]

More important to the directorate was efficient liaison and the promotion of uniform policies with some fourteen denominational laymen's movements, and three "affiliated movements."[62] These were the bodies that could most easily distribute relevant literature, and were best suited to supervise local missionary committees and fund drives. Such cooperation also allowed the utilization of the existing staffs and organizations of the various churches, and avoided interdenominational jealousy and rivalry over the apportionment of fund drive receipts. Internal conflict over the LMM's unwillingness to promote the cause of home missions as well, however, could not be avoided, and led to such embarrassments as a Baptist magazine's call for a campaign to "stamp out" the Laymen's Movement.[63] The directors also had difficulty explaining why such prominent denominations as the Episcopalians, Northern Presbyterians, Disciples of Christ, and Congregational Churches failed to follow the lead of the seventeen who had federated with the national movement.[64]

With suspicion, jealousy, apathy, and divided purposes hampering the LMM's activities on the denominational level, its most spectacular accomplishments were made in situations in which it could direct and dominate the work. "The Movement stands for investigation, agitation and organization," summarized J. Campbell White after two years' activity.[65] Investigation referred to a Centennial Committee world tour of mission fields in 1908, and the general educational program of the LMM. Organization was accomplished through the denominational bodies and the city and church missionary committees using plans and material supplied from New York.

Agitation, which Samuel Capen had identified as the primary initial objective as well as the characteristic of any movement, took place most effectively through the hundreds of congresses, conventions, and campaigns sponsored by the Laymen's Movement during its final decade. The first coordinated drive was the National Missionary Campaign in which seventy-five separate conventions were held in major cities during the winter, culminating in May of 1910 in the Chicago National Missionary Congress.[66] Between campaigns, hundreds of mission dinners, special conventions to train workers, and even to wake ministers up to their missionary obligations were sponsored by the movement.[67]

The meticulously planned men's mission dinners and weekend conferences were successful, at least in part, because they provided a relatively inexpensive form of entertainment and social fellowship for urban men.[68] Prominent public figures, whom the average layman was unlikely to hear under normal circumstances, were included in the speaking teams made available by the movement. The teams were preceded by field secretaries who held both congregational and city-wide meetings, bought advertising space, and often succeeded in having laymen take over church services the Sunday before the conference. Whenever possible, prominent local citizens were included in city cooperating committees to utilize their influence in making a maximum impact on the community through such devices as the closing of factories, stores, and offices on the day of a meeting.

Although the Laymen's Movement was active throughout the United States during national campaigns, its leaders found it difficult to sustain interest or build up permanent committees outside of the east and the Chicago area. A survey of largely "unworked territory" in 1914 revealed the Pacific Coast, southwest and, surprisingly, New England, as the areas most in need of field secretaries and additional work should necessary funds be made available.[69]

By 1918 the Laymen's Movement had greatly expanded both its work and message. Permanent divisional committees hired their own field secretaries; a larger staff, fluctuating with the advent of campaigns, was supervised by a dozen permanent secretaries operating from New York. Cooperation with the personnel of the denominational groups extended the national committees' reach. The movement had embraced the promotion of home missions as a joint objective with its original purpose, and *Men and Missions* identified the LMM with patriotism, temperance, Liberty Bond sales, and anti-bolshevism, at least partially to confound criticism of its continued promotional activities during wartime.

Suggestions that the movement had run its course were strongly countered, on the assumption that the war's demand for sacrificial dedication and work from American men would only increase their zeal in pressing toward the spiritual conquest of the world. "The Laymen's Movement as 'an inspiration and a challenge and a spiritual dynamic' has only begun its work."[70] A year later the Laymen's Movement was completely absorbed by the Interchurch World Movement. Its publications staff moved to the journal of the new organization, and the secretarial staff was reassigned to similar positions under new auspices. Even a large proportion of the members of the LMM's governing boards moved into comparable Interchurch committees. Since the Interchurch Movement proceeded rapidly toward its spectacular collapse a year later, the merger decision turned out to have been the LMM's death sentence.

The American foreign mission movement at the turn of the century produced no more characteristic innovation than the Laymen's Missionary Movement, nor one with greater potential significance. Its accomplishments were listed in Cornelius Patton's retrospective testimonial when he called it:

> The movement which gave us the every member canvass and the church budget; which at a critical time for the Kingdom was instrumental in aligning tens of thousands of businessmen in missionary belief and activity; which in hundreds of churches reenforced pastoral leadership by bringing to bear

upon the problems of the Church the brainpower and enthusiasm of practical-minded business and professional men; the enterprise which . . . inaugurated a new era of missionary incentive and support.[71]

The question remains, however, whether the movement's death after twelve years represented failure or success in realizing its potential.

A legitimate evaluation of the Laymen's Movement and its campaign and convention techniques can only be made in relation to the movement's professed goals. And in trying to identify these, one is surprised by the ambivalence with which its leaders identified their objectives. They sought a spiritual revival as a means toward a more rapid realization of the Kingdom of God, and yet they wished just as strongly to be practical, modern, and businesslike in conserving the fruits of the reawakening. This trend can be seen in the unprecedented employment of advertising and other promotional techniques as well as in J. Campbell White's insistence that "prayer gains power by definiteness": that praying for specific missionaries, projects, or fields was more productive than the old-fashioned inclusive Concerts of Prayer.[72] Practicality is also reflected in Patton's summary of the movement's contributions, and in John R. Mott's tribute to the Laymen's Missionary Movement for its effective methods "of getting the newly interested laymen to use their fresh knowledge, interest and enthusiasm," and for affording "a multitude of men practical outlets for new-found vision and passion."[73]

On the other hand, there was the recollection of a participant to the businessmen's prayer meeting in which the Laymen's Movement was conceived: "Mr. J. Campbell White facing his audience, swayed by a great emotion, with tears upon his cheek, challenging the men present to their immediate Foreign Mission task." Sitting in a sanctuary suffused with a "tense spirit of earnestness, the deep spiritual tone, and the manifest presence of God's spirit," the men responded positively.[74] Samuel Capen was seeking a similar reaction when he addressed a Student Volunteer

convention and quoted Horace Bushnell's prediction: "One more
revival, only one more, is needed, a revival of Christian stewardship,
the consecration of the money power of the church under God;
and when that revival comes, the Kingdom of God will come in a
day."[75]

Whether Capen was speaking hopefully, or descriptively, he
ignored a further pertinent observation of Bushnell's. "If a great
scene must be compassed; if a preacher who is noted as having a
wondrous faculty to convert men must be sent for as indispensable";
the Congregational theologian had written more than a half-century
before, "If a mill of mechanism must be planned it would not seem
that the church has much to do with the contrivance in any way."[76]

Bushnell's warning had been delivered during a period of
professional revivalism and perfectionist reform which was predominantly an eastern urban phenomenon, usually originating in men's
prayer meetings, where experts applied special techniques to effect
conversion in an atmosphere charged with excited group emotions.[77]
The rapid growth of the urban population, and the increasing influence of laymen in the churches at the beginning of this century,
provided a broader area of effectiveness for the professionals who
developed these techniques and offered a "revivalism which reduced
regeneration to a method for drumming up church members."[78]
Methods effective in signing up church members were also useful in
soliciting pledges in an every member canvass or at a men's mission
conference.

The professional religious administrator, who values businesslike expertise in the operations of his organization, will not discard
this orientation when it comes to "marketing"—approaching his
potential constitutency for financial support. The answer to the
riddle of the Laymen's Movement's true nature probably lies in
different conceptions of the means by which a common goal could
be reached. The part-time directors sitting on the movement's committees hoped to see a national awakening of men, a general revival
in American Protestantism, from which foreign missions would inevitably benefit. But they expected this to "happen," as the LMM had
happened in a winter prayer meeting. Some thought it had happened

in 1910, when the providential coincidence of the World Missionary Conference in Edinburgh and the first National Missionary Campaign in the United States produced Laymen's Movements all over the British Commonwealth, in four continental countries and even in Egypt. But the enthusiasm of 1910 did not become the predicted mighty torrent. It required more national campaigns, more imaginative advertising, new regional organizations and secretaries, and hundreds of conferences and speakers merely to keep it alive.

The professional secretaries recognized these facts long before the gentlemen on the committees. So they talked about a national campaign whose theme would be "a challenge to prayer for the inauguration of a national spirit of awakening."[79] They also regularly organized prayer meetings in communities about to receive convention speaking teams, and testified that habitual prayer would double "the total efficiency of the entire missionary propaganda . . . without adding another worker."[80] But they put their efforts into the General Secretary's trilogy of organization, education, and agitation, and both wearied and confused many of their supporters in the process.[81]

The men's missionary conference or dinner was the most effective tool developed by the Laymen's Movement to bring its message to American Protestants. At these meetings didactic facts were interspersed with prayer, and promotion combined with worship. Teams of speakers exhorted and promised more than they demanded or received from the participants. And this ambivalent merger of objectives and means explains the mixed impression the movement made. On the one hand is the testimony of a "cigarette smoking, champagne drinking Christian" converted to abstinence and preaching the cause of missions; of a Buffalo layman averring that "the city had been stirred spiritually better than by any Evangelistic meetings."[82] Some remembered truly spiritual meetings with addresses so unworldly that an American Board secretary recalled convention speakers "too orthodox and too close to a literal interpretation of the commands of scripture to be well suited to Congregational congregations."[83]

Others recalled the sticky atmosphere of Rotary luncheon

camaraderie that emerged from sessions addressed by "a one time railroad man who knows a thing or two about life as it really is," "a manufacturer of preachers hailing from Chicago," and an expert "fresh from the Armenian massacres." "There was Fisher, Fred B., the very same," read the account of a Kansas City convention, "fresh from the mission fields of India, who arrived at the convention . . . fuller of information than a barrelful of peanuts, and on fire with ambition to tell everybody about it, including newspaper reporters and convention delegates." The dynamic Mr. Fisher, who served the LMM, Methodist Centennial, and Interchurch World Movement in various secretarial roles, was "the platform manager, team leader, and general boss of everybody and everything, and knew how to do the work, and did it. His chief assistants consisted of one lusty lunged Naftzer . . . and two secretarial side-partners . . . ," and all ten thousand men in the audience reportedly returned to their homes secure in their faith and irrevocably committed to the evangelization of the world in their generation.[84]

Both of the impressions illustrated here are correct, although each reflects only a single aspect of the movement. The same is true of the debate over the submergence of the Laymen's Movement in the Interchurch World Movement. That step made sense from the point of view of gentlemen directors who held that "every now and then in the life of the church we need a movement,"[85] and who were willing for various reasons to defer to the most inclusive and massive one ever envisioned in the United States. It was equally attractive to religious professionals who saw the Interchurch World Movement as a well-financed opportunity to apply the techniques they had developed on a truly national basis and to all Protestant communions. From one point of view a movement had run its course, from the other an experimental beginning was now to move to a greater stage.

Movements are evanescent, and their transformation into more lasting form takes place with or without planning. When did the student volunteer movement, begun by inspired youngsters traveling from campus to campus at their own expense to tell others of the cause they had discovered, turn into the Student

Volunteer Movement that died of disinterest in 1955? Had not the apparatus of national committees, Volunteer Bands, quadrennial conventions, magazines, newsletters, study courses, and millions of pamphlets perpetuated a movement beyond its time? The leaders of the Laymen's Movement were also perplexed over the problem of determining the point at which a movement ossifies and loses its distinctive spirit and direction.

In 1910, the Executive Committee heard a paper dealing with this question, and was led into a far-reaching debate on the continued existence of their venture. The eventual consensus was to continue the work for a few more years before coming to a decision. Robert E. Speer pointed out that, not only had its objective not yet been reached, but that for the time being, the LMM had not yet become a formal organization. "It has the unique characteristics of being the unincorporated embodiment of a great living principle," observed the Presbyterian board secretary. John R. Mott agreed that the movement was just finding itself and reaching the point for which it had come into existence, "that of touching the conservative men who had been watching the Movement critically to see whether it was merely sporadic."[86]

John R. Mott, the organizational and administrative genius of this century's foreign mission movement, personally embodied the conflict manifested in so many areas of its activities. He remarked on the chilling effect that young volunteers grown old in office had on the enthusiasm of the SVM, but continued to supervise that movement's work for four decades. He lauded both the Laymen's and the Student Volunteer Movements for remaining movements, but participated most actively in perfecting their organizational structure and promotional plans. "We need one more society, and we need that very badly," he said in 1906, "a society which will have as its object the prevention of the formation of any more missionary organizations."[87] The same man was instrumental in forming the SVM, World's Student Christian Federation, Foreign Work Department of the International Committee of the YMCAs, Interchurch World Movement, the conversion of the Edinburgh Continuation Committee into the World Missionary Council, and

closely involved in the leadership of additional groups ranging from
the Laymen's Movement to Near East Relief. At the same time that
he recognized the danger of organization, he appreciated the need
for it. He preferred spontaneous spiritual motivation, but, with experience and impatience mitigating faith, he was at the same time
instrumental in perfecting and transferring the promotional fund-
raising methods of the Laymen's Movement to the IWM.

It was probably inevitable that a dynamic man with his ability
would avoid too close a confrontation of this general dilemma,
while also finding it personally painful to consign the instruments
he had organized to their fate, or to surrender their control to less
able hands. In any event, it scarcely seemed important to mark
precisely the arrival and departure of new enthusiasm. "Movements,
so-called, pass over the surface of life like waves," observed Frederick DeLand Leete in his survey of proliferating men's religious
associations in 1912. "When they have passed, comes the trough,
and then another wave." Their span was less important than the
fact that inevitably new ones would appear. "The tide is produced
by the constant operation of Christian influence upon the minds
of men," he concluded, "and the activities of the regular institutions of the Church are the streams which bear fullness to the
ocean of evangelistic success, of religious development, and of
abiding usefulness."[88] The passing of the era of the religious trust,
in other words, could ultimately be viewed with equanimity, but
not until those involved in its construction had experienced the
failure of the ultimate expression of their plans.

The Interchurch World Movement

A former missionary and LMM secretary wrote in 1919 that
the Interchurch World Movement "will prove the wisdom or un-
wisdom of our methods by the supreme test of efficiency."[89]
After collecting only $3,000,000 of the over $8,000,000 expended
on promotion in a campaign designed to net $336,777,572 for 31
denominations in 1920, but producing subscriptions totaling only
$176,000,000, the directors decided upon an immediate cessation

of activities.[90] Subsequently another former missionary and board secretary described the test as a "failure pitiful to behold," and the movement as "one of the most colossal fizzles that has ever befallen an effort of the combined churches of America."[91]

The Interchurch Movement represented in part an effort to federate or coordinate denominational mass fund raising campaigns that had first been organized in response to the dawning of a new century, and which were more ambitiously revived at the end of the war in such drives as the Presbyterian New Era Movement.[92] The vastly successful Liberty Bond and service organization wartime campaigns provided further examples to church functionaries. Many Interchurch Movement spokesmen shared Woodrow Wilson's idealism, and publicly supported the League of Nations. They ordered a survey of the task of postwar reconstruction and evangelization, accepted the one billion dollar figure Protestant church agencies declared it would take to win this campaign,[93] and undertook to provide it in a religious equivalent to the war to end war.

The Interchurch Movement also resurrected the supervisory and coordinating functions that the LMM had assumed in the 1913–1914 United Missionary Campaign, a precedent that the outbreak of the war and denominational rivalry had prevented from being perpetuated in a prospective United Missionary Council.[94] From the LMM it borrowed not only personnel, but the every member canvass, publicity, convention and advertising techniques, and the principle of not becoming involved in the direct collection of contributions, or of publicly appealing to church members to finance its activities.[95]

All of these precedents were hastily combined, and applied on a grander scale. Thus, instead of reliance on the movement's staff, two leading New York advertising agencies were retained to mount a national publicity campaign. A long-term lease on a $500,000-a-year New York office building was arranged to house the secretarial and administrative staff. Professional canvassers were hired instead of reliance on locally trained amateurs, and the younger Rockefeller made his contribution as star of a speaking team which toured the country and attracted over 10,000 to a single meeting in Kansas City.[96]

The objective was "the allied strategy of a Christian offensive," wrote Associate General Secretary William Foulke. "The marshaling of the whole Church of Jesus Christ in North America for its whole Kingdom task, individual, national and overseas."[97] And J. Campbell White, who surrendered the presidency of the College of Wooster to join the IWM, described it as "the most deeply significant and promising" religious development of modern times.[98] In more practical terms, the final report of the organizing committee of the movement conceived of it as "primarily a Home and Foreign Missionary Movement . . . to be broad enough to cover all those interests in the United States and Canada outside of the local church budget which are naturally related to the missionary enterprises through national agencies—denominational or inter-denominational."[99]

"In my judgment, for the first time that I have ever lived," declared the initially dubious John R. Mott at a planning conference for the new venture, "it is possible for Protestant Christianity to have a plan that will be literally world-wide. That . . . shall shake the United States of America to a degree that has never before been done in any piece of planning that has been conceived."[100] His role in the planning must have been negligible for much later he agreed that the movement had been largely a failure due to the preponderance of "the promoter type, and . . . lack of prophets, statesmen, and wise master builders" among the personnel.[101]

Although Mott may indeed have had his reservations in 1919, he was probably caught again in the conflict between spiritual objectives or motives and businesslike means which characterized the Laymen's Movement. "The Inter-Church World Movement had its origin I verily believe in the Mind of the Spirit," wrote a secretary of the Southern Presbyterian Board. "Every discussion of its plans and aims has been characterized by such unanimity of opinion that we may assuredly gather that they meet the mind of the Spirit Who gives unity."[102] This attitude contrasts with or at least mitigates against a wholly businesslike campaign, and also permits the uncritical acceptance of expert advice and guidance. And when that expertise fails to achieve the divine objectives, recriminations and cynicism follow.

Like "all disappointments, the Interchurch debacle lends itself to a providential interpretation," maintained the editor of *Christian Century.* "It has made clear the bankruptcy of the promoter's type of activity." Interchurch methods were only the application on a slightly more comprehensive basis of the same principles that had come to characterize most religious programs. "This method was that of the promoter," he maintained in summary, "with its promise of a short-cut to great results, its use of the technique of secular publicity, its dependence upon mass psychology and its adoption of highly specialized organization as an instrument for putting extraordinary pressure upon the feelings of the Christian public."[103]

Yet, in view of inauspicious postwar conditions, frenzied management, and persistent interdenominational friction, it was difficult to maintain that the Interchurch failure proved anything regarding the basic idea of a united Christian front for missionary work. Since neither promotional expenses nor receipts were pooled, it turned out to be not ecumenical or cooperative as intended, but "a concurrent effort on the part of leading Protestant denominations of the United States, each one conducting its own campaign and sharing its ingathering with no other."[104] It was thus possible to maintain the objective, and to rationalize the disaster as a sturdy moral exercise which had gone awry for many unavoidable reasons, but which was not nearly as portentous as critics suggested. And increased contributions to missions and larger numbers of volunteers during the immediate postwar years seemed to verify this conclusion.

Nevertheless, it was a long time before the big campaign and the bigger plan received another trial. The Interchurch Movement was the climax of the promotional approach to religious giving. It provided an opportunity for the churches and the bright young professionals to demonstrate what they had learned from the business world. The abysmal failure of the campaign to end all campaigns indicated that they had learned less than they thought or claimed. Or possibly it provided a demonstration that salesmanship and high-pressure promotionalism were not necessarily appropriate for raising the funds required for the benevolent work of the American churches.

The Expanding Superstructure

The zeal for organization and institutionalization displayed in the flowering of mission agencies, and the creation and coordination of allied groups, had its counterpart in the professionalized superstructure of the movement. Bodies were created for consultative and administrative purposes that had no direct contact with either the home constituency or the non-Christian masses abroad. In part this trend reflects changes in the contemporary business community, in part simply a practical response to the problems posed by the physical expansion of foreign mission activity. "The Scriptural idea of missions is first individual," admitted the Reverend J. N. Murdock at the first meeting of what became the Foreign Missions Conference of North America. "But the great need, as I take it, of our modern mission is general organization." What the church cannot accomplish by itself scripturally, argued the American Baptist Missionary Union secretary, can be achieved by these means. For "when you undertake a large business you must have combination, say what you will against overgrown corporations."[105]

The outreach of what was called the foreign mission movement of the Christian churches had consisted in fact of the highly uneven individual efforts of particular churches or groups of enthusiasts. The sending boards had worked in isolation with virtually no auxiliaries to coordinate or assist their approach to separate constituencies. The only regular contact between these uncoordinated cells of the movement occurred on a personal basis—between clergymen or secretaries attending conferences called for other purposes than consideration of their peculiar work, or in the form of correspondence between school friends, or missionaries meeting in the field. To achieve greater cooperation between these organically separate cells, the movement's leaders created first an organization for consultation on the national level, and then the International Missionary Council. It is suggestive that men sharing a common preoccupation with a specialized function of the Protestant churches successfully created such agencies decades before their denominations could agree to form their own consultative councils.[106]

The Foreign Missions Conference of North America was the unexpected result of an interdenominational meeting of foreign board secretaries and officers at New York's Presbyterian Mission House in 1893. British and continental societies had been holding similar sessions regularly for some years. It became an annual conference of the representatives of United States and Canadian boards, although a formal name was not adopted until 1911. The conference reports reflect businesslike meetings, generally devoid of stirring sermons or ringing oratory. Every conceivable practical problem of mission work was treated in a paper or discussion at one point or another, but corporate statements or declarations were made hesitantly, if at all, during the early decades. Samuel Capen recalled in 1913 that most denominations had been reluctant to join and that many of the early discussions were aseptic if not insipid, "there being topics of denominational character which if introduced would have broken up the Conference."[107]

By 1907 the loosely organized and largely informal conference agreed to establish a Committee on Reference and Counsel to arbitrate problems of field comity, negotiate with governments, and provide a single voice for the movement in emergencies. Its powers were jealously restricted, potentially controversial policy questions being declared beyond its scope and any action infringing on the internal administration of any board or society prohibited. Even though its decisions were not binding, it became a respected spokesman for the mission movement between annual conventions.[108] By 1923 this committee had become an incorporated executive body of the conference, holding regular quarterly meetings and served by a permanent staff. The conference had become "the most inclusive organization in Protestantism," embracing denominations that did not cooperate in any other way. Despite the absence of sanctions, Cornelius Patton reported that no board would think of acting independently on any major matter without prior consultation through the conference.[109]

Committees and subcommittees on various geographical fields, governmental relations, missionary training, and other mutual concerns, did most of the work of the FMCNA. Representing a pooling of talents, their reports were the product of specialists whose advice would not have been available to most member societies.

Even before "management" had begun organizing, the missionaries formed an International Missionary Union. Initiated by a returned missionary at a Niagara Falls camp meeting in 1884, the union thereafter held annual conferences at a rural New York sanitarium. The week-long meetings were initially treated as an opportunity for furloughed and retired missionaries to socialize, pray, and exchange experiences. After 1902, however, a formal agenda of addresses and working sessions was introduced, and recent board appointees were sent by the societies to receive special training from the veterans.[110]

Despite the union's cooperation with the boards in the preparation of new missionaries, it never became an official auxiliary of the sending societies or lost its predominantly social atmosphere. Board administrators often addressed and participated in the conferences, but membership was "limited to evangelical Foreign Missionaries who were or had been in active service."[111] No significant interest in developing a professional association or a corporate body that could represent missionary interests to the boards or to the Foreign Missions Conference ever developed in this fellowship. A paid secretariat could not be maintained with the nominal dues collected, so continuity was provided largely through a core of retired missionaries permanently settled in Clifton Springs. Although "international" in name, "natives of foreign fields" were never allowed to attend as guests except by prior arrangement.[112]

A major step toward international cooperation between Protestant mission agencies was the World Missionary Conference held in Edinburgh, Scotland in 1910. The mere fact that some 1200 delegates from every Western sending nation and seven Oriental countries or colonies could come together to discuss the mission of the church instead of the work of the 159 separate societies they represented seemed a providential omen. With new movements springing up, and old ones expanding across the world, the assembly seemed to mark a new day for missions. Here was planning on a grand scale and the public attention that mission leaders had so long sought for their work. Guarded optimism pervaded the sessions. The contemporary claim that there had never "been such a gathering in the history of the Kingdom of God on earth" reflects this sentiment.[113] But even a later and more objective assessment found that Edinburgh "marked the beginning of a new era in world missionary co-operation and thus become a singular event in the life of the whole church—the root-symbol of the Ecumenical Movement in the twentieth century."[114]

What was unique about Edinburgh, beyond its scope and the publicity it received, was the convergence of the enthusiasm of the student Christian movement with the professional interests of missionaries and administrators.[115] The conference featured such prominent laymen as William Jennings Bryan, who participated actively rather than serving as ornaments at an opening ceremony.[116] Professional discussions of missionary topics had been held both in the field, and under the auspices of the Foreign Missions Conference in the United States. But the specialists and professionals had not previously been brought together with the "great missionary demonstrations fitted to inform, educate, and impress" such as the Centenary Mission Conference held in London in 1888, or the New York Ecumenical Missionary Conference of 1900.[117]

As an unprecedented spectacular, the New York conference had been a well-reported success.[118] Its lasting contribution to mission work or the movement's organization, however, could only be traced through individual inspiration or personal contacts made between leaders and spokesmen. The delegates could neither legislate, nor did they establish the executive council that had been recommended since the 1880s. They did, however, become convinced that both the public and the movement would benefit from regular meetings of this sort called at least once each decade. And when the Foreign Missions Conference politely declined the honor of sponsoring the next gathering, British mission leaders began preparations for the Edinburgh spectacular.

Robert E. Speer and John R. Mott were among the organizers of a North American preparatory committee which met with British leaders in 1908 to draft plans for the next convention. Mott was primarily responsible for eliminating the traditional pattern of restricting discussion to the content of formal addresses. He headed one of eight commissions which investigated assigned topics thoroughly, consulted by correspondence with hundreds of experts, and then presented carefully prepared reports to the conference as the basis for further discussion and work in open forums.[119] The result was that, unlike previous meetings which had been oriented toward capturing public attention, and which provided little occasion for serious discussion between addresses, receptions, and sermons, Edinburgh became a working conference.

To this end, the international preparatory committee proscribed all resolutions involving questions of doctrine or church polity, and asked each society to send several of its outstanding missionaries and "if practicable, one or two natives."[120] The word "missionary" in the conference title, of course, had the tacit modifier "foreign." The same orientation is reflected in the curious willingness to hold a "world" conference including only seventeen members of native churches of mission lands, and these not direct representatives but "native" members of society delegations. Even the criterion for assigning credentials emphasized achievement at home rather than in the field, delegates being selected by a formula that recognized the size of the budgets of the sending societies.[121] Perhaps inevitably, given the size and youth of the non-Western churches, these implied and specific restrictions made Edinburgh an assembly of the sending agencies of the West. Here officially designated delegates of recognized societies, selected on a proportional principle, met in a consultative conference to survey the work remaining to be accomplished, and the resources required, to reach an optimistic conclusion.[122]

The results of this strategic survey were published in nine volumes and formed the basis of much additional commentary and planning by individual leaders and agencies during subsequent years. To its contemporaries, Edinburgh 1910, was to missions what the Hague conferences had been to the peace movement: both accomplishment and promise of an imminent successful end. Four years before the Great War, neither group suspected, let alone anticipated, the cataclysm which was soon to make a mockery of peace societies and to dash the dream of the world's evangelization by that generation. In surveying the events of the succeeding decades, John Mott looked back to the 1910 assembly as "the high-water mark of popular missionary interest," partly because the lay leadership of the churches was more widely represented than at any subsequent international missionary meeting.[123]

At the time, however, no decline in popular interest was evident, and some of the conference leaders held high hopes for the Continuation Committee of the World Missionary Conference which the delegates had unanimously ratified in the only official action taken by the conference. Prominent among these leaders was John Mott, whose initiative and preliminary planning, as well as efficient performance as presiding officer of the formal Edinburgh sessions, had brought him into the limelight.[124]

Mott was elected chairman of the forty-member International Continuation Committee, which was intended to continue the more scientific study of missionary questions initiated at the conference, and "to preserve and extend the atmosphere and spirit of the Conference."[125] With characteristic energy, he quickly organized a series of twenty-one conferences of missionaries and native Christian leaders throughout Asia, which he personally attended and directed in order to get grassroots evaluations of methods and plans for an area containing three-quarters of the world's population.

In the aftermath of his 1912–1913 swing through Asia, local organizing committees or national continuation committees were formed, which eventually became the National Christian Councils of China, India, and Japan.[126] Since each of these bodies was organically related to the Continuation Committee, it occupied a unique position in the missionary structure. Instead of forming just another nondenominational independent auxiliary of the churches, such as the Student Volunteer or Laymen's Movements, it provided a channel through which the missionary societies themselves could function jointly and effect policy in the mission field, albeit on a limited basis.[127]

When the war interrupted the work of the committee, the Foreign Missions Conference and its British counterpart established an Emergency Committee of Cooperating Missions. This predominantly Anglo-American body made a gesture in the direction of internationalism by providing for the participation of "each other country, the missionary societies of which would be willing to appoint representatives."[128] Despite the resultant exclusion of societies in the Central Powers, their work in the field was protected with varied success by the Emergency Committee.

The executives of the wartime committees were virtually the same as those in the Edinburgh group; they moved on intact into the 1920 World Missionary Meeting at Crans, where plans were drawn up resulting in the birth of a permanent International Missionary Council at Lake Mohonk, New York, a year later. The new council was based upon national bodies, the Foreign Missions Conference, for example, providing the single delegate apportioned to the United States and Canada. It built up an effective secretariat, continued publication of the quarterly *International Review of Missions,* and appointed an interim Committee of Reference to handle its affairs between sessions.[129]

As a body representing mission boards and seeking to mediate and solve their problems, the International Missionary Council indicates a recession of lay influence. The laymen's auxiliaries had had their day of prominence, and their support would continue to be deemed useful. But the new national and international boards of directors of the mission movement granted them no seats or direct role in the making of policy. Professionals such as John Mott, who had served as chairman of all three post-Edinburgh commit-tees, or J. H. Oldham who had served each as official secretary, thus took over the direction of an international coordinating and policy-making council of the mission movement which had orig-inated in the 1910 conference they had helped to shape in a new direction.

In addition to achieving a new level of supradenominational professional bureaucratization, the international missionary leader-ship began the adjustment to new developments in the mission field. In 1910, less than a score of representatives of the non-Christian world had been allowed to sit in on a meeting of over 1000 Western delegates. At the enlarged International Missionary Council meeting in Jerusalem in 1928, nearly half the delegates were what was now called "nationals" from the younger churches in the mission fields of the Western societies.[130] The International Council thus represents a unique development in the mission move-ment which both expressed and helped transform the nature of Protestant missions. It provided a workable means for Protestant mission cooperation, particularly in such areas as preventing the collapse of European mission establishments during the two world wars. At the same time it gave recognition to the developing churches of former mission areas, and helped to coordinate their efforts through a network of National Christian Councils.[131]

Before 1920 the terminology of missions reflected a concep-tion of Christian expansion by conquest. Both the fact that Chris-tian nations could engage in the mutual butchery of the greatest war the world had seen, and the self-conscious growth of national churches in mission lands, forced reappraisal and accommodation during succeeding decades. Mission leaders had equated conquest with unity, only to be forced by the success of their efforts to grant a voice to mission stations that had become churches.[132] Both recognition of this fact and significant cooperation occurred earlier in the field than in the churches at home. Similarly, the movement's agencies were pressed by secular hostility and a sober reappraisal of their resources to cooperate more extensively than they had in the past.

The organizational changes that occurred in the mission movement in the decades before World War I were less a response to
theory or theology than a pragmatic reaction to necessity. There
was no new theological imperative pressing toward an ecumenical
ideal and the lowering of denominational barriers to cooperation.
But the exigencies of meeting a common foe and raising sufficient
support did dictate such cooperation and the increasing employment of inter- or nondenominational agencies. The Laymen's Missionary and the Student Volunteer Movements, the Foreign Missions Conference, and the World Missionary Council reflect prag-
matism more than an ideal, although it would be fatuous to deny
the coexistence of both a dream and pedestrian necessity. The
proliferation of agencies and auxiliaries, coordinated by both
formal and informal means, had created a stronger and more effectively organized Protestant mission movement during the decades
before World War I than during any previous period in the movement's history.

There were indications, however, that one former element of
strength had been lost in the process of organizing the movement.
The dynamism of a spontaneous movement based on religious conviction and compassion for non-Christians who were eternally
damned had become imprisoned by the last quarter of the nineteenth century in denominational agencies paying perfunctory
obeisance to the old spirit. Stirred by the idealism and enthusiasm
of youth, an effort was made during subsequent decades to transcend bureaucratic and creedal restraints and to relaunch a true
movement. Instead the existing agencies absorbed the dynamism
to become bigger and more powerful, while an interdenominational
superstructure developed that became equally bureaucratized and
antithetical to the unrestrained and uncalculating enthusiasm that
characterized a true movement. When promotionalism no longer
sufficed, and an economic depression forced retrenchment, the
young people required to work another renaissance were busy with
other causes.

Chapter 2

SUPPORTERS AND STAFF: THOSE WHO STAYED HOME

I'll go where you want me to go, dear Lord
Over mountain, or vale, or sea,
And I'll stay where you want me to stay, dear Lord,
You can always depend on me.

I. T. Headland, variant of "I'll go"

In 1916 a small executive committee elected by the twenty-eight member Board of Managers of the American Baptist Foreign Mission Society arranged the distribution of $1,364,268 to the 127 mission stations and dozens of related schools and hospitals maintained by the society. The travel, supplies, and salaries of 712 missionaries in every part of the world had to be supervised, and indirect administration exercised over 6054 native laborers and 2841 churches in the field. A similar committee, aided by a small staff, paid the 1276 missionaries and 5863 native workers of the Northern Presbyterian Church their share of the Board's $2,262,061 income, and allocated the remainder to some 163 principal stations, 1678 outstations and their attached medical and educational facilities. The twelve-member Prudential Committee of the American Board disposed of $1,207,126 to 664 missionaries and 4877 natives assigned to 106 stations and 1461 outstations.[1] In addition to stewardship for funds collected, the boards, committees, and secretaries of some thirty major American foreign mission agencies were concerned with planning for the future, maintaining general support, and raising over $19,000,000 for the next year's work.

Clearly, therefore, by World War I missions had become a unique form of big business. The administration and supervision of such large-scale philanthropic enterprises on an international basis could no longer be entrusted to clerks and retired clergymen. The secretariats of individual societies continued to consist largely of such men, but they were joined by educational, business, and promotional specialists, and drew a larger number of laymen from business and professional circles to serve on their agencies' governing boards. The traditional mission-board functionary also tended to be excluded from the new interdenominational and international service organizations and auxiliaries of the movement, and to be replaced in the public eye by dynamic missionary statesmen acting as spokesmen for the entire movement.

Both the expansion of the movement and bureaucratic specialization within its agencies thus created a perennial personnel problem which forced a reassessment of the traditionally restricted use made of laymen. Mere willingness to increase the number of laymen serving on boards or employed in responsible positions in the home offices was not enough in what turned out to be a highly competitive quest for their services. The expansion of the social and philanthropic work of the churches had created similar staff problems for other evangelical agencies. Meanwhile thousands of new white-collar jobs were provided by the rapid growth of business and governmental bureaucracies. Both professional and avocational mission agency personnel thus had to be recruited from the same pool of educated Protestants from which these competitors, as well as various progressive reform groups, were already drawing. Under the circumstances, the ability to attract the caliber of personnel that directed the movement's unprecedented expansion at the turn of the century was both crucial and surprising.

The mission boards achieved their objective in part through effective publicity that changed the traditional image of the foreign cause, and in part because many laymen at the turn of the century were not waiting to be invited into participation in church service. Theodore Munger described a new spirit as the result of which the American churches were graduating from mere awareness of their social obligations to action, and usually at the instigation of young Christians rather than the clergy. "There is thus coming about what has been called the 'Priesthood of the People,' who are returning to the primitive idea of religion, and are taking the work of the Church into their own hands," he wrote, "and—for the most part—are dealing with it in wise ways."[2] This activist spirit was not only reshaping the church, but making the claim of a Christian America more credible, and it led the young into both domestic and international reform movements.

The Christian Laymen

Since foreign missions remained the preoccupation of a minority of even Protestant church members, the laymen willing to serve these specialized voluntary agencies were a select group with peculiar characteristics. Whether professionals who eschewed more prestigious opportunities in denominational affairs, or unpaid board trustees who made an equally conscious decision to ignore fresh air funds or the National Municipal League to concentrate their spare time and money on foreign missions, they opted out of the normal patterns of their peers. What they shared with them was membership in the confident and self-conscious one-third of the American population in 1900 who were formally affiliated with the Protestant churches. Although the unchurched and even non-Christian majority might outnumber them, they were certain, as a popular mission lecturer asserted in 1912, that their "thirty-three millions, most of them women and children, control the sentiment of the United States and make it a Christian country."[3] Being identified as a member of this Protestant minority scarcely distinguished the reformer from the conservative, or the businessman from the mission board or YMCA secretary. It did, however, identify a group of men who, regardless of their professions, organizational affiliations or special interests, confidently applied moral and evangelical standards to public life and social issues in a manner that would strike the current generation as both quaint and impolitic. Whatever its theological deficiencies, the New Theology fit their times, explained surviving problems, and provided the dynamic for a mild revolution.

The reserve corps of supportive laymen included some to whom religious activism was more a matter of tradition or noblesse oblige than of a newfound activist spirit.[4] As a group such men were more likely to contribute their money than their time. Some, however, in an effort to add meaning to life, reinforced tradition with personal conviction and made a more considerable contribution. John D. Rockefeller Jr.'s deep interest in foreign missions and the ecumenical movement, for example, seems to have been based in part on the desire to participate in a historic reshaping of society. "I see the church moulding the thought of the world as it has never done before," he wrote in 1918, "leading in all great movements as it should, I see it literally establishing the Kingdom of God on earth."[5] To a sincerely religious young man trained in the art of philanthropic giving by the former Baptist minister Frederick T. Gates,[6] the scope and potential of an international movement seemed to capture the imagination more than prosaic charity, even of the scale practiced by his father.

In a period when public figures had not yet acquired their modern reluctance to be closely identified with particular denominations or to promote the work of Christian evangelization, politicians with an evangelical background could also be expected to lend their support with little regard for political distinctions.[7] Theodore Roosevelt, at whose death America "lost her most powerful lay-preacher,"[8] agreed to serve as an official delegate to the Edinburgh World Missionary Conference until pressing obligations at home forced his reluctant resignation. His political opponent, William Jennings Bryan, both wrote and spoke in favor of the work and, according to Frederic C. Howe, declared that, if he were only young enough to begin a new career, he would choose to dedicate his life to foreign missions.[9] And Alfred T. Mahan, "than whom there is not in the country a man whom we can more appropriately designate by the fine and high phrase, 'a Christian gentleman,' "[10] served on the Board of Managers of the Episcopalian mission society and later on the General Committee of the Laymen's Missionary Movement.

But supportive statements and honorary committee memberships did not solve the movement's personnel problems, nor did such old-line evangelicals represent the new laymen who volunteered for more active service. The new breed tended to be younger, and to become involved in church service earlier in their careers. They were the product of easier access to higher education, and of the local church clubs, leagues, and associations which had taught them the duty of providing leadership in such organizations in order to make similar opportunities available to a larger proportion of the next generation.

As the progressive movement was characterized in part by an unprecedented influx of interested and well-meaning amateurs into areas previously monopolized by professionals, so in a period of declining clerical influence practical young laymen moved into leadership positions in Bible leagues and Sunday schools, home and foreign mission groups, YMCAs, Epworth League, Christian Endeavor Society, and a host of others.[11] They were not unduly loyal to specific institutionalized forms of Christian duty, and less interested in respecting denominational lines than the venerable placemen they began to shoulder aside.[12] Impatient and confident, they took their religious commitments for granted and concentrated on progress made synonymous with growth. In their emphasis on methods, they most often took the business community as their model. "We are in a period where capable businessmen are preferred in movements of this kind," wrote Minneapolis Mayor David P. Jones to the American Board's president. "Confidence is inspired where businessmen are taking hold of the work of missions and other religious lines."[13]

The laymen tended to be conservative in politics, a characteristic of which they gave oblique evidence by affiliating themselves with traditional evangelical endeavors such as missions, rather than joining equally moralistic Christian gentlemen in the progressive movement. An at once more subtle and basic distinction than that provided by vague political categories, however, separated the two types of activists. Daniel Aaron sketched the composite progressive as a man "who combined a zeal for service with a curiosity for facts, who worked for the gradual displacement of the obsolete by the new, who understood the relationship between human conduct and unjust economic conditions, [and] who believed in 'purposeful change.' "[14]

The lay officers, trustees and directors of mission societies shared this outlook, but not the proposed means of achieving the objectives. They identified many of the same dangers and social ills as the progressives, and were just as moved by humane compassion for the underprivileged. They also advocated a scientific approach, and purposeful, not radical, change. But the evangelicals were not interested in political solutions. Salvation, not politics, presented the best hope for a cure in their eyes. And, despite increasing social awareness in certain quarters of American Protestantism, salvation was still largely viewed as an individualistic process. Personal commitment or conversion to traditional Christian values by a majority would thus eliminate the problems that had resulted from national material progress outstripping spiritual advance. This did not preclude some participation in social, economic, or political reform, but it also did not admit any of these approaches to be of primary importance or sufficient by themselves.

Christian reformers had earned nothing but opposition for their efforts in the past, declared Samuel Capen the year before his election as president of the Congregational Sunday School and Publishing Society. "They found that it was regeneration, not reformation the people needed, regeneration included reformation, reformation was a failure without regeneration."[15] Similarly, Capen's biographer Chauncy J. Hawkins, pointed out in 1914, that, while the "fight for social righteousness has never enlisted so many brave hearts nor been so intense as at the present hour . . . , yet in spite of this fact, it is also probably true that there were never more men living on the outside of things than at the present hour." Faith in the dollar, materialism, and distrust of ideas reigned supreme because of a positive belief "that the teachings of Jesus are impossible for practical use in the realm of affairs."[16] Political action or the social sciences could not prevail against problems that could be overcome only by applying the gospel. Surrender to God's will counted more than planning or organization.

The general distinction between these points of view is illustrated in the lives of two men born during the Civil War decade, both concerned with reform during part of their careers. Municipal reformer Frederic C. Howe moved from a small Pennsylvania town where only Methodists and Republicans were granted respectability to a denominational college staffed largely by retired missionaries and ministers. At Allegheny College he absorbed the evangelistic "morality of duty, of careful respectability," and little else.[17] Together with classmates preparing for some phase of ministerial service, Howe "felt a sense of responsibility to the world. I wanted to change things." Unlike them, however, he was unsure of how to proceed. "It had to do with politics. Also with economics," he recalled. "My mind found new authorities," he wrote of the graduate school experience when the crucial change occurred. "They were intellectual rather than moral, social rather than personal."[18]

Even after receiving a federal appointment, Howe continued to identify with the idealistic young liberals and reformers who wanted to go beyond the New Freedom or New Nationalism. These were the very people Chauncy Hawkins had condemned for their preoccupation with the material world—for "living on the outside of things." Ironically men like the Reverend Mr. Hawkins could not see that the nonevangelical reformers were attacking the same foe. "I was part of this liberal movement," wrote Howe of the outsiders. "To me it was a renaissance of America rising from the orgy of commercialism."[19]

Just as disillusioned with commercialism was Henry W. Frost, who helped establish and became the director of the North American Branch of the China Inland Mission. A reform-minded businessman coming from a comfortable urban middle-class background, he found his life empty until he was converted to orthodox evangelical service. "I was in politics in those days," he wrote about the 1880s, "and intent upon reforming the United States, if not the world." After hearing a fiery evangelist preach, however, it became plain to him "that reform activity would never satisfy my soul." Subsequently "I renounced politics and gave myself to the furtherance of those things which would make for the salvation of men and the coming of Christ as earth's Lord and King."[20]

For the first time in a comfortable and economically successful life, Frost seems to have felt personal fulfillment when faced with a handful of converts after a summer's adventure as a lay preacher in an upstate New York village. "I drank at that moment the sweet nectar of soulwinning," wrote the Princeton-educated mill owner. "Henceforth, I would give myself to God, as I might find it possible, to bring precious souls and lives to Him."[21] Because his convictions were not supplemented by formal training, Frost was refused appointment as a missionary, and made his considerable contribution to the foreign mission cause as a lay volunteer.

The ability of the movement to attract sufficient laymen depended on its success in publicizing the unique aspects of the foreign mission enterprise. In making their appeal to the public, mission publicists placed less emphasis on traditional evangelical or humanitarian considerations than on secular themes. Patriotism and the ability to influence world history and policy making were offered to the small-town businessman willing to serve on mission committees. Just as Richard Hofstadter found the expansionist leaders of the 1890s disillusioned with reform, and eager to discover a larger, more statesmanlike, less restraining theater of action than domestic politics, so the mission leaders offered an opportunity to magnify influence on a broader horizon.[22] Addressing a commission of the Men and Religion Forward Movement in 1912, Samuel Capen declared that the most crucial problem was to present men with an ideal in life that was worthy of their manhood. The missionary purpose met the requirement best, he argued, for "the greatest power in the world today is the missionary. It is not commerce or diplomacy that is changing the world but the men who are preaching the gospel."[23]

The petty wars and diplomatic crises of the pre-World War decade led to more frequent assertions that the United States must bring her moral weight to bear in international relations. "The American type, the democratic type must be conserved not only for the type's sake, but for the whole world's sake," a Philadelphia newsman told a laymen's mission convention in 1913.[24] This theme was more stridently repeated once the European powers proved their moral weakness and need of guidance by blundering into a world war. For now the American churches could not only help guide them back to peace, but could also assume the duties the Europeans were forced to drop. "There is wider opportunity today than ever before for an ordinary life to touch world issues," a mission magazine editorialized in 1917. "Big things are not restricted to big men." Although the temperance, ecumenical, and peace movements all touched intimately upon world affairs, Christian missions provided the broadest avenue of influence. To be part of the recreation of one catholic church, to help shape the emerging nations of the Orient, this was the way to help make history as part of the world forces of organized Christianity. "Being small in these great days, letting the great movements go on without one's life, while one settles back into petty ways and parochial concerns," the appeal concluded, "is an offense for which excuse will be hard to find. At this time men should ask if their lives are helping to make a better world."[25]

The technique of clothing Christian service in dramatic dress to attract laymen who were discontent with ordinary lives provides additional insight into the motivation of the thousands who responded. Both mission societies and other evangelical reform agencies had in the past been criticized as the preserves of an elite at least partially engaged in serving their own ends. In trying to attract more personnel, they also provided access to social respectability if not membership in the elite. It would be difficult to prove that social climbing was the conscious motive of the average layman enrolled in the movement's work, but the opportunities were certainly made obvious.

Samuel Capen's ancestry, for example, was proper enough to allow his election to the Society of Mayflower Descendants and the Sons of the Revolution later in his life. Yet as the sickly son of a grocery clerk who had to make sacrifices even to allow his son to finish high school, young Capen showed little promise of joining his genealogical peers in Boston society. He dreamed of college and theological school, but was forced instead to clerk in a small Boston carpet store. At the age of twenty-two he was taken into partnership, and had reached a plateau in his business career above which he never rose. The people who counted in Boston society he saw only as customers until his service in local and denominational philanthropic agencies won their respect and an opportunity to sit at the same table with them. Later he was to be received in the White House by President Roosevelt, and to preside over several national conferences. His correspondents included Theodore Roosevelt, William Howard Taft, Henry Cabot Lodge, Charles Evans Hughes, Alfred Thayer Mahan, James Bryce, and other prominent contemporaries. In mission circles his acquaintanceship and renown were international. Although there is no evidence that Capen chose his service avocations in a conscious search for status, it must have provided some satisfaction to a grocery clerk's son who never rose above the economic level of a small businessman to be told by the Secretary of State of his gratification at having "won the confidence and approval of men like you."[26]

A similar effect operated among the clergy as a career in mission organizations took on some of the attractions of an elite service. Unless he was active during a period of reform agitation, the home-mission functionary was unlikely to meet people in public life or to receive general recognition for his work. At a distance, foreign evangelization seemed a less mundane business than dealing with immigrants, dirty reservation Indians, or even a normal country parish, particularly when serving as administrator or board spokesman in an Eastern city. Mission board secretaries like Arthur Judson Brown, who did not leave pastoral work to join the Presbyterian Board until he was in his forties, found themselves consulted by presidents, decorated by foreign governments, and widely acclaimed as statesmen of the missionary and peace movements.[27] James Bashford, a little-known Methodist clergyman whose career had apparently reached its high point in the presidency of a small denominational college, accepted the position of missionary bishop in China against friendly advice. Through the many books he wrote to report on his work in East Asia, Bashford was thrust on a much larger stage than offered by Ohio Wesleyan, allowing his biographer to write that it was only the last years of his long career that transformed the former pastor and educator into a world figure.[28] The promise of prestige was not the motive that drew such men from

pastoral work to the foreign mission movement, but one wonders
how their biographies would affect a young seminarian with un-
formed career plans.

The laymen who entered the service of their churches after
1900, then, were similar in background and outlook to the average
progressive. The primary distinction was that religion remained
central to their activism. They remained closer to the evangelical
tradition and were more apt to seek change through existing church
agencies. Beyond this difference, there is no justification for a clearcut distinction between conservative, liberal, and radical among
the men expressing either the domestic or foreign concern of the
American Protestant churches. Neither party allegiances nor mere
reactionary dissent distinguished these men, but individual interpretations of the duties prescribed by applying a common gospel
to the secular world. The more orthodox evangelicals may recall
the apparently hypocritical pomposity of early nineteenth-century
"trustees of the Lord" who also feared change and bewailed religious
decline amidst increasing secularization.[29] But if the socially concerned churchman of 1900 saw himself as a trustee of his nation's
heritage, so did the expansionist, the progressive, and the populist.

Trustees, Directors, and Benefactors

The administrative structure of an American university provides the closest analogy to the functional division of the laymen
who joined the home base of the expanding foreign mission movement. The careerists became either minor bureaucrats comparable
to department chairmen or assistant deans, or as spokesmen and
policy makers filled positions resembling those of college presidents, vice presidents, and deans. Meanwhile, established business
and professional men were recruited as trustees invited to engage
in long range planning and fund raising. Typically, the trustees
found their services most appreciated when they concentrated on
producing money, and left administration and policy to the professionals. And here the analogy loses its usefulness, because many
of the new board advisers were successful businessmen who
would not concede that the professional secretaries were superior

to them in either evangelical fervor or administrative expertise.

The largely successful campaign to dispel the traditional prejudice that foreign missions were the special concern of ladies' circles and idealistic youth, which culminated in the organization of the Laymen's Missionary Movement in 1907, thus produced a mixed blessing. The ambivalent reaction and motives were reflected in the debt-ridden American Board's selection of a Boston merchant as its new president in 1899. Denominational college presidents and clergymen, particularly Middle Westerners who might help broaden the board's geographical base, had dominated the list of nominees. The board's executives were also reminded that, since the incumbent vice-president was a layman, it would be unwise to exclude the ministry from both top offices.[30]

Samuel B. Capen, a partner in a Boston carpet store, was nevertheless elected. For seven years he participated vigorously in the board's management, ignoring both the tradition and the op- portunity of acting as an honorific figurehead invited by the regular staff to address and preside over occasional meetings. Then, in- fluenced in part by continued disgruntlement in traditionalist quarters of the board's constituency, Capen polled the most con- sistent ABCFM supporters prior to announcing his intended retire- ment. Without exception the surviving responses urged Capen to remain in office. Since not a single valid criticism of his administra- tion had been put forward, his correspondents agreed, it was simply his status as a layman that continued to perturb the old guard.[31]

The response of a Congregational pastor from Brooklyn sum- marized the attitude that led to major changes in the leadership of the foreign mission movement:

> The change in the economics of the Board as a practical organization, which warranted and called for the substitu- tion of a layman for a clergyman as its President, was in response to the changed aspects of Christian enterprise in our era, giving to such enterprise a more businesslike and less purely ecclesiastical character. . . . There has been no reversal in this current of affairs, no going backward to what was

characteristic of a former era. On the contrary, every argument for expert, practical handling, which existed when you took the helm, exists today with increased force.[32]

With this mandate Capen not only retained the presidency until his death in 1914, but proceeded the year after the poll to organize and assume the chairmanship of the national Laymen's Movement which was the most dramatic manifestation of the new trend.

A sketch of Capen's service career provides the simplest summary of the motives and preconceptions of his fellow mission society trustees. To the executive committee of his own society, he was "the personification of all that the board stood for at home and abroad."[33] To a prominent New York lawyer, Capen "represented perhaps the ideal of the business man, the Christian business man."[34] As sketched by Francis Peabody, that ideal was a man "not hard in business and soft in charity, but of one fibre throughout. His business is a part of his religion, and his philanthropy is a part of his business."[35]

His religion was also part of his politics in a fashion that at first glance made him indistinguishable from the average progressive.[36] Only a persistent uneasiness bordering on fear of change separated those who finally ventured out of the evangelical tradition to join the more worldly progressives from those like Capen who made their peace with the world and their Christian consciences within the faith in which they had been reared. Capen's entry into state politics, for example, followed his discovery "that Massachusetts is not in the character of its population what it once was." To guard that character he advocated prohibition of alcoholic beverages by constitutional amendment, for "statutory law which may be changed by another Legislature does not give that permanence which should prevail in moral questions."[37]

His policies as president of the Boston School Board were guided by the belief that the chief aim of education was not the acquisition of knowledge so much as the formation of good character under the power of uplifting personalities.[38] Protective character building motivated his participation in efforts to

Americanize Boston's immigrant population as well. "We must either lift them up," Capen warned, "or they will drag us down."[39] His sense of morality overrode both practicality and sympathy in his political outlook. At Capen's memorial service, George S. Smith revealed that the deceased had often taken himself into the city slums from which so many public administrators had come. "He put himself in their environment and tried to picture their deprivation and the influences that they were surrounded by from childhood," Smith reported, "and he came to recognize that their moral standard was lower than our moral standard."[40] The amazing condescension of this discovery neatly disposed of the political opposition's point of view, and would seem to make a reform of living conditions unnecessary.

The Boston merchant's interest in political reform was largely a reaction to dangers posed by corrupt and demagogic politicians, ignorant immigrants, or unsound economic policies. The program developed in response was not derived from any political theorist or party platform, and consisted simply of exerting undefined Christian influences and establishing a reign of civic righteousness. When Capen subsequently identified the danger posed to his country by a hostile non-Christian world, he was drawn into the foreign mission movement in a similar response. "The East and West are touching each other politically, commercially, and socially as never before," he pointed out in 1909. "There is a new peril in all this unless the whole world shall quickly learn the Fatherhood of God as revealed in the face of Jesus Christ." Again the cure was spiritual or religious, although the threat was identified as " 'the chance of a dreadful future clash between two radically different and hostile civilizations.' "[41]

In meeting his civic duties, a spiritual diagnosis of society's disease had not kept Samuel Capen from political activities. Similarly, although the threat to peace and order presented by anarchic international relations primarily required broadcasting the gospel, it also drew the American Board's lay president into the peace movement. He was an active trustee of the World Peace Foundation at his death, and earlier had been one of the few businessmen who responded to an invitation to the original Lake Mohonk Conference. He remained an active participant and a firm partisan of international arbitration, but his primary concern was stability and security for his homeland. "We need courts of arbitration and of world peace to save the nations in the social revolution that is going on," he declared in 1912.[42] And ten years before World War I he pointed out that technology had shrunk the globe and given portentous meaning to the oneness of the world. "We need to save the world in order to save America spiritually," he declared, again revealing his priorities.[43] He made the connection between the peace and foreign mission movements in a curiously militant way. "In its spirit of conquest and in the courage and sacrifice it calls forth," the mission movement was the long sought moral equivalent to war.[44]

To claim that Samuel Capen's entire service career can be explained in terms of conscious reactions to clearly identified dangers of social or cultural conflicts would be an obvious oversimplification. In his own mind, his civic and philanthropic work constituted an interrelated unit based on the immutable principles of his faith. But he belonged to a generation so confident that it possessed the true religion and the blessings of providence that its members were more likely to verbalize threats than to fear them. A sense of *noblesse oblige* motivated efforts to eliminate the remaining flaws in their civilization.

A similar confidence underlay their mission campaign, however much they might speak of launching a revolution. Their interest in the non-Western world was not founded on a desire for revolutionary reform as much as a mellow self-satisfaction tempered by a sense of duty. The motive was not primarily a reaction to fears of rising heathen powers or unresolved international problems, but the assumption that all others must wish to be recast in the mission-sponsor's mold. After Samuel Capen's death, the Reverend Edward Lincoln Smith noted this aspect of his world view and identified it as the patriotic motive that had held a central place in his mission activity. "In vision, he saw American missionaries going to every people on the earth with open Bible," he wrote of the American Board head, "with school, college and hospital teaching them to speak one language, to read one literature, to think the same thoughts and to be moved by the same motives." As the result of this unlikely cultural homogenization, the human race was to be finally unified.[45]

If Samuel Capen gave more of himself to a wider array of causes than the average lay volunteer, he nevertheless typified the outlook of the Christian laymen dedicated to reform and adjustment to a changing world, yet unwilling to join the progressive movements in either American Protestantism or politics. To understand the contradictions between liberal and conservative in the careers of these Christian gentlemen, it is necessary to distinguish between objective and means. Capen retained the values and faith of his fathers, without question, until some tenet proved ineffectual in meeting a worldly problem identified by his Christian consciousness. His religious beliefs reflected the distinction between the traditional Hopkinsian theology and progressive orthodoxy or the Andover theology.[46] Instead of accepting such labels or positively embracing a new theology, however, he merely modified the old by reluctantly retreating from positions that reason made untenable.

What did not change was the objective of Christianizing America and the world, of making a personal contribution to the coming Kingdom. Capen's religiously motivated sense of social responsibility led him on a pilgrimage from civic to international concern. During this journey he constantly sought to recruit new men for the church's work and to have them share his sense of duty. He took for granted that, no matter what a man's profession, if he was Protestant he must feel the same call that led him to dabble at politics and reform, and to accept office in home and foreign mission groups. Even though it required much organized prodding, the fact that so many laymen responded indicates that his assumption was accurate.

The movement for a more vigorous participation of laymen in the work of the churches drew volunteers from all classes. Although national in scope, its most conspicuous examples and the bulk of the leadership were centered in eastern urban areas. Deno-

minational leaders were aware that some of the most successful
applications of the organizational techniques developed by the
Laymen's Movement to enlist males in active Christian work were
made in rural areas. The headquarters of these bodies and of most
of the major denominations, however, were in the eastern cities.
In the same area also was a far greater concentration of the
nation's wealth, which it was hoped the laymen would bring into
service with them. The result was the creation of an apparent
eastern establishment which had no relation whatever to the
superior piety or dedication to philanthropy of the region. A
number of boards recognized this tradition as a handicap to
enlarging their western and southern constituency. Their reaction,
however, consisted largely of the judicious selection of a few
western leaders to their governing boards, or the recruitment of
promising young men into the New York or Boston office.

Any detailed biographical survey of mission supporters is
made difficult by the regional divisions in American Protestantism
and the differences in social composition of denominations which
vary widely in the emphasis they place on foreign missions. Since
the inderdenominational Laymen's Movement both operated on a
national basis and incorporated the select minority of Protestant
laymen who considered overseas evangelization the most important
activity of their churches, a survey of its unpaid committee members provides the best means of characterizing the early twentieth-
century lay supporters of foreign missions. The typical committee
member of the Laymen's Movement during its thirteen years of
national activity before 1919 was a self-employed business or
professional man near the end of his career. Half of them had
received a college education, most of them were active in other
religious activities, the overwhelming majority were Republicans
in politics. Presbyterians dominated the denominational representation, New York the geographical base.

Most of them lived in the metropolitan areas of the Middle
Atlantic states, a lesser number in New England or middle western
cities. The south and west were proportionately underrepresented.
Although they were part of a group of successful and relatively

wealthy men, none seem to have been millionaires, and most had won their own modest fortunes rather than inheriting them. Although a minority claimed genealogical connections with the early settlers, the bulk of these men seem to have come from families of moderate means and no particular social standing.

As a group, they were more representative of the native-born, socially conservative *nouveaux riches,* than of any social or political aristocracy that had inherited a common tradition of trusteeship. The single common factor that united a Seattle lawyer with a British-born Chicago banker was the primary role that religion played in their lives. Whether Calvinist, catholic, or liturgical in background; banker, lawyer or railroad treasurer by profession, they felt a common drive to express religious commitment actively in the work of their churches or of broader interdenominational bodies. Whatever motive brought a particular individual to feel most strongly a sense of Christian duty, that incentive was also the most important determinant of a special commitment to foreign missions.[47]

The Missionary Statesmen

The influx of laymen into positions that had traditionally been the preserve of the clergy, and the development of new organizations depending on mass support, led to the emergence of a new type of hero in missionary propaganda intended for the American audience. Unlike the nineteenth-century literature in which the pioneer or martyred missionary held the spotlight, a handful of home board administrators, promoters, and organizers became the central figures in the movement's propaganda. Missionary statesmen such as John R. Mott or Robert E. Speer, whose overseas service at most consisted of an occasional tour, were decorated by foreign governments and accepted by the public as spokesmen for entire denominations or for newly created national organizations. The new missionary statesmen were predominantly laymen, but neither women nor the Christian gentlemen who served as trustees and committee members were eligible for this level of service.[48]

To a Capen or a Mahan involvement in the foreign mission

movement remained an avocation. They were part-time functionaries whose contributions and influence were channeled by the
equally businesslike professional secretaries who, after the turn of
the century, increasingly replaced the clergy in the administrative
positions of religious societies. In outlook, motivation, and background, these professionals resembled the part-time laymen more
than the missionaries they sent to the field. Their compulsion to
serve had been strong enough to turn them from other professions
at a time when career decisions were being made. And it was the
timing of this imperative, not ambition or ability, that distinguished
them from the Christian gentlemen who achieved financial security
first, and only then cast about for a service avocation.

John R. Mott, for example, rejected opportunities for both
political and business careers to become this century's most
prominent missionary statesman. His organizational abilities, personal persuasiveness, energy, and fund-raising genius would certainly
have guaranteed him a successful business career. It may be fatuous
to speculate about his political potential, but his Midwestern background was similar to that of William Jennings Bryan. Both attended
small denominational colleges intending to prepare for the law. If
Bryan was the better orator, Mott could claim intellectual superiority. Bryan made political capital by aspiring to play the role of a
Christian statesman. The positions he later held in the Presbyterian
Church, and the regret he expressed at having missed a life of missionary service, provide tantalizing material for speculations concerning life decisions.

John Mott had been trained for a similar vocation. Only at
the end of his college years did he decide not to follow the path to
a political career which his father had outlined in consultation with
Iowa's Governor William Larrabee.[49] Yet this decision was made at
Cornell, after he had left Upper Iowa University because that
"college became too religious for me, so much so that I decided to
go to another to get away from religious impressions."[50]

His subsequent career decisions reflect less a conscious choice
between alternatives than a somewhat reluctant drift into student
religious and YMCA work following the inspirational experience of

hearing a British evangelist at Cornell, reinforced by attending a series of Dwight L. Moody's Northfield conferences. Mott's evangelical work, his pioneering achievements with the International Committee of the YMCA, chairmanship of the Student Volunteer Movement and World's Student Christian Federation, capped by the Nobel Peace Prize and election as Honorary President of the World Council of Churches—all this was the work of a dedicated layman. Mott never felt compelled to find the time to follow a theological course or to seek ordination. This was characteristic of other important mission leaders of the period.

George Sherwood Eddy, another middle westerner who followed Mott's trail through Northfield and YMCA service before becoming a missionary in India, refused ordination by choice. "Although I had received a full theological training," he recalled, "I wanted to work as a layman in the broad Christian movements that brought me in contact with men of all religions rather than to be confined to a particular denomination."[51] His interests and ambitions also chafed at confinement to a mission station in India. Education, the fight for social justice in the United States, and publication of over thirty books occupied the long and useful life of this world citizen from Kansas. His younger brother, Brewer, served the mission cause as one of the most effective fund raisers in the history of the American Board.

Robert E. Speer's career provides another example of the idealistic layman who dedicated his life to a mission movement conceived in the broadest terms. Like Mott, he intended to go into law after college.[52] Like Sherwood Eddy he attended Princeton Theological Seminary without ever finishing his course or being ordained into the ministry. Although serving a number of interdenominational organizations such as the Student Volunteer and Laymen's Movements, the YMCA and Foreign Missions Conference of North America, his primary affiliation was with the Presbyterian Board of Foreign Missions. A secretary of this board for forty-six years, he found time to write or edit nearly seventy books, serve as moderator of the Presbyterian Church in the U.S.A., and president of the Federal Council of Churches in North America.

After sharing more than three decades of service with him on the Presbyterian Board, Arthur Judson Brown recalled that of all the public figures he had encountered during his career he counted Speer "one of the greatest men that I knew, surely a prophet of God."[53] Many others have testified to the inspirational influence and dominant role played by this Pennsylvania layman in the foreign mission movement during the first half of the twentieth century.[54]

In career mission leaders such as Mott, Speer, and Eddy, the line between layman and clergyman tended to become a technicality. Yet their prominence in the twentieth-century mission movement reflected the changes taking place after the 1880s. Among the many capable clergymen who continued to serve the movement, there was not one who achieved their general renown. Their influence was restricted to no particular denomination. Their concept of missions was a catholic one which tended to make that term practically synonymous with the church's work on earth. They saw themselves as Christian statesmen who could rise above political, sectarian, or even national ties. In technique and theology, they displayed the same disregard for divisions and categories. Although fundamentalist critics labeled them as liberals or religious eclectics and relativists, they were most concerned with accomplishments and with awakening in the American churches the same broad concern for mankind that their conscience had created in them.

The rural background of a surprising number of mission leaders seemed to have relatively little bearing on their general outlook or success. Mott, Eddy, and Bashford grew up on the waning agricultural frontier to become spokesmen of the movement in a period of rapid urbanization, industrialization, and increasing American involvement in world affairs. It would seem more logical for a New Yorker or Bostonian to direct the complex business and international affairs of missions than for a young man from Ft. Leavenworth or Postville, Iowa, to bridge the gap between two worlds. But those who survived the sifting process of religious service careers were the most flexible, and even in maturity the readiest students. Their colleagues who held too rigidly to the old values either failed or gained no prominence except with a minority of conservative followers in the denominations. Those who were too modern or liberal lost the confidence of their constituencies and were either denied responsible positions or had to leave the established societies to found their own leagues or organizations.

The men who succeeded in the established mission organizations often possessed exceptional intellectual curiosity but restrained their interest when it came to embracing a particular doctrinal point of view. Following a career in an area where only theological unsoundness constituted an insurmountable handicap, they were quick to adjust and keep abreast of change because they were preoccupied with their work, not with dogma. Combined with these assets was a driving ambition, tempered but not eliminated by a Christian conscience. As long as the stamp of Christian service could be used to sanctify ambition's proddings to achieve great things and act on a worldwide scale, these men tended to be blind to its existence. They were disturbed when they caught occasional glimpses of this drive and periodically, almost ritually, refused offers of advancement in other fields. Mott and Bashford, for example, both rejected White House offers of ambassadorships as well as prestigious college presidencies and high denominational offices. This self-denial helps to define the peculiar nature of their ambition. It does not prove, as many of their contemporaries maintained, that they were devoid of ambition merely because they persisted in following religious careers.

The missionary statesmen mingled the humility of a tool of supernatural forces with the normal human desire for grand achievements. They were, after all, directing a campaign to remake nations. Their decisions affected thousands of lives, and their agencies' budgets were calculated in the millions. Relatively free of immediate supervision, with constant pressure to increase staff and expenditures, they inevitably found it difficult to distinguish between personal ambition and the advancement of their cause. They were demanding toward their subordinates and elitist in practice, yet had no power that a democratically constituted voluntary society could not withdraw at any time. The ability to succeed under these conditions put an emphasis on personal ability to promote, manipulate, and conduct evangelical diplomacy.

Contemporary critics noticed only the incentives to pride and self-satisfaction. They underestimated the ability of religious dedication and conscience to temper the corrosive effects of power and to bridle ambition, or at least to channel it away from secular goals. Some restraints were institutionalized, as in the participatory prayer services which opened and concluded meetings of the governing board of the Laymen's Missionary Movement. But in most cases the checks were internal, revealed in a combination of acute self-awareness and dedication to some regimen for curbing ambition and restoring humility.

Robert E. Speer, for example, revealed, in his reply to a friend's praise of his accomplishments, that he was concerned lest he "drift into an almost flippant way of thinking about human abilities and achievements. There is a sense I suppose in which a man must believe in his own powers, and in the momentous issues that hang upon what he thinks and says and does if he is going to accomplish anything at all. . . . On the other hand," he speculated, "let him lose his balance just a little here, and at once, the pretension, the conceit, the disturbance of judgement which ensue, deprive him of his serving and undermine his influence, even with those who pretend still to hold him in respect."[55]

In the same letter, Speer admitted to some preoccupation with "the dangers that confront men in Christian life and work which grow more subtle as they go on." The solution he discovered for himself consisted of a curious combination of prayer meeting and sensitivity training session. He organized a group of men in similar work in the New York area whom he trusted intimately. They kept up a monthly prayer list, and once a year the group of eight or ten, which included John R. Mott, went off to a solitary place to pray and talk without restraint. We "have gone off alone, and just gone over the needs and experiences of the past year, the lessons we have learned, and new dangers and temptations with which we have had to deal."

Speer valued these sessions highly. Whatever their effect on the less prominent secretaries and ministers who attended, they reflected a demanding conscience and a keen awareness of the perils of fame which probably had no counterpart in men of equal power and responsibility in other professions. In the men who formed the front rank of missionary leaders, there was sufficient strength and humility to redefine ambition and success in Christian terms.

The New Missionary Bureaucrats

The proliferation of missionary agencies after the 1880s also created a distinguishable class of professional bureaucrats and specialists. Less well known to the public than the Motts or Speers, they filled the need for the movement's prosaic administrative and executive leadership in the United States. Although men had made careers as board and society secretaries before, in the nineteenth century they had tended to be ministers seeking an alternative to a life in the pulpit. Thus a post-Civil War diatribe criticizing organized religious benevolence had included the complaint that mission boards were merely the private preserve of clergymen and a few returned missionaries.[56]

During this century, the trend was toward the employment of men who were dedicated Christians, but specialists in some secular field such as accounting, fund raising, or public relations. The personnel qualifications for a Laymen's Movement secretary, for example, included such criteria as good education and health, attractive personality, and ability as a salesman, promotion-minded administrator, executive, and public speaker.[57] With the exception of the requirement for "missionary vision and commitment," the same description might have been made for an executive position by the personnel department of any contemporary business firm. That the men in the field felt estranged from these administrative specialists is obvious from criticism raised in 1931 during the Laymen's Foreign Missions Inquiry, and from the frequent suggestion that preference in staffing home board positions be given to returned or retired missionaries.[58]

Some of the new bureaucrats spent a lifetime in the service of a single organization; others were interchangeable and followed their opportunities through a series of religious societies engaged in quite different enterprises. J. Campbell White, for example, became a YMCA secretary after graduating from his hometown College of Wooster in 1890. After a year as a traveling secretary for the Student Volunteer Movement, he sailed to India as general secretary of the Calcutta YMCA. Back in the United States, he spent three years on the Ways and Means Committee of the United Presbyterian Church, then became executive secretary of the infant Laymen's Missionary Movement in 1906. Nine years later he resigned to return to Ohio as president of his alma mater. In 1919 he assumed the responsibilities of associate general secretary of the abortive Interchurch World Movement. A series of secretarial and administrative positions in seminaries occupied him until retirement age, and not until his sixties did he reverse the traditional pattern by becoming a Presbyterian minister.[59]

White's scale of living in this field was a comfortable one, certainly better than that of the average pastor or missionary in the field.[60] The peripatetic career of this sincerely religious man was not shaped by material considerations, but by a search for larger fields of Christian service. "I would be forced to question all of the intellectual and spiritual processes by which I have determined God's Will for my life during the past twenty-five years if I failed to accept this Call," he wrote the executive committee of the Laymen's Movement when offered the College of Wooster presidency in 1915. Dismissing financial and other practical considerations, he concluded that there was only a single question: "Does God ask me now to do this thing? I believe He does, and that should settle the question."[61]

White was one of the more successful professionals, although the upward momentum of his career was checked with the abysmal failure of the movement he surrendered a college presidency to direct. Thousands of others never achieved the prominence of even a J. Campbell White. They moved from Christian Endeavor Society to YMCA, or Missionary Education Movement to a board secretaryship. They viewed their careers as a form of service scarcely distinguishable from the ministry. Although most of them fulfilled their assigned tasks with dedication, they did not avoid the pitfalls of bureaucratic empire-building and intersociety rivalry. They had to contend with the jealousy of local ministers remote from national headquarters, as well as criticism from denominational members suspicious of change and the corrupting effects of power. The published critiques of men like Batchelder were only slightly more strident expressions of quite generally held suspicions, that even clergymen were not immune to the lure of philanthropic professionalism. A returned missionary might be a spiritual man before moving into a board office, Batchelder had warned, "but their official position educates them to be managers, so that, in time, they become as accomplished in all the subtlety of official craft, as ever did a professional politician."[62] How much more susceptible to the seduction of power were the laymen who had only their own consciences to protect them?

The cream of the college graduates going into this type of service was skimmed by the YMCAs and the Student Volunteer Movement. Cooperating closely, these two organizations regularly sent student secretaries to college campuses to speak, interview, and enlist men and women approaching graduation. Home mission societies and other sectarian bodies had no such organized recruitment system. They relied more heavily on personal contact through pastors or family connections, and on the graduates of denominational colleges unable to undertake or finish theological training. The Bible colleges and training schools, which were to be found in nearly every American city during this period, provided additional recruits with a smattering of training beyond that provided by the public schools.

Men with similar education and background were filling the expanding business and government bureaucracies at the turn of the century. What distinguished them from the religious bureaucats was largely the latters' desire to serve mankind as well as their own ambitions. The same is true of their superiors, and of the part-time volunteers who sought the satisfaction of a Christian service career in addition to their more mundane vocations. Among all these, a few subscribed wholeheartedly to the nineteenth-century slogan Samuel Capen quoted in his acceptance speech as the new business-man president of the American Board: "The American who does not believe in foreign missions, denies his ancestry, his country, and his God."[63]

Chapter 3

THE MISSIONARIES

There were no clear cut sociological or motivational differences between the men who administered the home base of the
foreign mission movement and the volunteers who went into the
field. They were all tangible products of Bushnell's Christian
nurture, and thus part of an idealistic and dedicated minority in
American life who chose mission work as the means of expressing
their religious convictions. If many board officers became all but
interchangeable with their counterparts in business and government bureaucracies, the missionary remained a distinct type who
created unique personnel problems. Unlike a professional who
anticipated lean years while building up his practice, a minister
who began his career in a rural church, or even a clerk or salesman
who hoped for promotion to a supervisory or executive position,
the missionary retired at the rank to which he had been initially
appointed. He was neither eligible for promotion nor likely to be
able to finish his career in the home office or as a policy maker.
Since neither the attraction of serving a particular board nor the
normal career incentives could be relied on by the mission agencies,
assuring an adequate supply of new recruits for the field posed personnel problems faced by no comparable organization in American
life.

The missionary was basically a minister or church worker
who surrendered home, family, friends, and opportunity for professional advancement to spend a lifetime preaching to, or working
with, apathetic aliens. Unlike his American colleagues, he was not
invited to serve a congregation that had freely chosen him. Furthermore, he accepted a tighter discipline in all areas of his work and
life from his mission board than any American pastor had to endure.
With these requirements added to the not inconsiderable sacrifices
demanded of a ministerial candidate, a chronic shortage of qualified
missionary volunteers seemed to plague the Protestant sending

77

agencies. A qualification is added only because it is difficult to separate the facts of personnel availability from the calculated pessimism of public appeals for volunteers.

Problems in Missionary Recruitment

An Adequate Supply?

The crux of home base administration was the procurement of personnel and money at levels dictated by the long-range commitments of a particular agency. Exclusive responsibility for planning and promotion in these two areas was usually assigned to distinct departments, with senior secretaries coordinating the overall campaign. At no level of the bureaucracy, and in neither the public nor private assessments of the responsible administrators, was there any agreement as to which type of resource was more difficult to obtain during the decades of mission expansion. Within a few years' span at the turn of the century, for example, a former Baptist minister pleaded for consecrated money to send out the thousands of volunteers he averred board secretaries had been forced to reject, yet one of the responsible administrators expressed the persistent anxiety of the Baptist Missionary Union over the inadequate volume of candidate applications.[1] In 1890 the Presbyterian missionary contingent in China was informed that no reinforcements could be expected, despite a flood of applications from the seminaries, because of insufficient funds.[2] Little more than a year later, the reason given by another Presbyterian secretary was the inadequate supply of candidates produced by the seminaries.[3] Even a full-fledged discussion of the relative demands for candidates and funds at the 1903 Foreign Missions Conference produced no consensus, but did reveal the basic reason for the persistent confusion.

It became obvious in the course of the debate that each denominational agency of the fragmented missionary movement followed different administrative procedures and applied its own personnel standards. While one board turned back applications until their budget allowed a position to be funded, others accepted candidates with faith in their denomination's ability to respond quickly to a demonstrated need for money.[4] Newer communions, without the tradition of a trained ministry, were likely to have more satisfactory candidates than they could afford to support. The established agencies of the larger denominations, however, often demanded better credentials from their candidates than were required by the average church at home. High personnel standards were in the interest of these boards, both because of the initial cost of outfitting and establishing a new missionary, and to preserve their reputation with their constituency as efficiently administered agencies deserving of support. "I would not seem to criticize the policy of any other Board," observed the American Board's new businessman-president in 1901, "but I am sure that the policy of some of them in sending out inferior men and women has often brought reproach upon Christian missions."[5] In a period when the proportion of college graduates entering the ministry began to dwindle, to insist on ordained men for missionary service was to court persistent shortages, despite new promotional techniques and organizations such as the Student Volunteers.

There seem to have been sufficient candidates for available positions at the turn of the century, even if the applicants did not always have the advanced training in education, medicine, and other developing specialties the administrators would like to have insisted upon.[6] The high point in the availability of candidates was reached immediately after World War I. "We look for a large increase of missionary forces as a result of the war," a missionary journal predicted in 1918. Men who had fought in the crusade by serving in Red Cross or "Y" contingents would not be content to return to pedestrian civilian jobs, maintained the editor, and their training and spirit should be employed. "These new-found recruits should not be demobilized," he proposed. "They should simply be re-distributed."[7]

To a considerable degree this hope seems to have been realized. The American Board sent more new missionaries to the field in 1919 than in any other year between 1900 and the Depression.[8] Most of the major sending agencies reached a peak in the number of missionaries in the field during the early 1920s which was not approached again until after World War II. The high point for Student Volunteer enlistment, as well as for the total number of new American missionaries sailing for the field during the first four decades of the movement's existence, was 1920. The largest number of Volunteers sailing during the same forty-four year period left in 1921.[9]

Changing the Composition of the Missionary Force

A number of strategies supplied the necessary volunteers at the end of the nineteenth century, the most important of which was a grudging redefinition of the typical missionary sought by the sending agencies. Administrators were forced to re-examine traditional policies and prejudices and to lower standards in some cases. Single women and laymen were employed in far greater numbers, as were natives of the mission fields. The mainstay of the mission forces, however, remained the ordained male missionary.[10]

With a few exceptions in the pioneer days at the beginning of the century, the ideal nineteenth-century missionary was an ordained minister expected to function with equal facility in all phases of his station's work, with the help of a wife who did not share his status. Despite the logic of filling teaching or nursing positions with laypersons, however, such personnel specialization was held to represent a deplorable diminution of standards.[11] Methodist Bishop W. F. Oldham provided another rationalization of this attitude for delegates at the 1914 Foreign Missions Conference, pointing out "that an ordained man costs no more than a layman and that until you come to specialization the ordained man can easily do all that the layman does, and do some things by reason of his ordination that the layman can not do."[12] By the time he spoke, however, the mission establishment in China had already become so complex that the major boards were required to surrender to specialization despite their proclivities.

To set an ordained minister to teaching elementary school was a waste of talent, as was making him a mission school principal or a college science instructor. Similarly, the medical work in East Asia had gone beyond the point where ministers with a haphazard knowledge of first aid could run a station infirmary. Yet qualified applicants for medical positions were discouraged if the administrators continued to insist upon postgraduate Bible school courses or even theological training. Many of the younger men also came to the field strongly influenced by the tenets of social Christianity, and refused to consider street preaching or tract distribution as their primary ministerial function.

Such objections, and the economies of using lay specialists for technical and educational tasks, led to their increasing employment. Printers, teachers, mechanics, and nurses began to receive full missionary status. The American Board added the designation "business agents" in 1916 to distinguish accountants, architects, and business managers sent to foreign stations from the traditional missionaries.[13] A number of boards adopted short-term enlistment programs to attract young college graduates, much as the Peace Corps or VISTA did for another generation. Although this was a convenient way to staff educational facilities, it was also criticized as a wasteful experiment producing inadequate returns for the investment in the transportation, outfitting, and training of the young laymen.[14]

Despite the fact that women composed a numerical majority of American missionary personnel from the beginning of the enterprise, they remained an underdeveloped source of recruits whose increased appointment at the turn of the century was viewed by traditionalists as another example of the general lowering of personnel standards.[15] Almost all nineteenth-century female missionaries had been the wives of ordained men. A combination of Victorian prudery, the public's overestimation of the hazards of foreign duty, and their inability to receive ordination explains the reluctance with which the regular sending agencies had commissioned single women. By 1900 American women had been accepted in areas of public life and employment previously closed to them, and had gained readier access to higher education. Since the dangers in foreign service had also markedly decreased, the regular mission societies found it easy to give in to the urgings of the women's boards to employ more of their sex.

The single woman missionary, however, remained a second-class citizen of the mission station for decades.[16] Often in combination with missionary wives, she served as teacher, nurse, or tract distributor but, lacking the opportunity for ordination, she could not administer sacraments or fulfill the ministerial functions of most of her male counterparts. Other reasons for board prejudice against spinsters were the opportunity for rumors which their presence at a station provided the Chinese community, and their disturbing willingness to marry eligible men, regardless of their denominational affiliation, with a consequent loss to the society that had borne the expense of sending them.

A marked increase in the number of native helpers used for tract distribution and other auxiliary purposes after the 1880s indicated the development of the most natural solution to missionary personnel deficiencies.[17] By 1902, for example, 1,037 missionaries of all types, including wives, were outnumbered by 2,906 native workers attached to the same thirty-three American Protestant mission societies active in China.[18] The development of a native ministry, however, was disappointingly slow. This was due in part to the lack of men willing or qualified to undertake the long course of study required for ordination, and to a lesser degree to the reluctance of some missionaries to surrender responsibility to native pastors before the churches they served had become completely independent of foreign financial support.[19]

Education and Missionary Recruitment

All missionary recruiting procedures rested on the assumption that the ideal candidate was the end product of a Christian education. Some societies relied largely on their own staffs and denominational channels to reach volunteers. Others chose to cooperate more closely with the Student Volunteer Movement or Foreign Missions Conference to obtain the benefits of general publicity and the centralized promotion of standards. In either case, the recruiters attempted to influence the twenty years of education that preceded the typical volunteer's application to a sending agency.

Children and Adolescents

The informal phase of education within the family was largely beyond the reach of religious agencies, but they were aware of the importance of proper early guidance in shaping future Christian workers. In 1880 the American Board investigated the family background of 140 of their active missionaries, for example, and determined that 122 "had both a godly mother and father." Only six, on the other hand, were the product of families in which neither parent was a church member.[20] One avenue into such homes consisted of the inexpensive mission magazines issued by virtually every denomination and many of the women's groups. As pious substitutes for dime novels to which no parent could object, they provided many a rural youngster with a romanticized introduction to the outside world.[21] In exotic descriptions of heathen depravity, interspersed with celebrations of victories by heroic soldiers of the cross, they could also plant in young minds an exciting image of the missionary career.

Handicapped by the lack of a Protestant parochial school system, mission promoters also experienced difficulties in reaching youngsters after they began their formal education. Aided by the development of such social sciences as psychology, however, some mission administrators became excited about the prospects of applying the science of "how God works in a child." "It is the first time that it has ever been possible for a new generation of the church to be trained from infancy for the world's great task along the lines of an assured science," T. R. W. Lunt told a panel on children's work at the 1910 World Missionary Conference.[22] Robert Wilder, one of the founders of the Student Volunteer Movement, reminded the same assembly that "boys and girls are at that optimistic period of life when they believe that the whole world can be reformed, and it is at that time that we should plant the seed of missionary information in their hearts."[23] The General Secretary of the Young People's Missionary Movement contributed the information that young people were most susceptible to propaganda near the age of conversion, which was usually sixteen. "If we postpone the training of those who might become missionaries until they have passed beyond the adolescent stage, and have had fixed upon them impressions of business and professional life," warned Harry Wade Hicks, "we shall have lost our opportunity."[24]

The calculated approach of these specialists was not generally adopted by a denominationally fragmented movement which lacked both resources and opportunity to implement such a program. Their analysis, however, supported a less intensive effort to bring the mission message into every area of religious education. Harry Wade Hicks's Missionary Education Movement provided the lesson plans, posters, and literature to plant mission study in Sunday school curricula, and to introduce it into the programs of such youth organizations as the Epworth League. It also provided plans and supervision for more ambitious efforts, such as the campaign to establish "a School of Missions in each Church" on the Pacific Coast.[25] Meanwhile Samuel B. Capen, who, like John Wanamaker, John D. Rockefeller, and hundreds of other prominent laymen, regularly taught Sunday school classes, read and distributed copies of the influential *Sunday School Times,* which published scores of articles on foreign mission topics under the editorship of Robert E. Speer's good friend, Charles G. Trumbull.[26]

Proliferating denominational youth groups at the turn of the century provided new opportunities for the foreign boards to distribute their promotional literature. And the founder of the older United Society of Christian Endeavor, which in 1918 encompassed 78,496 societies in over 80 evangelical denominations and practically every nation in the world, promised "to promote in every way intelligent and enthusiastic loyalty to denominational mission work."[27] By exploiting such opportunities, alert board secretaries could get their message to thousands of impressionable youngsters in church clubs, camps, and schools. They had not been reached by the nineteenth-century agencies, and were outside the scope of such better-known recruiting organizations as the Student Volunteer Movement.

The College Focus

The most strategic group for missionary recruitment, however, was the tiny fraction of evangelical young people who continued their education in the colleges. White male college graduates at the turn of the century did not approximate as much as 1 percent of the white male population past college age, and historically only 30 percent of our congressmen and 60 percent of our presidents had earned degrees.[28] Yet the preponderance of missionaries was drawn from this educated elite. After 1888, prospective volunteers could be reached on dozens of campuses through the traveling secretaries and regional organizations of the Student Volunteer Movement for Foreign Missions. The direct activities of the mission boards, however, were focused on the small church-supported colleges which had graduated well over 90 percent of all theological students in the United States at the turn of the century, and between 87 and 95 percent of the active missionaries in 1932.[29]

Denominational colleges were the most fertile hunting ground for missionary volunteers because they enrolled the type of students most likely to have been exposed to foreign mission propaganda in church youth groups and Sunday schools. When the religious pressures to which these students were exposed during four of their most impressionable years included a tradition of missionary service, they could be expected to be unusually receptive to the plea of a returned missionary speaker or traveling secretary. At the end of the nineteenth century, the proper atmosphere was most likely to be found in the newer western colleges which had themselves been founded as part of a missionary thrust.[30] If not there, it could usually be identified with the guidance of a founder or mission-oriented president.[31]

Once they had identified such colleges, the foreign mission boards tried to sustain interest in their cause by placing returned missionaries on the faculty, cultivating other sympathetic teachers, and providing free speakers and literature. The influence a single popular instructor could have on successive student generations made such efforts worthwhile, even if some of the older returnees found themselves alienated from their American students.[32] Sympathetic faculty members were also expected to further a campaign to make the study of missions a legitimate part of a liberal arts curriculum. As a major combining the study of history, comparative religions, and the social sciences, it was promoted as a broad cultural approach to international affairs, both superior to established disciplines and designed "to destroy narrowness and give men and women a world-consciousness."[33] Mission study as an academic framework for the subject matter of later area studies or international relations programs failed to make major inroads in the face of increasing secularization in denominational colleges, and because of faculty suspicion that propaganda and education could not be effectively divorced in presenting this subject. Nevertheless, such advocates as President Henry C. King of Oberlin described the introduction of mission studies in 1906 as an irresistible trend which every board of trustees and university faculty would have to confront in the near future.[34] However limited the overall results of the program may have been, its promotion and occasional acceptance marked a high point in the legitimization of mission advocacy during the prewar decades. Even the academic community was no longer to enjoy the luxury of ignoring a movement the churches had slighted for centuries.

Missionary Training

The problem of missionary training was closely connected with the promotion of recruitment and propaganda in higher education. The early view that distinctions between common ministerial and foreign mission work were senseless and a handicap in recruitment[35] changed later in the nineteenth century to require higher standards for potential missionaries and to provide at least some specialized training. The major boards maintained high standards because it was virtually impossible to devise an economical probationary system or to test a candidate's adaptability to work in a foreign land. Hence, the safest policy was to demand a somewhat better educational record, a stronger physical constitution, a virtually flawless character, and higher dedication than was considered necessary for the minister of a local church or the nurse or school teacher who could easily be replaced if she proved incompetent. When the seminaries and denominational colleges did not produce an adequate volunteer force with these qualities, and the mission agencies found themselves unable to establish educational institutions of their own, a largely unplanned compromise solution was developed. Specialization allowed the employment of religious workers with superficial general training, since these were certified in increasing numbers by institutions with questionable academic standards. At the same time, the sending agencies increased their efforts to introduce specialized missionary education in the seminaries that produced their regular missionaries.

The establishment of special training facilities began partly in response to enlarged opportunities for lay workers, and in part as a result of the antiformalistic enthusiasm stirred by the Moody revivals. The Moody Bible Institute in Chicago was initially designed to prepare evangelists for urban home missionary work, but later broadened its functions and sent home trainees to the foreign field. Moody called its graduates "gapmen," providing them with a minimum of formal theological training to do the work for which seminary graduates were either unavailable, or which they were unwilling to undertake.[36] It was a comparatively well-financed and stable institution compared to the dozens of transient Bible schools dedicated to meeting both the educational needs of the poor, and the personnel requirements of the evangelical churches. Also available in the same city, for example, was the Chicago Training School for City, Home, and Foreign Missions, which a devout former Sunday school teacher had set up in her modest home. Awarding diplomas after a year's exposure to Bible classes and elementary medical lectures, the school reported in 1890 that 54 young ladies had received appointments to the foreign field during its first five years. There is no indication that their course differed from that of the 234 girls prepared for the home field during the same period.[37]

The products of transient Bible schools and short training courses usually went to the smaller societies or to such rigidly evangelical bodies as the China Inland Mission, which valued spiritual sincerity over academic preparation. Arthur Pierson had suggested a shorter and more practical missionary training course in his *Crisis of Missions,* particularly favoring the omission of classical studies and linguistics. Intellectual standards often worked havoc with youthful dedication and spiritual ideals, Pierson explained, and long years in colleges and seminaries "not infrequently leave candidates with a chronic chill."[38] Few of the older boards were willing to accept either the diminution of personnel standards, or the anti-intellectual implications of such proposals. As a Presbyterian secretary tersely responded to suggestions that his board adopt the China Inland Mission's policy of sending out briefly trained laymen: "I do not believe that uneducated men are necessarily more spiritual than those who are broadly and thoroughly trained for the work."[39]

Pressure to provide more thorough training seems to have come from the field itself as much as from administrative standards. Although specialized training in addition to college preparation was first considered necessary only for medical and some educational positions, even the requirements for simple evangelists were raised in the pre-World War decades. A conference of Baptist mission secretaries and officers was told in 1917 that the high school diploma and a full course at a Bible training school of the first rank which were then required of evangelical assistants to regular missionaries, were no longer adequate. The Woman's Board had been unable to respond to an urgent appeal for reinforcements because the request had specified that only college women be sent for such work. Since all of the board's college candidates were preparing for either medical or teaching positions, no reinforcements were sent. The conference had to content itself with a resolution calling on all the agencies represented to select only the most able candidates in the future, "developed and fortified, whenever possible by the highest general training our schools can afford, and supplemented by the best possible technical training of each for his special work."[40] The lack of available facilities, and the cost of such training, made it difficult for mission boards to follow the policy hopefully outlined at this and similar working conferences.

The boards sought special training for the ordained missionaries by advocating the addition of mission courses to seminary curriculums, and even the endowment of chairs in the subject. A report to the Foreign Missions Conference of North America in 1896, however, found that only 4 out of 57 theological seminaries replying to a poll maintained at least one professor of Christian missions. Not quite half of these schools required examinations in missionary studies or provided special lectures in existing courses. A survey completed three years earlier had found even less official recognition of the subject, and also established that only 2 percent of the seminary graduates who actually became foreign missionaries were influenced in their decision by instruction in the seminary.[41] The rest had come to school already determined on the career, and there was reason to fear that others were diverted from their ambition by the lack of interest reflected in the absence of special preparatory courses. John R. Mott quoted a board secretary bewailing the negative influence of most seminaries where "from the beginning to the end of the course the whole presumption in the teaching and attitude of the faculty is that the men are all going to stay at home."[42]

Resistance to the addition of mission studies at theological schools was based largely on the additional time required of the students, or faculty reluctance to delete traditional courses in favor of the new field. Often consciences were salved or denominational requests answered by designating a Missionary Day, or requiring research papers on missions in existing courses.[43] Where traditional ties to a mission board existed, more progress was made in legitimizing the new field. At Hartford Seminary, for example, the initiation of a separate course in 1911 culminated eight years later in the establishment of a distinct Kennedy School of Missions.[44] A number of boards encouraged their candidates to attend the Kennedy School for specialized training and to pursue area studies. Occasionally they even assumed the cost of this postgraduate study, but such a policy was initiated with even greater reluctance.[45]

Before World War I the resources of the mission movement were inadequate for the broader development of experiments with specialized training. With declining contributions in the 1920s, the boards found it necessary to concentrate once again on convincing mature and generally educated potential replacements to select a foreign instead of an American parish, leaving distinctive training to veterans in the foreign field and experience.[46]

The Student Volunteer Movement

As a dynamic mass organization separate from, and supplementing, the efforts of the traditional foreign mission boards, the Student Volunteer Movement for Foreign Missions represented the most significant innovation in missionary recruitment and education during the expansive period. It was born in 1886 in the revivalistic atmosphere following Arthur Pierson's address near the end of a Dwight Moody conference for student Christian workers. Two years later, it was formally organized by students associated with the Young Men's and Young Women's Christian Associations, the American Inter-Seminary Missionary Alliance, and the Canadian Inter-Collegiate Missionary Alliance.[47] The independent organization that resulted was carefully designed to avoid overbureaucratization. Professional staff was kept to a minimum, regular use being made of volunteers for a year or two before they were sent overseas by denominational boards.[48] Campus Volunteer Bands were grouped into state and regional Volunteer Unions, but these remained autonomous and free of direct control by the national organization. Every four years the movement's focus shifted from the local Volunteer Bands to spectacular international conventions attended by thousands of enthusiastic young people.

Students generally became aware of the existence of the movement through a lecture sponsored by the campus Volunteer Band. They might join a mission study group organized by the band, using literature and inexpensive texts supplied by the national movement. If these exposures and the prayers and personal urgings of friends and visiting Student Volunteer secretaries were successful, the next step was signing the Volunteer declaration: "It is my purpose, if God permit, to become a foreign missionary."[49] The immediate effect of this commitment was inevitably dynamic, providing a personal focus which separated the volunteer from his classmates. "College days for us students were enriched with the constant picture of the future, 'when we are on the field'," recalled

Sherwood Eddy, "and 'the evangelization of the world in this generation' was accepted as a personal responsibility."[50] The remainder
of the volunteer's college career now became a matter of preparing
for the field. He read about the work and mission lands in the collections the movement had contributed to his college library, and
studied more in non-credit courses devised by experts at national
headquarters.[51] He contacted his denominational board for suggestions, and spent his spare time trying to induce others to share his
commitment. Finally he attended the quadrennial international
convention to be addressed by leading churchmen and missionaries
in a distinctly revivalistic atmosphere designed to cement his convictions and commitment.[52]

The subdued criticism and friction which characterized relations between the established mission boards and the Student Movement make it difficult to evaluate the movement's actual contribution. Criticism was sharpest in orthodox circles where there was
mistrust of both "the YMCA minds" rushing toward Christian unity
by ignoring, rather than confronting, the issues that divided Protestantism, and of the social gospel emphasis with which the movement became thoroughly imbued.[53] There was also persistent opposition, most stridently voiced by Continental European mission
leaders, to the presumptuous and misleading implications of the
volunteer watchword. John R. Mott stubbornly defended it throughout his career as "the most distinctive, original and daring contribution of the Movement," but could not induce the Foreign Missions
Conference to endorse it.[54] Official disapproval never daunted the
student leaders, however, for Mott suspected that the attitude of
the older generation was summed up in a major board secretary's
warning to his colleagues that "we must bank the fires of the
Student Volunteer Movement."[55]

More telling, but equally ineffectual in banking youthful
enthusiasm, were disparaging official assessments of the Volunteer
Movement's primary function. The Rev. A. B. Leonard of the
Methodist Board told the Foreign Missions Conference in 1894
that the Student Volunteer Movement was not living up to his expectations. The reasons, he suspected, were techniques relying on

"a kind of hot-house influence which is brought to bear for the purpose of inducing persons under a moving speech to offer" their services without any clear understanding of the meaning of a life commitment. Another secretary admitted his board had been unable to accept more than one out of every ten or fifteen volunteers who applied, but he pointed to the propaganda value of the dozen who stayed home to spread the message.[56]

Student Volunteer spokesmen made a far more positive evaluation of their accomplishments. The 1936 convention was told that the movement had the names of 13,000 North American missionaries known to have sailed while Student Volunteer Movement members.[57] Shortly after World War I, John R. Mott estimated that "for some time" 75 percent of the men missionaries, and 70 percent of the unmarried women missionaries of North America had been volunteers.[58] But these apparently inflated estimates were not necessary to document the movement's accomplishments. The Student Volunteer Movement both nurtured, and was based on, an enthusiasm for the mission cause that was largely extraneous to the established agencies. Its propaganda efforts awoke interest on an unprecedented scale, and directed it into existing channels. It provided for the boards both a broader constituency and the opportunity to select candidates from a far larger number of applicants. Thus if the quantitative contribution to missionary ranks was uncertain, there was at least a qualitative impact.

There is some question, however, about the Student Movement's larger significance. Its leaders persistently referred to the events in which they participated as "the student missionary uprising," a claim reinforced by the interpretation that depicts the Student Movement primarily as a revolt against the formalistic and sterile expression of religious feeling characteristic of the older denominations in the late nineteenth century.[59] As revolts go, however, this was a harmless and peculiarly gentle one. Its effects were almost exclusively channeled through long-established, regular denominational agencies beyond youthful control. The discontent was directed into a cause which had long been an expression of the more conservative wing of American Protestantism, not into the potentially more radical camp of the social gospel movement. The suspicion persists that, although the students may have prodded their elders into moving a bit more rapidly in a direction in which they were already traveling, the danger of any significant youthful revolt was successfully diverted in the process.

Even if the Student Volunteer Movement became the most important single factor outside the established denominational channels in securing missionary personnel, it never replaced or controlled the agencies existing prior to its organization. Carping criticism of the Student Volunteers' youthful activism was never more than an undercurrent in contemporary religious circles. The boards welcomed the movement's work, borrowed some of the techniques developed by the less conservative young enthusiasts, and developed a closer liaison with the youth group's officers. But since the sending agencies alone made the decision to allocate resources to send a missionary to the field, the direct influence of the Student Volunteer Movement ended when the volunteer dropped his application in the mail box.

Missionary Candidates: General Characteristics

Decades before psychological testing and rationalized employment standards were introduced by educational, business, and other large-scale employers of college graduates, mission board administrators applied rudimentary versions of these techniques to select a peculiar American elite. The personnel secretaries had been saved much labor, however, by the extended process of institutional and self-selection which made the average applicant part of an educated and religiously motivated elite to begin with. What remained was largely a matter of checking credentials in order to discover the potentially outstanding missionaries, of whom it could justifiably be said that they were "men of native force who would probably have made their mark in any calling."[60] "Character" was the collective word for the characteristics the boards were most interested in, and the possession of what their peers considered good character was also a distinctive part of the missionaries' background.

Character was at least as important a criterion as academic

and physical requirements; this can be seen from the opening sentences of the standard American Board form for references:

> The candidate should sustain a *good character* among those who know him. Any gross neglect of duty, any transaction that has brought him under suspicion, is a disqualification, as it might, should he enter the missionary service, bring reproach upon the cause. His standing should be such that when his intention is announced, the common sentiment of those who know him will be, that he is well qualified for the work.

Within this context, admission by the candidate that he either drank or smoked was usually enough to bring him "under suspicion." Behavior toward the other sex was an extremely sensitive area. The American Board, for example, held up the appointment of an otherwise qualified candidate for several years until he married and disproved his college landlady's allegation that he would never wed because he was "so silly about girls."

Hesitation or qualifications voiced by a single reference could thus bar a candidate from service. The boards were diligent in displaying "a discernment which overrides the partiality of friends and the good opinion of pastors and theological professors." Glowing recommendations were commonplace, a Baptist secretary warned the Foreign Missions Conference in 1893. Whenever his board received three or four testimonials from professors in regard to a candidate and found one sending an entirely different estimate from the rest, "we follow the judgment of the one man always."[61] Against such odds, the man of questionable character or even minor personal idiosyncracies had little opportunity for service with an established board.

Any effort to establish an over-all pattern for the geographical origins of missionary candidates will be confused by the regional delimitations of most American denominations. In general, however, the supply of volunteers reflects a retarded version of the westward movement, with the thinly-populated far west making a negligible

contribution before 1920. Older missionaries still serving at the
end of the nineteenth century were most likely to have come from
the small towns and villages of central and western New England,
and upstate New York.[62] By the end of the nineteenth century,
however, the home mission efforts of an earlier generation began
to bear fruit. Colleges in the easternmost part of the middle west
provided the majority of Student Volunteers during the movement's first decade.[63]

A survey of the candidate papers of men and women sent to
the field by the American Board during the two decades at the
turn of the century provides no reflection of changes in contemporary American society. An overwhelming number were native-born
Americans, most of the foreign-born being children of American
missionaries. The middle west seemed to be replacing New England
as the birthplace of the majority of applicants. Fewer missionaries
came from farm backgrounds than expected in view of the still
predominantly rural nature of the population in 1900. A substantial majority came from small town or village homes. Surprisingly,
as many had been born in the larger eastern cities, however, as
were accepted from the far west. Southern candidates rarely
applied to the American Board, being recruited instead by the
regional branches of the larger denominations.[64] Scattered evidence, however, indicates that the same pattern of predominantly
small town origins applied also to the missionaries of southern
denominations.

Despite the prevalent assumption that missionaries were
largely the children of the poor,[65] the ABCFM personnel files
reveal a predominantly middle-class origin. The sons and daughters
of Civil War widows, farmers suffering from the agricultural depression, or low-salaried clerics and home missionaries did appear, but
in the society of their time they certainly could claim some shade
of middle-class respectability. Educational requirements also tended
to bar the children of the poor. Relatively few candidates, however,
came from families in "comfortable circumstances," and the rare
wealthy applicant was cause for much jubilation and publicity.[66]
In the eyes of the sending agencies, there was also some reason for

mistrust of the financially independent missionary. He was the source of potential discontent among his fellows, and possessed an opportunity to evade board discipline in policy matters dependent upon funds.[67]

The denominational background of American missionaries at the turn of the century is difficult to determine by referring to the records of the various sending agencies, since few were absolutely exclusive in selecting their personnel. Although the Student Volunteer records provide a convenient indication of denominational contributions to the overall movement, it must be remembered that only a minority of those signing pledges actually reached the foreign field. What does emerge from a comparison of the denominational affiliations of the 6,200 Student Volunteers reported on the rolls in 1891 is a rather unequal distribution of missionary zeal. Both the Protestant Episcopal and Congregational Churches counted slightly over 500,000 communicants in 1890, but the Episcopalians produced 2 percent of the volunteers, compared to the Congregationalists' 17 percent. Less than 100,000 Friends accounted for 1½ percent of the student pledges; thirteen times as many Lutherans contributed 3 percent.[68]

These differences are partly a reflection of theological variations between more or less evangelical churches, and partly the result of social factors. The Lutherans, for example, were still largely an immigrant church less likely to have a large proportion of their young people attending institutions where the Student Movement could reach them. Similarly, more than one-third of the three million Baptist communicants belonged to the "colored" branch of the denomination, with attendant socioeconomic barriers to either a higher education or the availability of missionary positions. On the whole, the Congregational and various branches of the Presbyterian Church carried a disproportionate share of the burden of the mission movement. These, plus the two largest Protestant communions, the Methodists and the Baptists, furnished the overwhelming bulk of the missionary candidates and the leadership of the movement.

There is considerable variation in the background of male

missionaries, but the young woman offering her services as an unmarried career worker was a far more consistent and predictable
type. As she emerges from the American Board's candidate files,
she came usually from a large rural family and had passed the age
at which she could reasonably expect a marriage proposal. Often
she had worked her way through normal school or college by inter-
mittent teaching. Once released from obligations to an ailing
mother or younger siblings, she decided to teach or nurse in the
foreign field instead. To a greater extent than the ordained male
missionary, who was normally accompanied by his wife, she cut
herself off from a familiar way of life and surrendered herself to
spinsterhood in an environment where eligible males were rare. Her
commitment was more difficult to revoke than her male counterpart's, and took on aspects of entering a Catholic order. This spirit
was reflected in the answer given by one young candidate for
China to the question why she wished to become a missionary.
"The desire to live a holy life and to help others to do the same"
read her plaintive reply, "and the fact that what once were plea-
sures and joys to me in the world are not so now."[69] To such a
woman, the work she could accomplish with hundreds of Chinese
youngsters seemed more significant than teaching in a one-room
country school.

Criticism of the drain of trained women was frequently voiced
by the candidate's references, and provides inadvertent testimony
to the qualities of such volunteers. "She is of strong mentality and
a great scholar," wrote a Minnesotan for one applicant in 1915.
"America needs her worse than Foreign Field's [sic]."[70] And even
a man who dedicated nearly a half-century of his own life to China
could worry at the end of his career whether the accomplishments
of the "remarkable line of consecrated and intellectually superior
unmarried women" he had worked with were an adequate compensation for the hereditary loss their celibacy had imposed on his
homeland.[71]

Personal Motivations
At the point of commitment, the missionary candidate's

dominant motive was a personally experienced spiritual dedication to Christianity.[72] Regardless of personal background or the route by which he approached the decision, complete submission to God's will was the catalyst that made possible the surrender of ambitions, homeland, and a normal way of life. If a desire for these things reasserted itself after the first flush of spiritual dedication passed, the missionary had nevertheless embarked upon a career far from home and difficult to abandon with an easy conscience.

The overriding religious dedication of the typical missionary candidate coincided with the procedures of the sending agencies. The uniformly accepted *sine qua non* among board secretaries screening applications were spirituality and the experience of a divine calling.[73] If the same secretaries had not also demanded college and seminary degrees supplemented by professorial recommendations, one might suspect the mission movement of harboring an anti-intellectual spirit. "Gifts and graces do not always go together," the Reverend Henry N. Cobb told an assembly of board secretaries. "And if the choice must be made between them, let the gifts go, and give us the graces of burning love to Christ and to the souls of men."[74]

If spiritual dedication was both expected and characteristic of the average missionary candidate, the only other uniformly applicable generalization is that this condition was never arrived at suddenly. The choice of a missionary career was neither rationally calculated nor the result of some Pauline vision. It was a trip down a progressively narrowing highway on which the exits became fewer and less sharply diverging from the main road before its terminus. The first step on the highway was an overwhelming personal experience of conversion.

The candidate papers of the period are filled with references to this experience, most dated precisely as an army discharge or wedding day in contemporary personnel records. Mention of the experience of conversion often seemed intended as a self-explanatory reason for the applicant's decision to serve. It was proof of election to an elite, and the beginning of a trip down a road different from that of ordinary men. "All my associates are Christian people," wrote a printer seeking appointment to China, "and with them only do I find enjoyment and congeniality."[75] Another applicant wrote that he had no intention of practicing medicine except in connection with evangelical work and in imitation of his master. "I regard my life as a failure just as *I* am known and loved *instead* of my God—if a knowledge of me does not imply a knowledge of my God, I live in vain."[76] Expressed by a medical student rather than a seminarian, this selfless dedication typifies the distinctive missionary spirit at its best.

Although an expression of steadfast faith and personal conversion continued as a characteristic of candidate papers after 1900, its form became both less precise and less orthodox. An American Board secretary wrote a candidate in 1915 that his doctrinal statement had been the first in some time that revealed a man growing more conservative in his theology since concluding his training. "We find so many men who do not know what they believe," complained Brewer Eddy, "who are drifting on an azure sea of general good hopes in the belief that Jesus was 'a perfect gentleman' (as one man said) and little more."[77]

The conversion experience itself became less often the result of a specific revival or camp meeting sermon than the product of a milder institutionalized process. George Wilder wrote in 1893, for example, that his conversion had been of that gradual kind which comes with a Christian upbringing, "so that it seemed only the natural thing to confess my love to Christ in the first revival meeting I ever attended."[78] Wilder had his opportunity when he was thirteen. Others registered their conversion at the annual revivals sponsored at most denominational colleges.

The later experience was likely to have a more direct effect on vocational plans, but it could also alienate the questioning student. Frederic C. Howe recounted the dreary experience of creeping forward to the mourner's bench during his sophomore year "to be prayed for by strangers for sins of which I was ignorant . . . I did what relatives, friends, and older college students expected me to do," he recalled. "And nothing happened."[79] Conscience-stricken at his immunity and failure, Howe later grew hostile to organized religion and avoided all further services and meetings. His home training had either been inadequate, or he had become so confident of his own abilities that he did not require the solace of conversion and could intellectualize the whole experience.

Such resistance required extraordinary means to overcome, and Dwight L. Moody proved his ability in this respect through his personal involvement in the conversion of a whole series of future mission leaders. Sherwood Eddy, for example, coasted happily through his career at Yale possessing an immunity similar to Frederic Howe's. He accompanied a friend to one of the Northfield conferences only because of the promise of a full social schedule and an opportunity to play tennis. Then he heard "huge and homely" Dwight L. Moody, "an uneducated man using bad grammar." He found himself intrigued by the man's power despite these obvious handicaps. Moody, whom he ranked as the most dynamic human being he had ever met, thus effected a turning point in the young engineer's life. "God became forever real to me," he recalled. "Religion was no longer a tradition or secondhand experience inherited from my elders."[80]

Whether by means of careful preparation in the home, or as the result of the overpowering personality of a revivalist, a personal conversion was only the first step in the missionary's career. The next involved the expression of a keenly felt sense of duty in some meaningful way. Compared with the convert who chose a successful career as a Christian businessman or professional, the potential missionary was a religious activist. Even revivalism or preaching in an established church did not provide sufficient scope for this need to tell the good news. Bishop James Bashford heard Moody early in his career, was struck like Eddy by the man's limitations, and yet inclined to follow him into similar evangelical work. Slowly the conviction grew on Bashford that "it is not sufficient for one to interpret himself from the pulpit, that the great problem is in the relation of one's ideals and life and that the great work of the Master consisted in personal life and in helpfulness to others."[81] These things Bashford could not adequately emulate as a pastor, bishop, or college president in the United States, but felt he approached while spending the twilight of his career in China.

Bashford's "helpfulness to others" was not simple humanitarianism. A majority of the missionary candidates before World War I, as a century before, described their need to serve in religious terms. They transposed personal convictions into an international policy. The young men whom we remember, said George Gates of the Haystack pioneers, were on fire with that same divine passion to help and to save that burned in the apostle Paul. "It is the passion for souls, only amplified into something more nearly approaching the divine ideal for all human life."[82] It was, in other words, an active participation in bringing in the Kingdom of God, a project requiring workers both at home and abroad. "We do not want all men to go out as missionaries," the Reverend G. T. Manley told a Student Volunteer Conference. "What we do desire is that all men should go where their Master wants them, and therefore it is really a question of consecration, rather than a question of vocation."[83]

It was only at this point on the road to a missionary's life that a distinction appeared between ministers, YMCA secretaries, and overseas evangelists. During the progression from conversion to the call to a life of Christian service, there was little to distinguish the participants. Only rarely was the desire to serve abroad consistently held from youth or early college days to departure for the field. Even when such dedication was fixed early by family ties or obligations, virtually every candidate accepted by the American Board at the turn of this century had first spent several years as a home missionary, YMCA secretary, or denominational functionary. Most of them considered staying with this work for the rest of their careers, often at the request of their superiors, and seemed to end up overseas almost by chance.

Thus, Horace Pitkin had no prevision of being martyred during the Boxer uprising when he wrote in his application that he "had always heard much of Foreign and Home Missions until there was a vague impression on my mind that some day I should be a Missionary." He had worked for the YMCA in college, and in New York and New Haven Rescue Missions during his summers. Even after signing a Student Volunteer pledge and entering a seminary, he retained "a vague notion of a few years' service, perhaps with a little romance connected with it, and then a return to an active pastorate in this country."[84] But as he pondered the needs of his future field, the vagueness gave way to a single-minded zeal and the dedication of his courageous acceptance of death in China.

The single most important factor that transformed the Christian worker into a foreign missionary was his conviction that there was a greater need for his services abroad. It is not impossible that some were disenchanted with unrewarding slum work or dirty Indians and sought a broader and more brightly lit stage for themselves. Without conscious dissimulation, even such feelings were expressed in terms of the heathen's needs. "I want to be a foreign missionary," wrote a California kindergarten teacher, "because God has given me so much that I want to place my life where it can be of most service to Him."[85] Another candidate summarized dozens of similar professions in attributing his decision to numerous factors, "but chief of them all was a growing and unescapable conviction that it was God's will that my life be invested where, so far as I could see, the need was the greatest and the forces meeting that need the least adequate."[86]

It was a traditional evangelical definition of need that these candidates responded to, and that made it so remarkably easy for them to give up social-service work in their homeland. It cannot be denied that some found teaching in a one-room school or working out of a settlement house too familiar to be as compelling an incentive as discharging the same duties within sight of the Grand Canal. For most of these religious young people, however, it was spiritual need which made the unevangelized Chinese more abjectly to be pitied than the tubercular sweatshop seamstress or the starving Navajo.

The personal transition from home to foreign mission work was also made easier by the advent of the steamship, telegraph, and regular sabbaticals. The nineteenth-century volunteer made a more permanent breach with past experience when he sailed. A rising gangplank was virtually the equivalent to a closing monastery door. By the end of the nineteenth century, however, the often used monastic analogy had been replaced by the simile of the frontier. Rather than psychologically severing all ties to his home- land as he boarded ship, the missionary saw himself in the vanguard of the Christian civilization that the United States represented. Home ties might be stretched, but they remained. The same dedi- cation that placed his classmate in a churchless mining town in Montana had brought him to Shensi. And he visualized China not as "something of a monastery where he could attain more fully his religious aspiration to be Christ-like,"[87] but as the most challenging, needy, and potentially rewarding field of activity. The key to mis- sionary motivation was activism, not contemplation. If initially there was a withdrawal from the secular pursuits of his generation, it was followed by the conscious choice of the most active and challenging religious vocation—a ministry to which only the ablest and most adventurous were called.

The simple religious motive that postulated foreign mission service as the most sacrificial and complete manner of meeting the duty incumbent upon a confirmed Christian was most characteristic of the candidates for ordained missionary positions. Among the printers, teachers, nurses, business agents, and medical doctors, Christian service was also the dominant value, but more trivial considerations were likely to be compounded into the impulse to serve abroad. What other avenue than missions were open to an idealistic young American who felt compelled to help people in other nations? Journalists and professors might urge them to take up the white man's burden, but there was no Peace Corps in which to enlist. No extensive colonial service was developed to recruit personnel for the territory acquired in the Spanish War. The developing professionalized foreign service had no room for graduates of small denominational colleges. Although increasing opportunities in world trade provided some openings, the objective there was profit, not service.

Meanwhile, the many propaganda agencies of the missionary movement and the Student Volunteers taught students to think in terms of humanity with a common need, rather than of politically divided foreign states. The YMCA and World's Student Christian

Federation ignored national and denominational distinctions and declared a brotherhood of Christians, if not of all men. To young people who were inspired with these visions and wanted to express their idealism, only the student Christian groups and the foreign mission agencies provided an outlet and an opportunity. For those attracted by the peace movement, here was a ready-made moral equivalent to war.

The sending boards usually did their best to dampen unrealistic enthusiasm by pointing to the mundane difficulties, low salaries, and physical dangers of mission work. No foreign duty bonuses, hardship pay, or commissary privileges were offered. The boards were chary of sending enthusiasts who would later demand to be returned, or whose disenchantment might disrupt a formerly harmonious station. Recruitment agencies and friends of missions, particularly the student groups, however, were not above using the appeal of exoticism and dramatic service. Yale Professor Harlan P. Beach, for example, recommended the challenge of the foreign field to the "man who chafes at the monotony of a home pastorate, who, in the phrase of Mills, 'is pestered in this pinhole here.' "[88] Even more unexpectedly, Groton School's Endicott Peabody announced that "missions are the grandest work in the world, and the missionaries are the heroes of our times. . . Boys," declared the man who had taught and strongly influenced Franklin Delano Roosevelt a decade earlier, "I would rather you would each one be a foreign missionary than President of the United States."[89]

Under the influence of this type of propaganda, it is not unexpected that some candidates went into the field possessed of romantic, and sometimes naive, notions despite the boards' efforts to weed them out. As a Princeton undergraduate, Henry W. Frost had gone through a period of "romantic interest in India," but the Presbyterian Board turned down his application when he proved unwilling to test his interest by going to the seminary.[90] Under the more serious motivation of his later life, he rose to the position of deciding which candidates to send himself.

At the end of the average candidate's progress from youthful conversion to commitment to the foreign field, the choice of areas came almost as an afterthought. Although more applicants specified a choice of fields than offered themselves in a general way, the reasons they expressed in no way reflected the serious thought they had given to their primary commitment. In the decades before World War I, China was the most popular choice as reflected both in the Student Volunteer Movement's statistics and the records of individual boards.[91]

Few of the grandiloquent pronouncements about the strategic importance of China ever found their way into an application form. A prominent church leader like Bishop Bashford might decline tempting offers to return home in terms of Christian geopolitics, insisting that he could do most for the Kingdom by offering his life for a great nation like China and maintaining this offering to the last. "It is lonely on the Yangtse, but the Yangtse, not the Hudson, is the seat of power."[92] The average missionary candidate, however, rarely displayed the same kind of vision or ambition. He usually felt he could accomplish more with his skills overseas. Like a young New Hampshire minister, he might prefer still-independent nations, "feeling that these countries are in the world current so to speak, and that the gospel is of more critical importance to them in that sense than to others."[93]

Most of the applicants who selected China, however, gave almost capricious reasons for their preference. Thus one candidate chose China because he had experienced cordial relations with Chinese acquaintances in college, and because he wanted a complete change of environment.[94] Another mentioned that her mother's friend had gone there, and that a Chinese vegetable man had told her about the country when she was a child.[95] A young Mt. Holyoke student was won to the cause after hearing Horace T. Pitkin speak on campus as a traveling Student Volunteer secretary. She never met him again but recalled the experience clearly some sixty years later. Upon completing her education she had gone to China simply because Horace Pitkin had gone there, and never gave the slightest thought to any other field.[96]

Family contacts were another frequent basis for the choice of fields. Often a classmate or relative had preceded a candidate to the field. Those missionary children who were drawn to the career themselves were frequently attracted by childhood memories and the advantage of a foreign language already mastered. Such second-generation commitments were rarely automatic, however, and sometimes led to a deliberate avoidance of areas in which comparisons with parents or their supervision were likely. Childhood influences, the memory of exotic stories, a chance acquaintanceship, a college course, or the personal request for aid of a missionary in the field—all these were given as reasons by candidates opting for a particular area. The decision for a specific field, in any event, was usually the least important and most lightly made of the series of commitments that led a young man or woman into missionary service.

Like his predecessor of the previous century, the missionary in 1920 was first of all a religiously dedicated man or woman. His or her ultimate motive was religious, not the service of commerce, imperialism, pacifism, or the other causes which were invoked by the movement's propagandists. Yet this generation differed from the pioneers in representing a religion that carried more cultural baggage than in the past. The kingdom they strove for was sketched in more familiar detail. The stern and demanding theology that impelled the first American missionaries to surrender their comfort, friends, and homeland had been modified. Judson and Rice and Mills had sacrificed willingly because they felt a duty toward souls that would be lost eternally but for their intervention. In the process they assured their own salvation and helped carry out God's plan for the world. They had gone out with no assured salary, no prospect of returning home on leave, and no mission board apparatus dedicated to their comfort and security.

The twentieth-century missionary tended to qualify, if not deny entirely, the doctrine of eternal damnation of those who had had no opportunity to hear the gospel. As a result, some of the urgency of the missionary motive was dispelled. Doing good was not an imperative for haste or sacrifice in the sense that irrevocable damnation had been. The new missionary had a more inclusive conception of what was involved in Christian service. Eventually the missionary became difficult to distinguish from the social worker who stayed at home, and demanded and received more of the perquisites of such professionals. He took as a matter of course living conditions and salaries that his predecessors would not have dreamed of. His sacrifice consisted mainly of being separated a while from friends and homeland. Occasionally enmity and disease created hazardous working conditions, but statistically these were probably no more dangerous than those faced by the home missionary in Hell's Kitchen or Virginia City.

Thus, technological progress narrowed the difference between giving service abroad or at home, while the intensity of the theological imperative to save damned souls was waning. This explains the efforts to discover other inducements and to harness a variety of marginal motives to improve the popular image of the mission movement. The organized revivalism of the youth movement and the complex and businesslike ministrations of the mission boards to their agents combined to secure more volunteers than had formerly been attracted by a grim and rigorous theology.

Chapter 4

FINANCIAL SUPPORTERS

American foreign mission agencies were far more vulnerable
to fluctuations in the flow of the financial life blood of the movement than to variations in the availability of new personnel. Totally
dependent upon voluntary contributions to meet their financial
commitments, the boards had no alternative to curtailment of activities when the necessary funds fell short. When several nineteenth-
century economic recessions produced a series of annual deficits,
the effects were quickly felt by missionaries who were forced to
close facilities or stations, work without reinforcements and at
temporarily lower salaries. The return to the former status quo in
the field was always slower than economic recovery at home, partly
because the payment of debts could be a condition to renewed
largesse by budget-minded contributors. For not only was the
board fund raiser dealing with a base so small that approximately
nine-tenths of foreign mission contributions came from one-tenth
of Protestant communicants, but that productive minority was also
highly susceptible to economic reverses since "people in average
circumstances are proportionably the greatest givers."[1]

The Laymen's Missionary Movement with its penchant for
figures and dramatic illustration summarized the situation at the
turn of the century:

About two out of three in the United States and Canada are
outside the membership of all Christian churches. Two out of
three people in the world live in non-Christian nations. Two
out of three people in these non-Christian nations are beyond
the reach of the present combined missionary agencies of
Christendom. And, in spite of these appalling needs, about
two out of three of the church members of North America
are contributing nothing toward the aggressive missionary
work of the church at home and abroad.

109

> Manifestly our first business is the enlistment of the other
> two-thirds of the members of the church as intelligent,
> systematic missionary supporters and workers.[2]

Broadening this base became the primary objective; enlisting what
an American Baptist spokesman referred to as the majority of
nominal Protestants to whom "the message of the Christian Church
means a life of responsibility with no contributions."[3] As embodied
in a favorite Laymen's Movement slogan, the end product of this
ambitious campaign would be: "The whole church enlisted in behalf
of the whole world."[4] And enlisted not only in numbers that would
make the body of the movement's supporters coextensive with
church membership, but in a spirit that would substitute sacrificial
for token gifts.[5]

The Loyal Supporters

Even after the advent of interdenominational campaigns and
sophisticated fund-raising techniques, each foreign mission board
continued to depend heavily on an identifiable base of loyal supporters. Most gave their gifts to their own churches; the proportion
of its income that a society received from this source depended
upon its constitutional relationship to the sponsoring denomination. An additional source of funds was provided by the separate
efforts of various women's organizations. Finally came the quite
unpredictable gifts of individual donors, some repeatedly, most in
the form of legacies. Only the last category might provide the
board with the reserves necessary to meet special needs or to tide
it over a decline in regular contributions, yet these funds were
peculiarly subject to the personal whims of potential donors.

The foreign mission supporters among American Protestants
consisted predominantly of native-born Caucasians, with women
more active in their support than men. Denominational differences,
however, make it difficult to generalize about the movement as a
whole with proportional financial contributions as uneven as the
offering of missionary volunteers. Again, the evangelical bodies
uniformly exceeded the per capita contributions of the liturgical

churches. The small United Presbyterian Church, for example, served as a model for other denominations before World War I because its members consistently contributed a disproportionate share of total giving for missions.[6] In 1913, the Protestant Episcopal Church maintained 168 missionaries in the field, supported by contributions of $677,975. The slightly less numerous Congregational Churches contributed $1,044,688 for the maintenance of 615 missionaries by the American Board.[7]

Creedal differences were supplemented by socioeconomic variations in some instances. That Afro-Americans made no contribution to foreign missions commensurate with their numbers, despite their evangelical traditions, is explained by economic deficiencies which barely allowed them to support their own churches' extension work in this country.[8] Similarly, the contributions of such liturgical bodies as the Lutheran and Orthodox churches were negligible, probably because a majority of their members were recent immigrants. Like the Roman Catholic Church at the turn of the century, they were preoccupied with reorienting the new arrivals and building their churches. Extension of their activities into foreign missions was the work of succeeding generations which were no longer foreign to the United States themselves and had risen above the economic level of the unskilled worker.

The most obvious effect of geography on mission support resulted from the regional restrictions affecting such immigrant churches as the German Evangelical Synod and the major denominations which retained the sectional divisions associated with the Civil War. Even the unified older denominations, such as the Episcopal and Congregational churches, however, reflect a pattern of decreasing support the further one moves from their geographical point of origin.[9] The East had been settled long enough to allow both the development of a tradition of support and of the family fortunes more characteristic of a mature economic base. Within a particular region or state, furthermore, the boards found money much easier to raise in cities than in rural areas. The larger urban congregations, whose members were more likely to be aware of international affairs and thus suceptible to propaganda identifying a crisis in some mission land, provided a natural point of concentration for the mass promotional efforts of such groups as the Laymen's Movement. Not only could more men be reached by holding conventions and rallies in large population centers but, "in the nature of the case, the city churches are generally able to give much more than those in the country."[10] The immigrant influx into Eastern cities modified this generalization, however, and led to complaints as early as 1901 that the development of suburban churches was not proceeding fast enough to make up for the contributions lost from the shrinking city congregations.[11]

In an era when only a scattering of women could be found in business, and club membership opportunities were few, the feminine supporters of foreign missions proved to be remarkably efficient fund raisers and propagandists.[12] Their contribution, however, was obscured by the male-dominated societies and received only indirect acknowledgement in the intense campaign of such organizations as the Laymen's Movement to remove the aura of women's work from local promotional efforts. The moderately successful campaign to promote male participation incorporated more hope and specious sloganeering than recognition of the significant contribution women continued to make in every area except total donations and national leadership.

A significant traditional source of income for foreign missions consisted of a group of loyal supporters impossible to define nationally, but well known to individual boards. Rarely wealthy by modern standards, their families had usually been associated with a particular locality and church for generations. Denominational loyalty and a sense of duty and propriety combined in them to create a tradition of regular contributions and generous bequests. Their gifts were not a reaction to new promotional techniques or the theology of stewardship as much as they were an inherited habit. To the dismay of board administrators, the steadfastness of the old guard and the volume of legacies began to wane at the end of the nineteenth century. "We need to return to the good old New England days," an ABCFM finance report concluded drily, "when no one was supposed to have died properly who did not upon death leave something in his will for the Board."[13]

The older societies were most dependent upon legacies for their operating income and reacted most sharply to the decline. "If our legacies had kept up to the old average," reported the American Board's president in 1901, "we could show now a surplus of $30,000 instead of a debt of $102,000."[14] Although it was traditionally far less dependent upon such income, the Northern Presbyterian Board also observed the decline with concern since legacies often made the difference between debt and solvency. "Those who are responsible for saving us from debt," a committee reported to the General Assembly in 1902, "are the dead, not the living!" To continue merely praying for an adequate income "is to commit the horrible impiety of praying God to take home more of His servants, that the stinginess of the Assembly on earth may be atoned for by the generosity of the Assembly above."[15]

More than any other agency, the venerable American Board had depended upon this type of support, and suffered as a new generation proved unwilling or incapable of maintaining its traditional allegiance.[16] The passing of what President Capen called the Old Guard, "a wonderful group of men of great consecration and missionary zeal, united to large financial ability," was noticeable also in the decline of large annual gifts. Most of these men who "could be depended upon every year to give their money by the thousands" had gone on to heaven. "Thank God, there are some royal givers of great means to whom we can now always turn," he concluded, "but their number is not sufficient to make good the great gifts of those who have gone."[17]

The reasons for the decline seem to be a compound of the dissatisfaction of older supporters with the broader activities and social concern of the mission agencies, and the submergence of the old fortunes in an industrial economy.[18] Whether driven away by theological innovations, or merely succumbing to age, the Old Guard was disappearing at the end of the century. A new generation of liberal givers had to be educated and won or the movement would languish. Some administrators put their hopes on new fund-raising techniques and mass promotional campaigns; others continued the effort to create a new guard of substantial supporters. The American Board, for example, compiled a select list of several thousand potential contributors who were personally solicited once each year. Their gifts did not come to the board through regular channels and by the 1920s amounted to as much as $200,000 a year. But this was during a period of $2,000,000 budgets and reflected the fact that large individual gifts never became a significant part of normal annual receipts.[19] The average church member who dropped his coins in the collection plate on Mission Sunday, or stuffed a few bills into a special envelope, remained the financial mainstay of the movement. Like the generous contributor who remembered the board in his will, he might also be a creature of habit. But either the typical contributor's income was inadequate or the waning strength of tradition made it seem so, for few of them were recruited into the select group so carefully cultivated by the boards, and so insignificant when compared to the mass of loyal church members.[20]

The Ideology of Giving: Stewardship

More insight into the composition of the foreign mission movement's constituency can be gained from an examination of the themes employed in fund raising at the turn of the century. The leading themes in a campaign to raise support for a religious enterprise were such traditional Protestant concepts as stewardship and tithing. Yet the tangible results of sounding these themes had never been adequate and led to an emphasis in the fund-raising literature on mundane and timely motives which threatened to obscure the religious nature of the work for which support was requested. "There is no lack of money," the Episcopal Board's Rufus Clark assured a conference of mission administrators in 1902. "It is the easiest thing in the world,—not the easiest thing, but easy enough,—to get money when people are interested."[21] Arousing interest became a preoccupation in which all allies were welcomed.

The focus of the campaign, and the theoretical basis of mission fund raising, was the principle of stewardship. Although stewardship had no special relationship to the foreign mission cause, it was necessary to promote its acceptance to loosen the purse strings in the interests of the foreign boards.

The idea that man is only a lifetime trustee for a portion of God's property is expressed in both the Old and New Testaments, and was reflected in the primitive communism of several early Christian communities. It received renewed emphasis and a broader interpretation, however, during the period of missionary expansion. "All life is a stewardship," wrote David McConaughy in a widely used church school study book. "Vital energy in whatever form— whether physical or mental, moral or spiritual—is a trust from God."[22] Not only was the biblical conception of stewardship at the heart of the Christian experience, but it was an absolute and all-encompassing obligation which could be used to solicit money, missionary candidates, and service by laymen.

Convinced of the validity of this theme despite evidence that the ideal was too demanding for the rank and file supporter, mission spokesmen adopted stewardship as the text of hundreds of sermons.[23] At a meeting of the American Board, for example, members found themselves castigated by President Capen for condoning a spirit of disloyalty to the expressed command of Christ. Too many Christians held erroneous conceptions about the ownership of money, he said, acting as if personal choice or inclination could determine their contributions in the way it might when they decided to buy a concert ticket. "This is the worst possible heresy," he thundered. It was not a question of how much of mine I shall give, but what part of God's I shall keep for myself. "Stewardship is the great idea in the New Testament," he concluded, "and the Christian who does not recognize this is, in plain language, stealing trust funds."[24] Not that this is a layman pleading for support of the mission cause without any reference to mundane motives. Giving was treated as an integral part of the Christian life, and a character-building spiritual exercise. Stewardship would protect the young businessman from the whirl of worldliness he would encounter since "our children cannot be safely left to breathe the materialistic spirit of the present age without first being made spiritually immune."[25] Stewardship for missions was even raised as a test of Christian piety. "A gift for missions in proportion to our ability," said Capen in 1910, "ought to be a test of discipleship."[26]

Ultimately, stewardship became the means of realizing the kingdom on earth, and to achieve such an objective the sacrifices had to be just as inclusive. "Jesus insisted that membership in his kingdom was to be predicated upon a unitary experience in which the whole personality as a unit was involved," wrote Edwin M. Poteat. There could be no partial allegiance, no calculation of membership in the kingdom on the basis of the amount of time or money surrendered. "The kingdom demands all, and the true believer gives *all*," warned the president of Furman University, "or he *gives* nothing."[27]

In the translation of these ideals into fund-raising techniques a fundamental distortion occurred. Those developing the stewardship theology looked toward the coming kingdom, sought a national religious revival, or preached of sustaining individual character. But the promoters talked of pledges, every member canvass teams, duplex envelopes, and quotas oversubscribed. Posters, rallies, and mass campaigns were always discussed as a means of stewardship education, but the emphasis lay elsewhere, and the results were counted in dollars. To mission leaders closer to the true meaning of stewardship, money was only an incidental by-product of dedication to the ideal. "If the Church is to roll in wealth and luxury, is to go back on the simple principles of the New Testament," wrote Dr. F. F. Ellinwood, "and expect that out of such a moral and spiritual icehouse, tender plants of righteousness with Apostolic zeal will spring up and make the world as a garden of the Lord, then the Church is more a dupe than even Satan in his most sanguine expectations could ever have anticipated." Hoarded wealth would corrupt the American churches, and more important to the veteran Presbyterian Board secretary: "A cold, rich, dead Church will not convert the world."[28]

The effect on individuals was discussed in similar terms. David McConaughy defined stewardship as God's most important device for the training of the human race, "one of the divine kindergarten methods of developing human life." Primary emphasis in his text was not placed on fund raising or the benevolent work of the churches. Instead, "the main consideration is given in this course to the reflex effect upon character." "Stewardship is not a mere method of raising money," concluded McConaughy, "it is one of God's schools for raising men. . . In this process, giving is made an acid test of character."[29]

The bridge between character building and fund raising rested on a peculiar definition of money. To the inner-directed man, wrote David Riesman, property was merely an extension of the individual self; a kind of exoskeleton.[30] "Money not only measures the things exchanged but in a very real sense it affords a measure, likewise, of those who exchange them, wrote McConaughy as if in corroboration. "It is coined personality."[31] This identification of character with currency made it relatively easy to profess stewardship while practicing promotion. If money measured the man, then the amount he contributed indicated the depth of his Christian character. The most blatant type of high-pressure promotionalism in fund raising could thus be explained as being in accord with a traditional Protestant doctrine. Giving to missions could become an equivalent of buying indulgences, for it served the function of making the subtle distinction between wealth that spelled materialism and wealth that betokened character. In practice, the tendency was to use stewardship rather than define it.

Educational efforts promoting the sacramental nature of giving and the universal obligation of stewardship unquestionably met with some success. It seems likely, however, that it was successful precisely with those dedicated church members who required no additional rationalization to contribute. There has long been a pattern of greater per capita giving to benevolent causes by the newer denominations, and those evangelical bodies that are closer to theological orthodoxy or a revivalistic tradition.[32] It seems likely that the greater role played by religious beliefs in the lives of the members of these churches helps to explain their closer approach to the stewardship ideal. Capen's observation that people in average circumstances were proportionately the greatest givers may also reflect piety or religious loyalty as an important factor. But this is not necessarily stewardship, and does not contradict the fact that the promotional literature of the period was often directed at attracting potential contributors by other means.

The model stewards and the group most aggressively approached were men of wealth. The occasional wealthy convert to the stewardship principle was held up as an ideal Christian gentleman, whose example, it was hoped, would be emulated. John D. Rockefeller, Jr. apparently took seriously his father's comment that God had provided him his millions, for he described himself as a trustee, and habitually defined his relationship to wealth in terms of stewardship. To have a man of his prominence observe that "giving . . . is the secret of a healthy life," was a godsend for fund raisers.[33]

More frequent subjects of publicity were businessmen who tithed. Tithing, as a Methodist Convention declared in 1919, was simply "the acknowledgement of God's ownership."[34] The well-publicized tithers, such as Robert G. LeTourneau, combined their example with a general zeal for evangelism, often exercised on their colleagues and employees.[35] President John H. Converse of the Baldwin Locomotive Works, for example, not only tithed and prevailed on his business associates to make additional contributions during hard times, but also wrote and published pamphlets to win wider support for his convictions.[36]

The same thin line that divided the dedicated layman from the professional missions administrator seemed to divide the generous contributor from the mission movement's lay functionaries. As a planning conference for the Methodist Centenary declared, a "stewardship of life, character and possessions" was "fundamental to Christianity."[37] Consequently, an offering in any of these areas met the test of loyalty. John Wanamaker was a Sunday School worker and Philadelphia's first salaried YMCA secretary before he turned to accumulating his department store millions. "I would have become a minister," he later said, "but the idea clung to my mind that I could accomplish more *in the same domain* if I became a merchant and acquired means and influence with fellow merchants."[38] Similarly, Samuel B. Capen's biographer attributed to the man who dedicated his last twenty years to inter-denominational and Congregational mission organizations the ambition of becoming "one of the great authorities in the world of finance, to accumulate a fortune, not for the sake of the money, but that he might use it in the bringing of the Kingdom of God on earth."[39]

Although there were such examples, more often the promo-tional methods used to broadcast the stewardship idea seemed to obscure the principle in the trustee's mind. Personal advantages were emphasized over duty, and immediate benefits were expected as if the steward had just enrolled in a correspondence course. "About twelve years ago I awoke to the blessed fact that the Lord was willing not simply to save my soul and my spiritual being," one H. A. Etheridge told a laymen's convention in 1914, but "that He was willing to come down and enter into partnership with me in the practice of law." The offer was appealing, and so Etheridge decided to ask the Lord to become his silent partner, offering to hold in trust any material blessings that might come to him as a result. The final contract specified a ten-cent contribution from every dollar and included the services of a missionary thus sup-ported. The Etheridges prayed daily for their missionary, and "he says he is doing the same thing for us." Despite the possibility of breach of contract, there was reason to believe the fellow was living up to the bargain. "That man is interested in my material prosper-ity," concluded the model steward, "because he gets a share of my prosperity."[40]

If nothing else, this approach does violence to the biblical doctrine of justification by substituting personal standards of charity for God's. As offered for emulation to several thousand businessmen at this conference, it may also have been a perversion of a slightly different concept. Partnership is a larger word than stewardship, the chairman of the Laymen's Movement suggested in 1912. "Stewardship as has well been said, suggests duty; partner-ship with Jesus Christ suggests privilege and opportunity."[41] But partnership also suggested equality of status and a guaranteed share of the profits, and in this sense ran counter to traditional interpretations of Christian duty and trusteeship.

The Laymen's Missionary Movement undertook the most vigorous promotion of stewardship and is most frequently cited as evidence of success in the campaign to naturalize stewardship among Protestant men. Its Stewardship Commission drew on leading laymen from every denomination, seeking their guidance in formulating a policy that would win wider support for missions from American business. Its promotional methods were viewed as an educational campaign to impress the duty of regular support of missions on the average church member. "Giving as an act of worship had to a degree been lost," a Laymen's Movement spokesman said as he recalled the period before 1906. "It had become spasmodic rather than systematic."[42] The movement issued numerous pamphlets on this topic, and vigorously promoted the sale of McConaughy's *Money the Acid Test* as a text for study groups. It stressed the theme at its conventions, and sent its agents to help organize denominational stewardship commissions.

When this constant emphasis on the divine mortgage that lay on all worldly property proved to run contrary to too many traditional and contemporary American values, it was the stewardship principle that was accommodated. The 1918 Laymen's Movement campaign slogan, for example, represented the unlikely marriage of "Patriotism and Stewardship." At a time when Laymen's Movement publications stressed an increasingly conformist patriotism, and professed abhorrence of half-hearted patriots who drank and were seduced by Bolshevism, they also advertised stewardship as "the only justification for the doctrine of private property."[43]

Throughout its history, the Laymen's Movement leadership was torn between evangelism and activism, between preaching stewardship and waiting for the results, and organizing to achieve them. "From the beginning the message of the Movement has been intensely *practical* and vital," wrote the general secretary reflecting this ambivalence. "Emphasis is first of all upon the *spiritual.*"[44] Prayer, "the mightiest power God has permitted humanity to wield," was prescribed to achieve a national spiritual revival and to defeat the invidious influence of worldliness and materialism in an era of unprecedented prosperity. After the scheduled fellowship for prayer, however, came the personal appeal for funds. Fund raising was developed into a science, and the trained solicitor confidently demanded a "worthy" contribution rather than coming hat-in-hand. Preliminary surveys and advertising preceded highly organized dinner meetings and conventions at which professional secretaries mocked the mite society or Mission Sunday giver. Business methods were pressed on the churches and mission agencies, not only for the sake of efficiency, but because it would earn the respect of businessmen.

"Let us never forget that the work we are trying to do under the name of the Laymen's Missionary Movement is not a business enterprise," warned Samuel Capen reiterating the original goal, "for if it is only that, it will surely fail. It is trying to urge men to be loyal to Jesus Christ."[45] The Laymen's Movement preached stewardship but practiced modern promotional advertising. If education in stewardship was the only thing required, what need was there for the professional fund raiser and sophisticated methods for separating men from their money? The Laymen's Movement may have had a spiritual aim and even provided spiritual meaning and satisfaction to many of its adherents, but in method it was led down the path of high-pressure promotionalism instead.

Both the Laymen's Movement and other efforts to promote stewardship failed to move America's wealthiest men, the group that mission leaders were most anxious to win over.[46] The Laymen's Commission on Stewardship presented a report which revealed that only 5 percent of $90,932,000 given in the United States during 1908 to various benevolent and philanthropic agencies in amounts of $5,000 and over had gone to religious objects.[47] What made this a particularly disheartening example of disloyalty to Christ in the eyes of the movement's president was the fact that the majority of identified contributors were regular in their church attendance.[48] Even this $4,500,000, of course, was shared among dozens of denominational agencies and with such organizations as the YMCAs. Foreign missions continued to receive a trifling share of the funds contributed for religious purposes by American Protestants, a group supposedly including the people motivated by the stewardship principle.

Beyond Stewardship: Secular Themes

Even if the stewardship principle had been effectively taught by the Protestant churches, it would still not have solved the basic problem of the mission agencies. Since obligations could be discharged as faithfully by contributing to organ funds or settlement houses as to the evangelization of Hunan, some further means of enticing the practicing steward into a commitment to foreign missions had to be found. The employment of other appeals for mission contributions reveals a similar ambivalence between spiritual ends and secular means.

"Nothing that is not instinct with the life and motives of the gospel can either fully comprehend the work of missions or effectively promote it," maintained the American Board's foreign secretary in 1891.[49] But each generation has its own instinct regarding the motives of the gospel, and what the expanding missions machine most desperately required in the eyes of its engineers at the turn of the century was money with which to purchase fuel. In 1908 Samuel Capen returned from the Toronto Student Volunteer convention convinced of the accuracy of a Methodist bishop's assertion that the rapid conversion of the world had become simply a question of money. Even if not entirely valid, this was the truth that had to be constantly and vigorously pressed. "We have the money in the pocket-books of the churches," he wrote John Mott, "how shall we reach it?"[50]

It was reached by appealing to the layman's interest in the exotic, in participating personally in great enterprises and leaving his mark on history, and on strictly humanitarian grounds. It was extracted by efficient new business methods, and the appeal of economic motives. With the influx of laymen into the mission agencies, a trend toward worldly emphasis was likely, if not inevitable. The exploitation of these motives in fund-raising propaganda, however, should not be confused with the basic forces behind foreign missions. The object of this literature was raising money, not justifying a traditional Christian duty. Stressing various material benefits does not necessarily reflect a wholehearted commitment to secular goals. To meet the perpetual and harrowing lack of funds the mission forces might countenance selling kisses in the church bazaar, but they did not stoop to prostitution. The fluctuation and variety of these secular justifications of the cause, the ease with which one attribute or slogan was dropped for another, all indicate the lasting primary concern of converting the neglected non-Christian.

One of the most natural and traditional subsidiary themes exploited by the foreign boards was the exotic appeal of their field. Usually coupled with attention-getting descriptions of native customs was a warning of urgency demanding immediate action.[51] When fund raisers exploited the romance of missions, they rationalized their emphasis as an educational task. In competing for public attention, however, they often found their perpetual crises overshadowed by more spectacular and immediate events. In 1896, for example, the ABCFMs Interior States Cooperating Committee found it "unusually hard to raise very much enthusiasm in this field on the subject of missions except for helping Armenia."[52]

After nearly four years of economic depression and unusual financial stringency for the board, there were still generous donations available for suffering Armenia and some from precisely the men who had declared themselves unable to continue contributing to the ABCFM. The same conditions obtained in 1908 when Capen listed floods in Texas, the San Francisco earthquake, and even recent volcanic eruptions in the West Indies as examples of the types of disasters that inevitably drew generous contributions. Since every appeal to humanity proved that the money was available, he maintained, it became only a matter of dispelling public ignorance concerning the day-to-day humanitarianism of missions. "If we can only make real to our churches at home the desperate need of our brothers across the sea, who are groping in the dark with no knowledge of the true God," said Capen, "then there will be money enough to properly support our missionary work."[53]

Dispelling ignorance usually took the form of emphasizing native aberrations from familiar American values. Ironically, exploiting the uniqueness of the work with exotic natives created friction which made the naturalization of foreign missions in the over-all program of the churches more difficult. Since a differentiation between home and foreign missions had first been made, the romance of foreign lands had been considered as providing an unfair publicity advantage for the overseas agencies. The endurance of this prejudice, and the companion charge that the more aggressive pursuit of dollars by the foreign mission societies misled laymen into making false distinctions, is reflected in the recriminations directed at the Laymen's Movement for refusing to include home missions in its promotional activities.

Animosity continued when foreign mission advocates in turn criticized other church agencies for riding on the foreign movement's coattails. Methodist Bishop James Thoburn, for example, disparaged the practice of ministers who took a collection for all denominational benevolent work after the annual missionary sermon, thus using "the most popular of the so-called benevolent causes to serve the interests of other causes which have nothing in common with it."[54] And a Presbyterian Board secretary noted a similar state of affairs in his denomination's practice of holding simultaneous meetings for fund raising. "In this as in all other movements that have been made in the last twenty years in the interest of Foreign Missions," observed F. F. Ellinwood, "the cause of Home Missions soon comes forward and embarks in the same boat, and in a short time is in possession of the saloon accommodations." Still, there was no point belaboring the issue. "We are much better satisfied with the privilege of going hunting with the lion," he concluded philosophically, "than with having no attention at all paid to the cause of Foreign Missions."[55] But others could not resist baiting the lion, whichever enterprise they identified with the royal beast.

Such feuding alienated potential supporters and drew ridicule from secular sources. Added to the charge of rivalry and duplication of effort among the agencies of the various denominations, such bickering alienated exactly the type of generous laymen to whom the movement hoped to appeal. "The multitudes of men and the millions of money wasted on sectarianism in Protestant countries are sufficient," wrote John D. Rockefeller's philanthropic adviser, "to evangelize the whole world."[56] Foreign mission spokesmen thus tried to gloss over the difference and emphasize the catholic nature of their work. The therapeutic value of the missionary spirit became a subsidiary promotional theme.

The Laymen's Movement endlessly reiterated the proposition that "the surest and speediest way to solve any local financial problem of the church is the generation of a healthy missionary spirit."[57] Regular accounts of spectacular increases in giving for local church needs on the heels of a Laymen's campaign were cited in the movement's publications. Laymen's Movement methods and the spirit of sacrifice aroused in giving for the foreign field were depicted as transforming entire communities or, as the movement's chairman told the Edinburgh Conference, "in helping to evangelize the world abroad we are revolutionizing the church at home."[58]

The acceptance of foreign missions as the bellwether of benevolent causes rarely transcended denominational lines. Corroboration was more likely to be a matter of denominational mutual aid than the expression of a generally accepted principle throughout the Protestant churches. Samuel Capen, for example, placed particular emphasis on this aspect but substantiated the claim in a number of addresses only by repeating the single statement made by the president of a Congregational home mission society. "I say without hesitation, that when interest in foreign missions is maintained in a church to the normal point," Dr. William M. Taylor had said, "all other activities and agencies at home will go of themselves and as a thing of course; while if there be a lack of devotion to that noble enterprise, nothing else will be prosecuted with either enthusiasm or success."[59]

The note of denominational loyalty struck in this cooperative appeal tends to mitigate the claims of interdenominational union through missions, and points to another subsidiary promotional theme. In the practical work of fund raising each board was expected to till only its own field. The Laymen's Movement, despite its nondenominational emphasis, directed contributors to support none but the regular agencies of their church. That there were divergences from this custom is illustrated by a resolution adopted by the General Assembly of the Northern Presbyterian Church in 1902 confessing that "we view with no little apprehension the readiness of Presbyterians to contribute to outside enterprises . . . while making insufficient provision for the work of our own Boards."[60] "We ought to feel ourselves, we should instruct our children," Samuel Capen said a decade before joining the American Board, "that fidelity to our denominational missionary work is a most solemn trust, received from any father."[61] When support was solicited on the basis of loyalty to a particular church instead of dedication to Christianity's mission, the contributions of foreign missions to ecumenicalism were more hoped for than actually achieved.

Among the least consistent of the minor promotional themes was the contribution supposedly made to American diplomacy by overseas missions. Secular appeals for foreign mission support were inconsistent, both because of the varied constituencies of the boards, and because of their efforts to stay abreast of change. Thus the fascinating idiosyncracies of the heathen were featured in one appeal, while another issued a humanitarian call emphasizing the brotherhood of all men. The churches' participation in American expansion demanded support before the turn of the century, but this was replaced by dedication to world peace as a primary goal during the decades before World War I. Once the Anglo-Saxon's religion was held to be an essential accompaniment to his civilizing mission, but by 1906 Lyman Abbott could criticize the Haystack Centennial audience for acting as if their religion was national property rather than worldwide in its validity. Jesus Christ is the son of God and the son of man he reminded them, "not a son of the Germanic race, not a son of New England, not a son of the Orient."[62]

Instead of using racial or cultural superiority to justify the crusade to civilize backward nations, the unique transforming power and universality of Christianity were stressed. "We would give the whole world a Christian civilization with everything which this includes," pledged President Capen in 1910. And while he transformed heathendom into Christendom, the missionary was removing the bases for war. "If the Missionary Boards could have one-fourth of the cost of the navies of the Christian nations we could plant Christian institutions which would help mightily to bring universal peace." Or if Mr. Carnegie would only invest his millions in missions, observed Capen, how much more would be done to secure the peace for which he stood.[63]

Missions as a panacea in international relations were only one aspect of another widely used theme. The fund raisers offered Americans an opportunity to participate in an epochal enterprise in which they could leave their mark on history. A style familiar from commercial advertising was borrowed to describe evangelization. "We want to mobilize the men of today for the last great struggle. Our times are for 'big' things," wrote Samuel Capen. "We are coming to a 'big' time in missions, for the time of formal praying and petty giving is about over. It is a 'man's job' to organize and finance the evangelization of a thousand millions of people."[64]

This celebration of bigness and epochal enterprises became a keynote of the Laymen's Movement's propaganda. The movement addressed itself to the "responsible Christian business and professional men . . . who, in the management of large business and political responsibilities, have been greatly used and honored." But for the small store-owner or insurance agent tied to his routine and neighborhood, who also read this declaration, the effect was one of subtle flattery. Our appeal, a 1908 promotional leaflet continued, is made "on the ground that these sturdy, brainy, capable and competent men who run the machinery, guide the enterprise, and hold the purse strings of the world take but little stock in missions, and that they need the cause as much as the cause needs them."[65]

The call to participate in great things was hopefully directed toward the wealthy. "If they will," observed Capen, "our rich men can plant Christian institutions everywhere in the East and rule it for Christ."[66] But at the same time this approach sought to make the small businessman feel he was one of the mighty also. The world's one hundred and twenty million Protestants control most of the world's wealth and brains, a Laymen's Movement pamphleteer assured his readers. They formed a heroic, optimistic, enthusiastic army ready to carry Christ to sin-cursed millions. "To fight in its ranks would be glorious, even in a losing cause, for it would be to know the joy of living. But to fight and win, as win they must— what soul of any appreciable stature can resist the inspiring inducement?"[67]

Since only a contribution was required to enlist, many did sign up and provided testimonials to the enlargement of life experienced after becoming liberal givers to missions. "There is nothing provincial about me since I have done that," reported an Atlanta attorney. "I am a citizen of the world."[68] Although the effectiveness of this particular approach can only be guessed at, it is significant that both the Laymen's Movement and most denominational agencies continued to stress in their propaganda the opportunities for personal enlargement and truly significant service promised to the liberal contributor to their crusade.

Since the prewar decade was characterized by an unprecedented campaign to enlist the support of Christian businessmen, it was inevitable that the most popular of the nonspiritual appeals for foreign missions be phrased in economic terms. Pamphleteers and preachers sought to identify the movement with the business outlook and dynamism of the day, and insisted that foreign commerce and missions were natural and mutually beneficial collaborators. Since evangelization was also presented as a vital ingredient in a crusade against materialism, there is irony in the use of material motives to mount the proposed expedition. The jeremiads warning of prosperity came from all directions. "Waning Christianity and waxing materialism are the twin specters of our age," declared President Jacob Schurman of Cornell. "The love of money and the reckless pursuit of it are undermining the national character."[69] "I doubt if any one of the Christian ages," agreed Dartmouth's William

Tucker, "ever needed as much as we need the balance and corrective of foreign missions to match the overwhelming appeal of the material world to the imagination of men."[70]

This theme marked a switch from the period when the Conwells, Beechers, and Lawrences had reminded businessmen of their Christian duty to make money. Whether on the advice of eminent divines or not, they had accumulated wealth and now stood accused of covetousness and corruption. They were made uneasy by assertions of preoccupation with money, and uncomfortable by charges that their only contribution to American life was a materialistic one. Philanthropy provided an answer because their money advanced the finer things in life, and even an opportunity to further spiritual ends.[71]

For church members, the foreign mission movement stood ready to convert materialistic contributions into laudable service. "We believe we must lose ourselves in this foreign work," said Samuel Capen for the other businessmen of the Laymen's Movement executive committee, "in order to save ourselves from materialism here at home."[72] Well before the laymen had organized, Capen had urged American businessmen to consecrate their businesses to God and support personal representatives abroad as the only means of protecting their Christian character from the peril of the contemporary "surcharged worldly atmosphere."[73] Here was a confident new sanctification of moneymaking, perhaps even the substitution of works for faith. "I am going back home resolved to be the very best lawyer ever I was in my life, and to make all the money I can," wrote an enthusiastic attorney after a Laymen's convention, "and send it out to help preach the Gospel throughout the world."[74]

This attitude was less a matter of ambivalence about two sets of values than a voluntary wearing of blinders. To make money and glory in the making was sinful. But if a reasonable proportion of the profits was dedicated to spiritual goals, no questions would be asked about the method of accumulation. The social gospel followers provided an antidote to the earlier justification of acquisitiveness by confronting industrialism and trying to mitigate its evils. Walter

Rauschenbusch explained his interest in the economic system by pointing out that it was "the strategical key to the spiritual conquest of the modern world."[75]

Mission leaders made a similar identification, but were not concerned with the system itself, which they would neither challenge nor specifically praise. They criticized only its success, and sold indulgences to those willing to apply the stewardship principle to their profits. The closest they came to studying business operations was to borrow as many modern administrative techniques as could be applied to their own enterprise. Beyond that, business was an abstraction—a neuter productive force to be harnessed. Bishop W. X. Ninde confessed to a Student Volunteer convention in 1898 that perhaps the clergy had made a mistake in lamenting the business frenzy of the times and the manner in which it preoccupied young men. Rather than be trampled in trying to stop the runaway, might it not be better to put a new motive in the saddle?

> Oh! it seems to me that the Elder Brother sometimes comes to these active, busy Christian young men and says to them: "Listen to me; that business appetite and habit of yours is not necessarily wrong. It may be your talent for service. I have great plans, vast enterprises, for bringing this world to my feet. I need vast outlays of money. I need your business capacity . . . Come with me, enter into my councils, sit down on my throne, become my partner."

When a man heeds that voice, maintained the Methodist bishop, his conception of business is revolutionized and "the line between the sacred and the secular vanishes forever."[76]

Mission spokesmen not only neglected to apply the critique of social Christianity to the economic system, but it was largely under their auspices that the business-justified Protestantism of the 1920s received its start. Bruce Barton's Galilean salesman, and Milton Hershey's recommendation of Bible study as a course in salesmanship and business English, were not mere reflections of

postwar cynicism and the death of progressivism.[77] Their counterparts and predecessors were actively promoting foreign missions at
the turn of the century. "It has been found that many men can be
reached through the presentation of the commercial effects of missions at home and abroad," wrote the editor of one of Capen's
economic homilies, "who are untouched by higher motives. . . Any
motive which will arouse men from indifference and neglect is
valuable," he concluded lamely. But habitual use of just "any
motive" was also bound to leave its mark on the cause it was used
to promote.

The more general connection between commerce and
evangelization had a long and respectable history which seventeenth-
century Englishmen traced to St. Augustine, and which had been
integral to the European voyages of exploration and the settlement
of North America.[79] The assumption of inevitable and happy col-
lusion was rather uncritically maintained as long as there was no
alternate means of spreading the gospel. It was reflected in early
mission sermons and as late as 1871 the hypercritic of the organized
mission movement, James Batchelder, assured his readers that
"GOD will work, overrulingly, through commercial enterprises, and
all the avenues of trade, for the realization of His grand designs."[80]
To Batchelder, this meant that mission boards were extraneous. To
the boards themselves, it meant that they had a reliable ally in
trade. But critic and supporters agreed in assuming that Christian
commercial activity would automatically extend Christianity.

As both the numbers and resources of mission agencies expanded during the nineteenth century, the necessity for maintaining the fiction that all or most merchants were also pious Christians
diminished. "Commerce is going everywhere," admitted Samuel
Capen in 1903, "and commerce without Christ is a curse. It means
firearms and the slave trade and rum."[81] The soaring generalities
prophesying universal progress and brotherhood in the wake of the
profit motive more and more commonly provided no place for the
gospel. Contemporary businessmen might maintain that "selfish
huckstering trade was the meliorator of the world," and "the most
powerful agent of civilization and progress,"[82] but mission leaders

tended to be unconvinced. Commerce might remain a useful ally, but it was increasingly seen as another facet of their civilization that needed Christianizing. "The doors are open all over the world and the commercial traveler is entering everywhere," complained Samuel Capen. "It is to be an open door for all kinds of business and a closed door for the Gospel of Christ?"[83] The old identity of interest was obviously gone.

The churches became increasingly reluctant to acknowledge the merchant as their agent, and were less interested in gaining passage for their missionaries on his vessels than in receiving a share of his profits to spend independently. Mission leaders wanted the businessman to pay tribute to the traditional relationship in a different coin, but it became increasingly difficult to convince him that he had anything to gain from the association. Laymen and their money were always more important to the mission movement than missions were to business. This fact produced a sometimes brazenly opportunistic type of promotional literature which sought to demonstrate immediate commercial benefits in return for business support to missions. Since religious interests took the initiative and played the role of supplicant in this approach, it is erroneous to cite this literature as proof that the missionary was the "running dog of imperialism." The businessman did not ask the missionary to be his salesman. He was bombarded with propaganda which tried to convince him that the missionary inevitably helped him also.

Nearly every book written by missionaries or mission publicists during this period included at least a plug for the patriotic economic potential of their work. A mission college professor, asking for corporate gifts to stations and facilities in China, promised that this would turn every missionary into a drummer and their home churches into advertising agencies for the generous companies.[84] Another educator predicted that the missionary's unconscious contribution to the revolution of rising expectations produced more customers for American business in China than converts to Christianity.[85] Even a distinguished old China hand like W. A. P. Martin felt it necessary to support this claim, though reluctantly, by holding up the prospect of millions taught to wear imported shirts washed in foreign soap.[86]

Men and Missions was making an effort to convince skeptics when it informed its readers that Sears Roebuck, Standard Oil, and the Singer Sewing Machine Company owed most of their market in China to missionary promotion. "There isn't an American missionary in China who would stand back a minute in recommending to his Chinese friends the purchase of American merchandise," a newsman assured a laymen's audience in 1919. "For this reason the all-too-well-developed tendency among a certain class of American foreign trade representatives to ridicule and belittle the work of missionaries is not only the height of ignorance, but a real knock at American ideals."[87] The American Board considered it worthwhile to reprint an item from the New York *Journal of Commerce* which commended the missionary's civilizing task, and also credited him with a tenuous economic role. The fact that English-speaking missionaries also taught converts the language of world commerce was taken to make "missions of paramount importance to the spread of British and American commerce."[88] A treaty-port journalist was employed to defend the missionary as a salesman. A mission board republished a trade journal's commendation for spreading the language of commerce. The economic utility of foreign missions seems to have been less than obvious to the American business community.

Still, this traditional sub-motive continued to find a place in the movement's propaganda. The addition of an adjective cured Samuel Capen of his fear of Christ-less commerce and allowed him to argue that it was simple self-interest for businessmen to support mission work: "When a heathen man becomes a child of God and is changed within he wants his external life and surroundings to correspond: he wants the Christian dress and the Christian home and the Christian plow and all the other things which distinguish Christian civilization from the narrow and degraded life of the heathen."[89]

After asserting that "we need to develop foreign missions to save our nation commercially," Capen supported his claim in terms reminiscent of Brooks Adams or Alfred Thayer Mahan. Without an increase in our overseas markets, he reasoned, it was inevitable that recurring business depressions would increase. Just as obvious was the fact "that only as we develop missionary work and create the needs which come with Christian civilization can we have these larger markets."[90] The remainder of this memorable economic discourse was laced with both graphic examples of profitable ventures and warnings of business depressions, such as the wholesale closing of American cotton mills which followed the Boxers' attacks in China.

Along with a more sophisticated presentation of missionary utility, the twentieth-century use of this theme was more brazen and widely circulated. A former consul illustrated the familiar argument with spectacular examples of missionary enterprise in a national magazine, for example, and concluded patronizingly: "No matter what church you belong to, no matter whether you drop a dime or not when the heathen hat is passed, you must admit it does look as if the missionary is a pretty good trade scout and publicity man for Uncle Sam, even if his own ballyhoo is a bit timid and lumpy."[91] The effectiveness of this line of propaganda is difficult to evaluate. Even in Christian business circles there were cynics who refused to take the argument seriously, particularly since the claims of mission publicists were so flatly contradicted by the realities of American trade with China.[92] Other loyal supporters of missions were offended by the exploitation of materialistic motives for a spiritual cause, and there is no evidence of self-serving business support for China's evangelization.[93]

The attempt to prove that the fringe benefits of missions were profitable had little relevance to the majority of the business community who were not engaged in foreign trade. Pandering to materialism was less necessary, and a far larger audience could be reached with a more subtle economic theme. Publicists increasingly attempted to identify missions with the mystique of big business, industrial progress, and innovation. Any American proud of his nation's rise to power, and thrilled by the achievements of gigantic new enterprises, was asked to recognize that the mission movement was mounted on a similar scale. Businessmen, in particular, were reassured that no corporation was more efficiently run or product-oriented than the agencies engaged in evangelizing the world. "We are not advising investment in a theory," wrote a board secretary, "we are seeking additional capital for a going concern which is a compelling, world-sweeping success."[94]

From this point of view, what had been castigated as a sin of the faithful in the past now became bad business and of concern to everyone. Thus the Presbyterian General Assembly was told in 1902 that by investing only nickels and dimes Presbyterians were guilty of playing at foreign missions. "Men are eagerly pouring their millions into great trusts for the gaining of other millions . . . ," a special committee explained, "while the Church of a million members, by hook or crook, manages to squeeze out a million dollars for the salvation of a billion souls! We make a plaything out of that which God gave us for our business, while we make a business of the things which He intended should be our playthings!"[95] Mission entrepreneurs sought more capitalists who would act on John Wanamaker's conviction, "that religion is the only investment that pays the largest dividends possible to receive, both in this life and in that to come."[96]

To attract such investors they engaged in flattery and built convenient bridges between formerly unrelated areas of enterprise. Laymen's Movement pamphleteers assured men who were used to big enterprises that missions were just as stirring and in need of the same talents. Meanwhile, others were reassured that "most business-men are not avaricious . . . often they are men of vision, of poetic temperament who love the exhilaration of large things. There is something sublime in the dream of a Cecil Rhodes."[97]

Board administrators also worked to dispel a lingering aura of other-worldliness. On the eve of a new drive to capture major contributors, a friendly retired banker warned the Secretarial Council of the Laymen's Movement "of the importance of keeping the stewardship campaign free from any machinery or ecclesiastical management to which big business men will not respond."[98] When the same movment's chairman sought the support of "the mature men of to-day who now have in hand the money which they can give if they will," he outlined a plan for avoiding denominational competition in the campaign. "This plan will appeal to the businessmen of to-day," he promised. "It is in harmony with modern methods in the business world. We want to utilize the principles of legitimate promoting."[99]

As president of the American Board and chairman of the Laymen's Movement, Samuel Capen was a leading practitioner of the business approach. He was sometimes criticized for exploiting an unworthy theme that was lacking in altruistic motives, but as a merchant himself he knew this was the strongest card he could play. "His arguments were thought out in the counting room," recorded his biographer; "his facts were gathered from the commercial world. He did not go to literature nor to history for his illustrations; he found them in his conversations with business men . . . and all his facts and illustrations and arguments were arranged to appeal to the businessman."[100] The professional secretaries of the Laymen's Movement agreed that this approach forced men to look up from their ledgers to confront the Great Commission. As never before, they saw businessmen "listening, not to the droning of mystic preachments, but to the hard logic of facts and the clear call of duty, coming from their own ranks, in the language of the market and the tea table, and they are striking hands to do the square thing."[101]

The business pitch for missions reached its apogee during the 1920s. The year after the *Saturday Evening Post*'s long treatment of missionary hucksters, Cornelius Patton appeared on the market with *The Business of Missions.* This book, by the American Board's Home Secretary, artfully summarized the whole economic appeal for mission support. It was dedicated to all who were both Christian and practical men. The approach was sophisticated and avoided the more blatant claims of economic utility. "This is a business view of foreign missions," the foreword warned, "but let no one suppose it is a view of foreign missions for the sake of business." Patton set a higher tone for his appeal without denying the efficacy of the practical approach. The idea that mission institutions "in foreign lands are beneficial to American trade has been sufficiently exploited. The contention is true enough."[102] With the confident air of a reasonable man talking business with his colleagues, Patton expounded to a more receptive generation what had traditionally been a minor theme of mission advocacy.

The business approach to mission financing was bound to attract some tainted money.[103] Suppressed discontent among the constituency of the movement over the various secular appeals that were employed found a focus when promotionalism brought contributions from unsanctified coffers. The controversy that erupted over John D. Rockefeller's $100,000 gift to the American Board in 1905 was only the most spectacular incident. Like unpublicized crises over lesser amounts, Rockefeller's offering drew fire from a curious alliance of traditionalists and liberals. Social gospel leaders, such as Washington Gladden, condemned the acceptance of the ill-gotten gains of monopolists. The old guard of the mission constituency, who basically resented the use of unbecoming appeals, agreed with the less controversial sentiment that "God's people in the world have got all the money that God needs, and He doesn't want, He doesn't need the money of ungodly men."[104] Part of the larger debate over means and ends in mission movement publicity thus raised the moral issue of justifying the acceptance of either ill-gotten gains, or the legitimate profits of otherwise disreputable contributors.

As they had with other potentially controversial issues ever since the pre-Civil War debate over the collection of money from slave owners, mission leaders sidestepped the question of whether all contributions to their cause were equally acceptable. The prevalent attitude among those not convinced by Bishop William Lawrence's rationalization that "it is only to the men of morality that wealth comes," and that "Godliness is in league with riches,"[105] was to either consider money a neuter factor, or one sanctified by proper use. Hoarded wealth, or cash kept merely to make still more, might raise moral questions. But if placed into the channels of benevolence the dollar both benefited the donor and lost its former character. Even if use alone did not accomplish the transformation, the churches stood ready to accept any "money sanctified by the motive which gives it."[106] Francis Peabody differed when he argued that "the first searching of a man's heart should not concern the Christian distribution of his gains, but the Christian getting of his gains."[107] But these and other disturbing questions raised by social gospel writers were either ignored or dismissed with comforting conundrums like Robert E. Speer's "You cannot serve God and mammon, but you can serve God with mammon."[108]

The classic test of these competing principles embroiled America's oldest foreign mission board, one of whose secretaries had quietly approached a wealthy Baptist steward with a record of generosity toward higher education.[109] The American Board crossed denominational lines because of its inability to provide for the increasing cost of maintaining mission colleges in the field with contributions from a constituency who could rarely afford a college education for their own children. There was jubilation in the board's rooms when two years of maneuvering and the careful cultivation of Rockefeller's secretary for benevolences, Frederick T. Gates, produced a $100,000 gift to the Congregational agency.

Congratulations were forthcoming not only over the large sum, but because the economic themes that mission propagandists had been stressing had apparently convinced the multimillionaire to make the largest contribution he had yet made to a religious enterprise outside his own denomination. "Quite apart from the question of persons converted," the former Reverend Mr. Gates had written Rockefeller in his customary analysis of the request, "the mere commercial results of missionary efforts to our own land is worth, I had almost said a thousand fold every year what is spent on missions." Citing supporting statistics, he elaborated on the "immensely profitable" by-products in supporting the American Board's request.[110]

Although Gladden was frustrated in efforts to force the money's return and in securing a resolution imposing a denominational prohibition on similar solicitations, he claimed victory because of private assurances that the spirit of his proposal would govern the board's future conduct.[111] There is no evidence, however, that the board learned anything but discretion from the entire episode.[112] Any thorough application of moral tests would have been illegal for an incorporated body, and inconsistent for an agency that had also accepted offerings from Moslems, Shintoists, and African savages. It also would have been paralyzing since it would require the wholesale resignation of wealthy corporate members who had provided solid support to their executives throughout the affair.[113] The prevailing view was best expressed by a canny Yankee who offered his advice as a long-time contributor to the ABCFM: "If the devil himself should give 100 M. knowing it would be devoted to the most noble cause known in this earth, as yours is," wrote old John Barry, "you would be a fool not to take it, and he would also be a fool to make an offer tending to undermine his kingdom."[114]

Whether the money came from fools, heathen, or monopolists, the prevailing need made it acceptable. To President Capen, acceptance of Gladden's strictures meant the loss of millions to missions and to other philanthropic enterprises. Other denominations and agencies wrote to support him in his insistence on "the right to solicit and accept from lawful owners, it being made perfectly clear that we pass judgement on no man and condone no one's faults." "There must be an 'open door' here," he wrote Lyman Abbott, "so that we as trustees may 'convert' money and put it to higher uses."[115] Rockefeller himself was assured that "the discussion of great economic questions will be in the end helpful and not harmful, and as a result of it all, the principle for which the Prudential Committee is contending will be clearly seen to be the only one that is tenable."[116]

Without doubt, the ABCFM stand was the only practical one. There is also little question that it was not based on a loftier moral principle than that of the protesters who briefly raised the issue, then lapsed back into passive acceptance of the practices of organized religious benevolences. Had Rockefeller not made his gift at the peak of muckraker preoccupation with his role and business operations, the gift might have passed virtually unnoticed. As it was, the public furor briefly focused the religious community's attention on the moral issues involved in mission fund-raising activities. The decision to seek contributions from America's wealthiest men, and the increased emphasis on economic motives for mission support, were both called into question. When only a minority of the movement's constituency displayed strenuous objections to these policies, mission leaders saw no reason to change their approach. They may have temporarily muted their appeals as a concession to hostile public opinion, but the campaign to enlist the businessman in missions continued. A year after the outcry died down, the president of the American Board helped found the Laymen's Missionary Movement, which became the most effective embodiment of the proposed linking of business with foreign missions.

Chapter 5

FUND RAISING AND FINANCIAL POLICIES

*Of those who give, some do it only from the impulse of
special occasions; some to save appearances; others systemat-
ically and from principle; though their consciences are too
often satisfied with donations so very small, that, but for the
account book, they might never know that they had done
anything.*[1]

Identifying the constituency and selecting the themes most
likely to attract its support were not the fund raisers' only concerns.
In the reciprocal relationship of the mission boards with their particular public, the volume of contributions received depended also on
the way in which money was collected and the manner in which the
societies' administration was conducted. The techniques and administration of fund raising provide additional insights into the
nature of the foreign mission enterprise and its relationship to other
areas of American society. The movement's base was determined
not only by who was asked, or the inducement employed, but also
by the asking itself.

The changes required by an expanding mission movement in
the development of new promotional themes were most obvious in
their practical presentation to the public. The traditional foci of
all efforts were the congregations and existing religious associations
and auxiliaries. As the source of the bulk of all contributions, the
cultivation of this captive constituency was vigorously pursued. A
second category consisted of the boards, or special departments
within them, acting as general fund-raising agencies outside denominational or organizational limitations. With other demands on their
personnel, and geographical and practical limitations on the scope
of these efforts, a third category of fund raising developed after the
turn of the century outside the established mission boards. Funds
could be raised through participation in centrally directed denom-

141

inational campaigns, or via the ministrations of such nondenominational national organizations as the Laymen's Movement.

Traditional Mission Board Fund Raising
Since the majority of American foreign mission agencies by
the end of the nineteenth century were departments of, or closely
affiliated with, the regular Protestant denominations, their appeals
for funds were made to a narrow constituency in competition with
other church agencies, and their freedom of action in seeking additional support was restricted. In trying to win their fair share, the
boards persisted in trying to educate church members to consider
foreign missions as more than a minor or occasional part of their
religious obligations. Missions were presented as the touchstone of
Christian faithfulness, "the center of the life of every church, the
supreme test of loyalty to the Master."[2]

That this remained more a hopeful slogan than accepted doctrine can be seen from the fact that barely half the Congregational
Churches in 1907 were making a regular contribution to their almost one hundred-year-old American Board. The report disclosing
this condition also showed that the noncontributing churches were,
for the most part, smaller congregations or those that existed
merely on paper. The board had little interest in raising this percentage, however, since it had discovered that "by far the most
promising source of income is the non-contributing element in our
contributing churches."[3] In confronting the problem of static support from Presbyterian churches, a similar conclusion was reached
and the average contributor identified. "If the bulk of the resources
needed for the world's evangelization are to come, as doubtless
they are, from the poor, or the modestly well-to-do," reported the
board, "they must come probably through an increase of church
offerings in the churches which now give moderately, or which,
if they appear to give generously, may yet be able to raise their
conception of generous giving to a higher level."[4]

To reach a higher level it was necessary to make a stronger
impact on congregations that often made only token contributions
out of habit or denominational loyalty. Traditional practice was to

follow an annual missionary sermon with a collection which represented the membership's sole contribution to the denomination's
foreign board for the year. A lackluster sermon, or poor attendance
due to bad weather, or vacations could thus directly influence the
budgets of the national boards. The limited funds produced by lone
annual services led the boards to suggest quarterly or more frequent
collections. They also offered speakers to relieve the minister and
used missionaries on home furloughs to address church groups for
the same purpose. In recommending this method to other societies
in 1902, an American Board secretary reported that over 800
addresses had been made by visiting missionaries sent to Congregational churches in a single five-state district.[5] Sometimes, however,
the collections they brought back to the board offices were less
than the payment for pulpit supply would have cost the congregation.[6] And resistance to more frequent Mission Sundays was strong
because the home mission, Sunday school, ministerial retirement
fund, and other denominational agencies all depended on similar
appeals and demanded an equal opportunity to present their cases.
The introduction of duplex envelopes to make weekly mission
contributions a habit seems to have had only limited success in the
prewar decades.[7]

Another technique used by mission boards in winning a
special place in local church benevolent giving was the sponsorship
of mite or cent societies. They were initially largely composed of
women banded together to contribute two cents a week or some
regular small gift to a special cause.[8] During the second half of the
nineteenth century they evolved into women's mission societies
effectively coordinated by national boards. Because they preceded
the formation of women's auxiliaries for most other benevolent
causes, they often maintained a virtual local monopoly of the most
active churchwomen and aroused scarcely concealed envy from
other denominational agencies. They had always been an essential
link between local churches and the sending agencies, but their
importance increased as feminine control of household finances
and individual ownership of property became more prevalent. "In
some churches," admitted Samuel Capen in 1900, "it has almost

seemed at times as though if the woman's work was taken out, there would be nothing left."[9] Such organizations were particularly susceptible to adopting particular stations, or missionary families, and supplying them with both necessities and little luxuries not allowed for in official budgets.

As Christian Endeavor Societies, Sunday schools, and denominational youth groups became more common, mission boards directed considerable attention to them as channels for their educational activities. The objective was less the raising of significant amounts of money than the training of a new generation of givers before they too became fixed in their habitual apathy.[10] Sunday school classes and young people's groups also provided a convenient means of distributing promotional literature with a high probability that the material would be studied. As late as 1902, a conference of board executives was advised that the traditional "missionary magazine is the most fruitful agent for collecting money that we have." It was promoted as virtually the only means by which direct news of missionaries in every field could be transmitted into American homes.[11]

The development of personal ties through letters or visits on furloughs was another productive method of increasing support. Sometimes the adoption of an individual missionary by an American church was a spontaneous gesture by a congregation eager to support one of its own sons who had volunteered for foreign service. More often the boards suggested that the church in which a candidate had been ordained, or served during his training period, might wish to assume part of the expense of maintaining him overseas. Foreign missions, personalized in the form of a familiar individual who wrote regular letters and sent pictures for stereoptican shows, provided a more immediate and dramatic object of support than general appeals sent from denominational headquarters. An enthusiastic speaker could bring the suffering of his flock, the lamentable needs of unevangelized thousands blindly reveling in hideous superstition and idolatry, and the smell of the primitive dispensary in the station storeroom into a church meeting as no brochure could. He might also forge a productive tie between himself and the congregation as a result.

Board administrators had mixed emotions about exploiting such personal contacts. By providing an opportunity to contribute to the support of a particular missionary, or to special projects or needs, they could escape the limitations imposed by infrequently scheduled fund appeals. Both personal identifications and the assumption of responsibility could produce sharp increases in congregational contributions.[12] Over 600 of the Northern Presbyterian Board's 700 missionaries in 1900, for example, were individually supported in this way.[13] But individual support rarely meant total or dependable support.

The payment of a token amount toward the salary of a minister in the field often satisfied church members that their whole obligation to foreign missions had been met. Meanwhile the boards had to pay the expense of administration, and supervise those projects outside their regular plans or budgets which they referred to as special objects. They also sometimes found themselves forced to finance work initiated through such gifts after the original donor had died, or as the project expanded beyond the ability of an individual or small group to support. "Special object giving is inevitable as people are now constituted," resolved a Foreign Missions Conference committee in 1899, "but . . . it should be regarded as prompted by a distinctly inferior motive, and that as far as practicable, such giving should be confined to objects which have been approved by the Boards, and which are within the regular appropriations for the year."[14] Board approval and supervision was absolutely essential since the societies were heavily dependent on the family and friends of their missionaries who formed a critical part of their regular constituency. "Manifestly, if each missionary encourages or allows his own circle to send its gifts directly to him," concluded a special mission conference committee, "the chief source of our supply would be dried up."[15] For those boards that depended on this relationship, achieving closer ties with individual congregations was not an unmixed blessing.

The Broader Outreach of the Boards

The traditional fund-raising activities were engaged in by all foreign mission boards in cultivating their normal constituency in the churches. It was expected that the churches of a particular denomination would support an appropriate overseas mission, and that the agency that administered this activity would primarily cultivate this base. The mission boards, however, were constantly searching for ways of expanding their base and reducing their dependence on local churches. The direction this effort would take was determined both by their constitutions and by the initiative of particular secretaries. In another sense, some of the broader fund-raising techniques resulted from the mission board's functions as an administrative agency, others from its functions as a professional fund-raising organization.

The administrative determination of membership conditions, for example, could be an important factor in board income. The extreme example is provided by the Foreign Christian Missionary Society, which before 1887 received no support from Disciples congregations, and determined the scope of each year's activities solely by the volume of life directorships and memberships sold at the annual convention.[16] Since the possession of cash was the only concrete condition for membership under these circumstances, criticism of this practice increased as denominations assumed closer supervision over their mission agencies. Memberships continued to be granted with an eye to improving support of the boards but in a manner more reminiscent of the selection of trustees and honorary degree candidates in contemporary college fund raising. An appointment might be made to attract potential contributors or leaders, or as a reward for increasing interest in a particular locality.[17] Secretaries concerned with long-range strategy paid attention to appropriate geographical and denominational representation and sought information concerning potential legators. With proper management, in other words, board memberships could continue to provide the source of income even when outright sale was prohibited.

Less formal means of recognition, such as publicity in denominational periodicals or at annual meetings, were also used to attract individual contributions. Even after World War I, the readers of established missionary magazines still provided the majority of annuity and legacy gifts, although cause and effect are not clearly discernible in this pattern.[18] Waning legacy receipts were met with various expedients which had the additional advantage of demonstrating the business acumen of board administrators to a broader constituency.[19] Board advisers developed conditional bequest and annuity plans, the most popular form involving the surrender of cash or securities to a mission society which in return guaranteed a fixed income from the interest during the life of the donor.[20] The avoidance of legal battles, inheritance taxes, and delays, commended the annuity plan to both parties.

After the turn of the century some boards also moved in the direction of investing funds rather than spending legacy receipts as part of the annual budget.[21] Endowment funds for missionary colleges, as well as such innovations as the Twentieth Century Fund initiated by the businessman president of the American Board, represented an effort by administrators to neutralize the effects of fluctuating annual receipts on long-range plans and commitments in the field. Since current budgetary needs were often too urgent to allow diversion of receipts for endowment purposes, such funds rarely lived up to expectations. Only a special drive or campaign could induce the constituency to make the necessary additional contributions, and many administrators were skeptical of these since they were often followed by letdowns and reduced receipts from regular church contributions in subsequent years.

Any voluntary organization staffing and maintaining a permanent physical plant scattered over several continents is bound to incur occasional budgetary deficits. The size of annual budgets was ultimately not determined by fixed costs or by the objective requirements of the work in the field, but by such imponderables as economic recessions, a snow storm on Mission Sunday, reactions by the constituency to a scandal or theological dispute, or unexpected fluctuations in exchange rates. Most of the periodic budgetary deficits incurred by the major mission societies were unfortunate accidents. Occasionally, however, there was evidence of an inclination toward a unique form of modern deficit financing.

This is not to say that fiscal irresponsibility was common, or that accounts were not scrupulously kept in the bastion of the Puritan ethic. During the nineteenth century, however, the majority of mission administrators were clergymen and not businessmen or professionals. Their training led them sometimes to take the parable of the fishes and loaves as seriously as the new business techniques recommended by well-meaning advisers. Would not the Lord somehow provide for a man willing to surrender his life to an idealistic cause? In addition to such faith, the practical psychology extracted from long experience provided hope that the faithful would ultimately respond to an adequately demonstrated crisis.

Solitary examples of individual missionaries who had exhausted their own funds and yet somehow survived in the field seemed to corroborate this view. Small "faith missions" also existed, representing either minor fundamentalist sects or organized for some special project initiated by individual missionaries. Only the China Inland Mission, however, operated on the faith principle as a matter of policy, sending missionaries to the field as travel funds were available and leaving their future maintenance to providence rather than to budgetary planning.[22]

No other major American sending agency displayed the same faith, and all tended to operate within planned budgets. When they were only departments of a particular denominational administration they had little opportunity for engaging in deficit financing in any event. Yet a veteran officer of the Disciples' Foreign Christian Missionary Society, which adhered to a strict policy of never undertaking anything without first having the required money in hand, claimed that many of the larger societies followed an opposite approach. They sent every man to the field who would go, he reported wistfully, and they prospered on credit. He attributed to an American Board secretary the observation that "all the advances made by that Board were made by getting into debt. The debt was paid, and the Board went on to larger things."[23]

In a policy paper prepared for the American Board in 1897, Secretary Hall indicated the utility of that year's deficit by pointing out that nearly half of the anticipated $85,000 debt had been removed during a three-week period in response to personal letters to certain "friends of the Board."[24] On other occasions special pleas to avert the shame of reporting a deficit at the annual meeting resulted in last minute pledges of thousands of dollars.[25] Similar techniques were forced on the Presbyterians, a special committee informing the General Assembly in 1902 that funds never came in regularly or as needed but at the conclusion of the year, "when the Board, growing desperate with the fear of a debt staring it in the face, is compelled to write tens of thousands of letters . . . and send forth its executive officers at their busiest time to organize conferences, and cry 'Debt, Debt!' until the churches make up the deficit."[26] Whatever the secretaries might feel about the moral value of balanced budgets, there is reason to believe they also used the leverage of their constituencies' firmer adherence to that principle.

A survey of the experience of leading American mission boards during the 1920s revealed that a majority had overexpanded in the field, appointed new missionaries in greater numbers than they had assurance of being able to support in the future, and raised salaries beyond their ability to continue payment after the advent of the depression. Requested to name other "policies which later proved unfortunate," the respondents listed borrowing in the hope of increased income or for special projects, failure to pay the debts before the depression, and bluntly: "our greatest mistake was made by operating with a deficit during the 1920's."[27] Whether these policies reflected an overoptimistic assessment of mission movement prospects, or a calculated challenge to the boards' constituencies, it is clear that deficit financing had become common practice with America's major Protestant mission agencies during the early decades of this century. Whether used consciously or inadvertently, this policy tended to increase total receipts.

That such policies could be openly debated is one indication of the increased importance in the mission movement of the professional administrator. Particularly in fund raising, an experienced secretary was of crucial importance to the efficient operations of a board. Employing someone of the caliber of a James L. Barton, who was credited with being the leading force in raising some $33,000,000 for mission-related colleges before his retirement in 1927, gave an obvious advantage to the American Board.[28] At the turn of the century board executives became aware of the significant difference in their income that the addition of a promotional specialist to their staff could make. But the nature of the work prevented simply recruiting such men from the business world, and academic institutions were not providing training in public relations or fund raising. The mission board fund-raising expert was thus usually a fortuitous accident, someone who happened to be on the staff and was allowed to specialize. He was a self-taught specialist employing a pragmatic psychology shaped by experience, and social grace, drive, or intuition were more likely to determine his success than seniority or training.

This new breed of secretaries had nothing in common except their work. The successful fund raiser often had his choice of similar positions with other benevolent agencies once he demonstrated his value. Denominational loyalties usually kept senior secretaries from accepting other offers and, as they remained in the same position for decades, they formed close ties with their counterparts in other societies. They encountered each other at various religious functions, and the club met regularly at the annual sessions of the Foreign Missions Conference of North America.[29]

It was in the cultivation of individual donors that the expert home secretary proved his value. Cornelius Patton estimated in 1924 that no less than one-third of the annual receipts of the major boards came in the form of donations apart from church offerings. A sizable supplementary income of this sort, however, resulted only from persistent personal contact and the cultivation of a select number of the boards' constituents.[30] Such appeals were usually shrouded in secrecy for practical reasons, and the boards tended to be apologetic about having to resort to such approaches. "Why should the widow give her two mites to foreign missions if Dives stands ready to wipe out the deficit at the end of the year?", asked Walter Rauschenbusch.[31]

After the furor over the secret appeal to Rockefeller had subsided, Patton's board found it necessary to admit that, although special appeals to individual givers were regrettable, "it must be remembered that there are thousands of friends of the Board who are not in touch with any Congregational Church, and who never hear of our condition except through this kind of personal communication."[32] The American Board was fortunate in having the services of outstanding fund raisers such as James L. Barton and Brewer Eddy; other boards found it necessary to employ outside agents with the proper experience in soliciting individual prospects.[33]

David Brewer Eddy, younger brother of the YMCAs' Sherwood, was an outstanding example of the successful practitioner in this individualistic type of fund raising. Through personal charm and individual interviews, rather than mass campaigns, he raised hundreds of thousands of dollars during his thirty-five years of service to the American Board. He was a patient man with a gift for gaining the confidence of his prospects. An insulting letter sent to the American Board offices by an eccentric old Yale man, for example, was turned by Eddy into an opening resulting in a series of checks in the thousands. The crusty old Presbyterian donor continued to disparage the useless extravagances of plush board offices and would not give a cent to the board. Yet he gave Eddy as much as $25,000 at a time to use as he saw fit. When he seemed sufficiently prepared for the suggestion of a $1,000,000 foundation gift, providence spoiled the secretary's plan and timing. The disconsolate Eddy reported that his old friend had left nearly $12,000,000 to various Presbyterian agencies instead, despite the fact that he had resolutely refused to see their agents for years. He "remains to me," wrote Eddy in retrospect, "a mixture of Santa Claus and of Mystery."[34]

In conjunction with Cornelius Patton, Eddy began shortly before World War I to compile a confidential file of names eventually exceeding 4,000 separate entries. Although an exceptionally high death rate made it difficult to maintain this private list, it contained confidential information which was employed to send periodic personal reports on the area or work in which each prospect was particularly interested. Every summer a personalized appeal reminding the potential donor of past gifts was mailed and rarely failed to produce additional contributions on an ascending basis.[35]

The approach here is essentially the same used by John R. Mott to achieve his even more spectacular fund-raising totals. He usually avoided impersonal campaigns relying on some common theme and tailored his appeal to a particular wealthy individual asked to contribute a precise amount for a specific object.[36] Winning sympathy or general good will was not the object of speaking tours and work with youth groups, agreed Brewer Eddy, sounding like a polished salesman; "the most effective missionary education was in securing a gift on the dotted line."[37]

Although the great mission fund raisers were masters of technique and shrewd psychologists who seemed to imitate successful stock brokers, their ultimate objectives placed them in a different category. Mott particularly was a superlative organizer and planner, but the money he secured was not the same coin sought by an equally adept security salesman from the same people. "To ask money of a man for the purposes of the world-wide Kingdom of God is not to ask him a favor," wrote Mott's friend and biographer; "it is to give him a superb opportunity of investing his own personality in eternal shares."[38]

Mott chose to consider money as only "so much stored-up personality," the product of a given number of days' labor, and thus accumulated power which could be used to extend that life beyond death. "When you try to relate an individual to Jesus Christ as his living Lord," he explained, "you are doing precisely what you are doing when you seek to relate the sacrificial gifts of rich or poor to the plans of His Kingdom."[39] Mott never approached an interview without first seeking guidance in prayer and considered the mystic power thus gained as the primary reason for his success. Giving, considered in the nature of a sacrament, transformed the money raiser into an enlarger of the Kingdom, an evangelist in a slightly different field. "Such service," wrote Mott recommending it to others, "involves a blending of sacrificial and joyous experience."[40]

On these terms, however professional the approach, fund raising for religious purposes took on a unique character. Its nature was best described in Mrs. John Mott's observation, that "ultimately you can raise money only for something for which you are really giving your own life."[41] Perhaps it was this restriction that hindered mission boards in promotional efforts that were aimed at a general audience. To ask the public to forget denominational lines and support missions was not the same as inducing a single oil magnate or department-store heir to make a gift. National campaigns, like the American Board's centennial celebration in which returned missionaries who toured the country were interviewed in the press and even the White House, rarely produced results commensurate with the expense.[42] Besides, catering to the public's taste for news of romantic mission fields could backfire when natives posing as theological students or recently converted maharajahs financed their travels on lecture circuits created by the mission boards.[43]

Bigger than the Boards: Fund-Raising Innovations

The mission board, acting as a fund-raising agency, was best adapted to cultivating the captive constituency in its own churches. Some had the personnel to move beyond this to solicit select men of wealth. To reach the occasional churchgoer or sympathetic Christian, however, it was found necessary to rely on specialized national and nondenominational organizations which represented both the culmination of trends in the mission movement and were independent of it. If organizations like the Laymen's and Interchurch World Movement sometimes ignored Mott's definition of the sacred calling of fund raising, the strictures at least did not harm the mission boards or reduce their traditional constituency, despite the fact that they provided an impetus to the new superstructure. Nor did the boards surrender control to the new national organizations. They merely employed them to implement techniques they had developed but were incapable of applying on a sufficiently large scale.

The keynote of the new national organizations and campaigns was the same fascination with bigness that underlay denominational plans for quick world evangelization. Taking their cue from business in an era of economic consolidation, mission leaders were not only interested in obtaining a share of the new wealth for their cause but also in imitating the methods of the corporate giants. Attacked for plotting the establishment of a religious trust in proposing the federation of several congregational mission societies, a committee chairman candidly admitted the charge. "If we can get nearer together, remove all rivalry and every possible chance for friction, collect and disburse the gifts of the churches more efficiently and economically, then why not have a 'Religious Trust?' "[44] Expressed here is the same desire to rationalize the mission constituency as reflected by the trusts in their respective economic fields. "In harmony with the highest business methods of our time," President Capen assured his board membership, "mission work is being consolidated in order to prevent waste and insure economy and efficiency."[45] Only a few years after the organization of the Standard Oil Trust, Capen had summarized his lifelong dedication to the businesslike operation of religious benevolence in a slogan equally appropriate for either enterprise: "Organization, efficiency and power."[46] If it worked for the steel, sugar, and tobacco trusts, why not for the trustees of the Kingdom?

Another contemporary development influenced mission leaders to think big. American philanthropy was shifting from reliance on traditional retail giving to the wholesale benefactions of the Carnegies and Rockefellers. "I gradually developed and introduced into all his charities the principle of scientific giving," wrote the older Rockefeller's secretary and adviser. "and he found himself in no long time laying aside retail giving almost wholly, and entering safely and pleasurably into the field of wholesale philanthropy."[47] Samuel Capen spotted this trend in 1908 when he wrote John R. Mott to inquire whether Andrew Carnegie's expression of disdain for the retail method in philanthropy did not provide an opportunity for a more audacious effort to reach men of wealth. "If only God would touch some man's heart and lead him to give a million dollars for Foreign Missions or even one quarter of it and make a break in this way," he wrote hopefully, "I believe others would follow."[48] Rather than waiting for hearts to be touched, Capen planned. In the midst of the tainted-money controversy he concluded that the time had come for the representatives of various mission boards to get together to "block out a plan which would cover the whole world and which might involve millions of dollars, and then bring this plan before the wealthy men of this country who would look at large things much quicker than at small ones."[49]

Two calculations entered into the development of the great plan. One was recognition that "the country is enormously rich, but the wealth is getting more and more into the hands of those who already possess," as a Presbyterian secretary informed a mission in China.[50] Whatever criticism this fact might have aroused elsewhere in contemporary America, it was carefully muted in the mission movement. "I don't mean that we need more preaching against the sin of covetousness," explained Bishop Ninde of his call for a new gospel of wealth, "but we need more preaching on the beatitude of luxurious giving."[51] The emphasis on reaching what Ninde called "Christian rich men" merged comfortably with the assumption that less wealthy churchmen would also respond more generously to an audacious challenge.[52]

The new direction and scale of mission fund raising had a reflex effect upon the movement. When men of wealth proved relatively indifferent to denominational distinctions, the pressure was toward interdenominational planning at home and cooperation in the field. To win the approval of successful captains of industry, a proposal also had to have an air of businesslike efficiency about it, and board secretaries became concerned with the image the movement presented. "Every year when it is suggested that some curtailment of the work will be necessary unless larger gifts come to the treasury," reported the American Board's J. M. Hall, "a motion is put that the Prudential Committee be directed to make no retrenchment in the work, and amid applause and singing the 'Doxology' it is carried. Now brethren," he chided, "this emotional method of dealing with definite and serious financial problems does not and will not appeal to the judgment of conservative men to whom the work is committed."[53]

Meanwhile, within the denominations, congregational dissatisfaction with multiple appeals expressed itself in pressure to federate benevolent societies or to present combined budgets during single campaigns. When home- and foreign mission societies were forced into combined appeals, they could demand in return that the churches fulfill their allocated obligations. Plans and statistics became focal points overshadowing individual needs or causes. Dramatic campaigns tended to provide the illusion that Christian duty had been satisfied for another year once pledges reached a carefully calculated and widely advertised dollar total. Whether it represented an imitation of the commercial world, or church reaction to too many requests, the shift from free enterprise competition to combination and joint planning among benevolent societies became increasingly obvious after 1900. It seemed to provide the best new hope for the mission movement in many decades. "When we Congregationalists wake up to business methods in missionary work, plan the work and work the plan," promised President Capen, "the day of debts in our Societies will be forever ended."[54]

The new business look in missions involved a number of techniques which were finally consolidated in the interdenominational Laymen's Missionary Movement but had their origins in various churches and missionary boards in the decade before 1906. Among these innovations the broadest favorable consensus developed for promotion of proportional, systematic giving by every church member. "Giving spasmodically and by impulse is usually small giving," observed Samuel Capen in 1903. "That which has thought, and plan, and method in it brings the largest results."[55] What he advocated five years before the Laymen's Movement began promoting the identical system for all Protestant churches was "some plan of systematic organization, with the purpose, by a personal canvass, of reaching every member of our churches and securing each year a definite pledge for our missionary work."[56]

A complementary forerunner of the Laymen's Movement approach was an effort to involve a broader group in missions through study groups, conventions, and membership on mission committees. Whether taking the form of open board meetings to attract interested outsiders,[57] organizing Christian service clubs, or calling denominational businessmen's conferences to provide advice, the objective was somehow to involve the noncontributing and inactive church membership.[58] Outlining the Presbyterian Forward Movement's plans to involve men more directly in all denominational activities, David McConaughy expressed a general sentiment when he maintained that, "so far as concerns the missionary enterprise, the layman has not been in it." The future charter member of the Laymen's Movement entertained the 1906 Foreign Missions Conference with a parody few found funny: "In the world's broad field of action / In the bivouac of life / You will find the Christian soldier / Represented by his wife."[59] The twelve-year career of the Laymen's Movement after 1907 was both a means of fighting this traditional apathy and proof that denominational efforts had made some headway since the nineteenth century.

Another approach to enlisting the public concentrated on the increased use of publicity, advertising, and showmanship. Press agents were added to staffs and newspaper advertisements initiated.[60] Mission spectaculars such as the World in Boston exposition in 1911 went on tour in major cities. Colorful exhibits, pagodas, temple gardens filled with idols, and even an opium den, were provided "to arouse interest in Home and Foreign Missions among the indifferent and careless." The awful and exotic were purposely emphasized and a spectacular "Pageant of Darkness" attracted large crowds.[61]

Although such spectactulars were rarely financial successes, they did involve hundreds of local church members in direct support of the cause and provided thousands of others with the kind of direct information that mission leaders considered the most effective method of popularizing the movement. The usual rationale postulated automatic and overwhelming support once the public understood the facts of mission work. But the facts were often distorted in the telling. The World in Boston deliberately emphasized "the darkest aspects" of heathen degradation. The Southern Prebyterian Church devised a catchy method of getting the facts to preoccupied businessmen by presenting the needs of specific stations in the same type of prospectus used by mining or manufacturing companies in floating securities. In this format a minister in Korea became a sort of salesman, and investment in his business venture was invited.[62] Whether either form of educating the public about missions had anything to do with Christianity or not, the approach was both new and temporarily effective.

Culmination: The Laymen's Missionary Movement

The outstanding example of new methods in mission fund raising after 1906 was the Laymen's Missionary Movement of the United States and Canada. It sought to tap more effectively the wealth created by industrialization, and to enlist American men in the mission cause. It tried to plan a practical, concerted attack on the non-Christian world, and to enlist all potential givers and transform them into habitual contributors. These were precisely the objectives sought during the preceding decade by board officials and mission leaders like John R. Mott, Samuel Capen, David McConaughy, and J. Campbell White, all of whom held strategic offices in the new organization.[63]

Despite the founders' wishes the Laymen's Movement became both an organization and a movement dedicated to religious principles. From its Madison Avenue headquarters came the pamphlets, books, speakers, and organizers of conventions and campaigns. A conscious effort was made, however, to keep the staff small and efficient and to avoid building up a bureaucratic organization. More than a dozen Protestant churches formed denominational laymen's movements, more or less directly reflecting the policy of the New York body. The directors or chairmen of the denominational movements were usually elected to the national body's General Committee. Liaison was also maintained by furnishing promotional literature or specialists for temporary assistance.

Eventually the national movement established seven regional divisions with subsidiary committees and locally financed staffs when necessary. Denominational suspicion of a new organization, as well as official emphasis on the spiritual nature of its goals, led the Laymen's Movement to stress its status as a movement. It had no membership beyond a few committees, no permanent nation-wide organization. It neither collected funds nor sent missionaries to the field. Instead it sought to enlist men in the mission crusade and to teach them the meaning of stewardship. "Information is the first word round which we gather," declared its chairman. "And the second is organization."[64]

Before long, organization dominated the movement's message. Its leaders spoke of launching a crusade the likes of which had not been experienced since the earliest days of Christian history. "The Laymen's Movement if it means anything," declared Vice-Chairman Mornay Williams, "means a new interpretation of the problem of life for the Christian." It was not just another campaign for money, he asserted, but an effort to show the men of the churches "what the vision of God is for each one of us, to see what it means to be a Christian."[65] Meanwhile, the movement's literature consistently exalted stewardship as the first principle and test of Christian faith; the act of giving to mission societies was elevated to the status of a sacrament.[66]

By no contemporary definition of spiritual revival or steward-ship could either objective be realized through advertising, social pressure, and professional promotion. Yet under the guise of edu-cation in stewardship the Laymen's Movement employed all these expedients as part of its plan for increasing mission-society income. A promotional pamphlet designed to win wider acceptance for the program, for example, provided a detailed outline of the fund-raising plan and mentioned its particular attractiveness to business-men. Examples of tangible success enjoyed by denominations that had already adopted it were followed not by a celebration of steward-ship or spiritual awakening but a standard product guarantee. For the plan had now been so thoroughly tried, concluded the pamphlet, "that success can be guaranteed on condition that the plan is accepted in its entirety and carried out according to instructions."[67] The perfect system devised at No. 1 Madison Avenue, in other words, had become the staple and preoccupation of a movement formed to teach men what it meant to be a Christian.

The core of the plan consisted of the formation of a local missionary committee which made the necessary preparations for an annual every member canvass. By 1913, the local committees formed as a result of Laymen's Movement promotion numbered in the thousands. Quite apart from their specific functions, the several hundred thousand laymen thus enrolled in the cause and transformed into active Christian workers were hailed by the executive secretary as "one of the largest fruits of the present missionary awakening."[68]

The committees were guided by New York to press for regular missionary prayer meetings and sermons in their churches, as well as sponsoring a Missionary Month celebration before the annual fund drive. They were to assure a prominent place in the every member canvass for foreign missions in the event that the financial campaign was supervised by a more inclusive church committee. The collection of preliminary information on each church member was suggested, including his income, past giving record, and relevant personal idiosyncracies. These data were made available to the canvassing teams who, forearmed with inside information, were prepared to press for a worthy contribution. Headquarters referred to this approach as an effort "to bring about more than ever before, what has been called 'applied personality.' "[69]

Applied personality in action revealed an admirable understanding of practical psychology. From the decision to send canvassers first to those least able to contribute, in order to have their sacrificial example to set before wealthier prospects,[70] to the insistence that all solicitations be made by teams, a pattern of exploiting weaknesses was followed. The mere presence of more than one fellow church member waiting to record a pledge made outright refusals or even token contributions embarrassing. A preliminary invitation to prayer or informal worship by the canvassers brought particular pressure to bear on those who had been lax in church attendance. Carefully compiled background information on each prospect enabled the canvassers to deal with excuses or to stir vanity or shame through subtle comparisons. If a prospect was known to have paid a large private or country club membership fee, for example, he might be asked how he squared this with a token contribution to missions. As proof that an individual possessed the "right kind" of money has sometimes been made the condition for membership in clubs providing higher social status,[71] so the every member canvass team was trained to demand tangible evidence of Christian faith and loyalty to the church.[72]

The pledges made in the annual campaigns were collected by the week during the remainder of the year, thus solving one of the problems of mission-board solicitation from the churches. Annual collections were inefficient, it was pointed out, because anticipation of a single cash payment undercut whatever appeal might be launched during the service. Quite simply, many a man who was willing to pledge ten cents a week would never think of putting as much as a dollar bill into the plate on Mission Sunday.[73] The Laymen's Movement also promoted weekly giving as the source of many other blessings. The system was described as scriptural, educational, equitable, a means of promoting prayer for missions, and of enlisting large numbers of givers. It made it easier to give more, provided continuous support without borrowing, and increased other offerings to the churches.[74]

Although Laymen's Movement personnel never participated in the implementation of their plan at the local level, they did promote its adoption by holding thousands of dinner meetings, conventions, and coordinated campaigns at which selected laymen could receive instruction and inspiration to organize their home churches. Nearly one million men had attended some three thousand such conferences at the end of the movement's first decade.[75] The national organization put its efforts only into strategically located larger cities where preliminary work had been undertaken by local committees and an adequate audience was assured as a result.[76]

The organizing teams were instructed to make these meetings an enjoyable and meaningful experience, as remote from the old-fashioned Mission Sunday affairs as possible. As a result only lay-men were normally used as speakers, although "live" ministers and missionaries were also employed and sometimes lent a decidedly revivalistic flavor to the sessions. Frequently the enthusiasm stirred up could be harnessed to ringing resolutions to double or triple the area's gifts to missions in the future. The results were then held up to subsequent conventions for emulation.[77]

Showmanship, gimmickry, and social pressure were blended with evangelism in these campaigns, and the wealthy supporter was never forgotten. Officials from the national organization sometimes asked a select group to remain after the mass dinners and offered to initiate them into the Four Square Club. A gift to missions in four figures was the first requirement; the recruitment of three men to complete a square the next. Each leaguer also pledged to quadruple both his gifts to missions and to his own church.[78]

Neither individual nor regional pledges, however, were the principal goal. The primary focus was on a system designed to involve large numbers in average circumstances. "The main drive of these teams," recalled a participant, "was to present the Every Member Canvass as a new method. It was their gift to the churches for raising church budgets to new levels and the addition of the missionary subscriptions in the use of the duplex envelopes."[79] Once this method had been adopted, the Laymen's Movement often sponsored simultaneous city-wide campaigns in all the churches. These provided greater publicity, more widespread use of the canvass, created a friendly rivalry between denominations, and would either convert or "press obstructionists to the missionary cause out of the way."[80]

A final objective of the Laymen's Movement was the develop-ment of a national missionary plan. The every member canvass was a means of introducing a budget and orderly business methods into religious financing on the local church level. For American Protes-tantism in general, the movement sought to implement the watch-word borrowed from the Student Volunteers, by making just as businesslike an approach to the task of evangelizing the world in their generation. This National Missionary Policy took the form of urging the various denominations to define their own foreign mission responsibility and to adopt an adequate policy for cultivating their chosen fields. In 1909 headquarters announced that responsibility for the evangelization of 549,000,000 non-Christians had already been officially accepted by twelve American denominations.[81]

The Net Results

The exploitation of new themes and motives, as well as the development of efficient promotional methods, transformed mission financing during the first two decades of the twentieth century. At least a rudimentary basis for supporting a far more aggressive foreign mission campaign had been created; both income and the number of contributors had markedly increased since the post-Civil War doldrums. Yet no one associated with the movement ever admitted a sufficiency, let alone a surplus, of funds for the work at hand. Greater income had to be measured against larger costs, with a twofold increase in both home and foreign expenses faced by most boards during the early decades of this century.[82] And there remains a basic question of means and results by which to test the leadership. Was income increased because of rallies, duplex envelopes, and the celebration of missionary salesmen for American products, or perhaps despite the new themes and techniques? Was the improvement in the movement's financial condition merely a reflection of general prosperity, or had the leaders correctly interpreted and tapped a native vein of support for Protestant expansion?

Neither in an absolute or statistical form, nor in a general comparison with other benevolent enterprises, can these questions be objectively answered. The reason is that the official statistics are faulty when available and incomplete for the movement as a whole.[83] The major boards rarely reported gifts for special objects. Numerous unaffiliated churches, as well as congregations in smaller denominations with an antimission tradition, sent and supported their own missionaries while avoiding all connections with the regular sending boards.[84] In denominations with substantial immigrant membership, contributions were often channeled through societies in their former homeland.[85]

There is no reliable record of the millions raised over the years for the work of the Student Volunteers, Laymen's Movement, Missionary Education Movement, and other groups promoting the cause of missions. No one can determine the value of clothes, books, organs, and financial gifts sent directly to board-affiliated missionaries by family, friends, and adoptive churches. Nor can one estimate the extent to which missionaries in the field were successful in obtaining private funds for such pet projects as schools, hospitals, or chapels, once a board had officially rejected their requests. Although they were usually spasmodic, such contributions were sometimes organized by establishing committees of "friends" of particular mission schools, or maintained through personal ties to American medical colleagues and institutions.

Bookkeeping inaccuracies, special funds, personal gifts, missionaries without board connections, and funds sent from the United States to foreign or international mission societies thus contributed to a sizeable aggregate of unreported mission movement income. An accurate determination of the relation of these funds to official receipts is impossible, but it is clear that millions of dollars were contributed to foreign missions that were never credited to the mission boards. A subjective analysis based largely on contemporary judgments seems as good a means of determining the financial status of the foreign mission movement as a statistical study of incomplete official receipts.

In going directly to mission leaders and executives for an assessment of the movement's financial health, however, one has to guard both against their long-range optimism and against reactions to temporary disarrangements. Overexpansion in a new field might produce a decade of deficits for a society, or a budget could be disarranged by temporary setbacks like the Boxer uprising or the silver-exchange crisis shortly after World War I. Income also has to be measured against realistic needs, for not even the U.S. Treasury's income would have been sufficient to support the National Missionary Plan. The most misleading element, however, arises from the private optimism and public pessimism traditional with board executives and spokesmen.

Since he had experienced it all before, the veteran board administrator could accept temporary setbacks philosophically. To do so publicly, however, might turn an occasional financial embarrassment into a permanent depression. To maintain the flow of contributions, he was forced either to exude hope or cry for aid in the face of an unprecedented crisis. To preserve the morale of his charges, he could rely on the self-balancing effects of time and assurances that public interest was cyclical, and that the churches had always responded generously to demonstrated crises.[86]

Whatever effect enthusiastic publicity had on potential contributors, it distorted the nature of mission work and eventually brought harsh public judgment to bear on the apparently ineffectual missionary. The propaganda was phrased in terms of crisis, and money was the panacea that would ward off calamities and convert millions. In mission magazines every minor success was publicized as the beginning of a trend, every casual official reference favorable to Christianity eagerly seized on as a portent. The boards had to show progress or the impatient constituency might lose interest. This was particularly true of the men attracted by the business approach to missions or the economic argument for their expansion. The job of the church leaders was not unlike the post-World War II ordeal faced by each presidential administration in its annual struggle to justify the foreign aid bill to Congress, while pork barrel legislation tended to pass unchecked and unpared. Sustaining missions was somehow unnatural for the average American Protestant. It required either an excess of piety, or the careful nurture of an interest in things beyond his personal horizon and without an immediate effect on his life. In discovering and developing such an interest the pre-World War I generation of mission leaders excelled.

Prior to the last quarter of the nineteenth century, the boards' only rivals for Protestant contributions had been domestic charities. Partly in reaction to growing public interest in world affairs, however, new agencies developed to challenge the traditional monopoly

of the foreign mission boards. In 1880, an American seeking to express his concern for the rest of the world could do this only by
supporting a foreign mission society; after 1900 he also had to
weigh the claims of church peace and disarmament groups, the
World Student Christian Federation, the International Sunday
School Union, and the International Committee of the YMCA, to
name a few. To this were added campaigns such as Near East Relief,
which in the decade after 1918 alone drew more than four times
the average annual income of the foreign boards of the eleven
largest American denominations.[87]

But the strongest appeal to the same constituency came from
a traditional rival. To the average church member home missions
seemed more natural than foreign missions because their rationale
included the utilitarian service of reforming American society. The
foreign movement, on the other hand, had to dramatize its fight
against abstract danger such as revengeful and resurgent non-Western
nations. "The work of Home Missions is continually reinforced by
the inspiration of patriotism," complained a veteran Presbyterian
secretary in 1889, "and it seemed to me during the month of April
that I could hardly distinguish between the services connected with
the Centennial of the Republic, and those which were held in the
interest of Home Missions."[88]

The same motives applied to a number of nonreligious reform
groups during the progressive period which took over and extended
what had once been part of home missions. Protestants also contributed funds for the fight against child labor and white slavery,
the Americanization of immigrants and Indians, or the promotion
of temperance, woman's suffrage, and conservation. With the press,
politicians, and churchmen all calling attention to such immediate
social issues, the plight of distant heathen would have drawn scant
notice without a vigorous missionary propaganda campaign. And
that propaganda was not effective enough to warrant the perpetua-
tion in our era of the old charge that foreign missions always
attracted greater support from American Protestants than domestic
benevolences.[89]

That assumption can be demonstrated during the period under

discussion only by making a narrow and technical distinction. During the decade after 1899, for example, the American Board received 39 percent of the average annual income of all Congregational societies; the Congregational Home Missionary Society received 30.5 percent. The same churches, however, also supplied the American Home Missionary Association's 15 percent, with an equal amount distributed among the Church Building, Educational, Sunday School, and Publication Societies.[90] Since all but the American Board were thus involved in some way in the expansion of the denomination within the United States, the balance between home and foreign mission income takes on a different aspect. A survey of twelve representative denominations in 1902 revealed expenditures of $45,700,000 for congregational or parish expenses, $5,138,000 for home missions, and only $2,442,000 for foreign missions.[91]

Foreign mission supporters were not content even with this demonstration of their country-cousin status for, by calculating their share of total denominational expenditures, an even more dramatic imbalance could be demonstrated. The prevalent ratio of contributions in the major Protestant churches during the three decades before the depression of 1929 was approximately four dollars for congregational expenses to one dollar for all benevolences.[92] Indeed, Lankford's study of twentieth-century Protestant giving found the Seventh-Day Adventists the sole exception to the pattern of expending more for nonbenevolent local objects.[93] Missionary propagandists utilized this imbalance to lecture the churches on their selfishness. Even more dramatic illustrations of the plight of foreign missions could be achieved with the selective use of denominational statistics by which ratios of ten or even thirty to one between giving for local objects and missions could be demonstrated.[94]

Although an increase in the movement's share of benevolent giving was a realistic objective, the conversion of entire denominations into missionary churches was not. The use of the every member canvass and other Laymen's Movement techniques, for example, raised the contributions of some 2400 California churches to $4.47

per member for foreign missions, which was twice the national average.[95] But to seek beyond this to transform the giving habits of Presbyterians or Baptists into those of the Moravians who, even during the 1880s, managed out of their poverty to raise $12.00 per member for missions, was unrealistic.[96] The number of Americans willing to accept a personal missionary obligation was not much greater than the total membership of denominations like the Moravians, Witnesses, or Latter-Day Saints, which required such duty in some form from all its communicants. To the rest, a comfortably furnished church and top-flight pastor were more important than the unevangelized millions abroad. This was a human fact which might have been recognized by anyone except those bent on a superhuman crusade.

The use of human enterprise, on the other hand, was held responsible for the progress that was made. Whenever any optimism about the movement's finances was expressed during the prewar decades, it was almost always in connection with the work of the Laymen's Missionary Movement. Both the Northern and Southern Presbyterian Churches reached pre-World War II peaks in benevolent contributions during the period of active promotional work by the Laymen's Movement.[97] In the face of declining contributions to foreign missions in every other Protestant nation in 1908, only the United States and Canada, where the new movement had been active, showed a substantial increase in gifts over the preceding year.[98] Despite a business recession, North Americans increased their gifts to foreign missions during the next two years at nine times the rate of the British, who now ranked second.[99] And in explaining the introduction of the new methods in the Congregational Churches, the man who was both the movement's chairman and American Board president noted the interesting fact that where the plan "has been at work the gains have been large; where it has not been worked there has been a distinct loss; apparently if it had not been for this plan the totals would have been diminished rather than increased."[100] Capen's testimonial to the Laymen's Movement also verifies the suspicion that the prewar surge of mission interest and support was at least partly an induced rather than a natural growth.

The Laymen's Movement's actual influence can not be precisely defined. It was the one new organization on the scene exclusively dedicated to raising gifts to foreign missions; these gifts did increase. A study of Protestant giving between 1900 and 1927 conducted for the Institute of Social and Religious Research revealed a peak in benevolent giving immediately after the close of World War I, followed by a marked decrease. The total foreign-mission receipts from living donors in fifteen major denominations did indicate a more rapid upward trend after the organization of the Laymen's Movement, but also an even sharper increase in reaction to the war.[101] Estimating a fourfold increase in men's contributions in some denominations, John Mott described a similar effect with unprecedented peaks in foreign mission giving reached between 1918 and 1927.[102]

The movement's own publications provide little information, since they tended to stress only such spectacular examples of success as the Southern Presbyterian board's twofold increase in receipts after the early organization of a denominational Laymen's Movement.[103] Not record keeping but the didactic use of such statistics to induce other churches to adopt the plan and increase their income was the objective of such reports. On a larger scale also, the Laymen's Movement tended to be nondiscriminating in accepting credit. The aggregate contributions of North American churches to foreign missions during the first three years of the movement's activity totaled almost $7 million more than the amount received during the preceding three, and this despite regional economic depressions in the country. "It is probable that there would have been a shrinkage in receipts during this period instead of an advance," a spokesman claimed, "had it not been for the wide-spread awakening on the part of men."[104] At the conclusion of its first decade, the Laymen's Movement pointed with pride to figures showing that the increase in North American foreign mission contributions during that period had been greater than the increase during the previous nine decades.[105] Certainly part of this spectacular upsurge must be credited to the movement's agitation.

The movement also deserves credit for several intangible contributions. Whether its policies were wise in the long run or not, they inspired unprecedented confidence among mission leaders. Veteran fund raiser Brewer Eddy admitted that he could not substantiate the impression with figures, but he felt that the movement's work had been responsible for at least a twofold increase in giving to foreign missions. In 1910, he recalled, the American Board had suffered a trifling deficit; then "for a decade after we never had a problem."[106] None of the board's secretaries seems to have had reason to record a similar expression of satisfaction during the American Board's first century.

By the end of World War I, another subtle change of attitude took place as the result of the laymen's labors. "I know it is not considered quite orthodox; or very profoundly spiritual to emphasize the money question," apologized the secretary of the Evangelical Lutheran Board during a 1903 discussion of home field problems. "I meet with people who feel when I emphasize that feature, that it has a commercial sound."[107] In less than two decades his words had taken on an unintended quaintness. Certainly no such accusation would have been forthcoming from the men planning to merge the programs of several national movements and all of the major Protestant denominations into the colossal Interchurch World Movement in 1919.

Both the statements of mission leaders and statistical surveys thus indicate a general increase in the financial support given by American Protestants to their foreign mission agencies before 1920. Between 1904 and 1914 communicant church membership in the United States had increased 25.3 percent; total contributions for all local church expenses had risen 39.7 percent; for missionary and benevolent work in the United States 62.8 percent; but contributions to foreign mission work were a startling 87.5 percent.[108] If foreign evanglization still lagged in total receipts, its relative improvement had been remarkable. Only the expected continuation of the upward trend in per capita giving to foreign missions failed to materialize.[109]

With exceptions in individual denominations, a high point of giving was recorded at the beginning of the third decade of this century, followed by a relative decline. In relationship to both ideals and gross-income figures the upsurge of support in the decade before 1920 did not perpetuate itself. Mission leaders such as Mott, Capen, and Eddy might express their gratification over increased support yet continue dissatisfied with both the total amount received and its proportion to the general giving of American Protestants. Although their personal assessments of the movement's financial health have to be discounted for studied overoptimism, the conclusions corroborate the results of statistical studies based on imperfect data.

The observations of several mission leaders also verify the impression that only the use of unprecedented energy and innovations in fund raising saved foreign missions from losing support during the first two decades of this century. They tended to interpret the development of colossal denominational fund drives, and the efforts of such groups as the Laymen's Movement which produced the increased financial support, as manifestations of a missionary awakening among American men. Whether a rising missionary spirit produced the new methods or promotionalism created the awakening can be argued as fruitlessly as the ancient riddle about the precedence of the chicken and the egg. In a period of increasing rivalry for funds from other benevolent agencies, organization and business methods were seen to work wonders in the commercial world. It would seem the leaders of the mission movement learned this lesson and put more effort into efficient promotion than into a campaign to effect a general spiritual revival in America.

EPILOGUE

Let us insist that every Christian shall feel that missions is
his one business. They have been regarded as an extraordi-
nary work; they are to be the ordinary. . . . It has been
regarded as a sort of supererogation to redound in special
credit to the doer; it needs to be made the test of
orthodoxy.

William Owen Carver, 1898

The second decade of the twentieth century was a period of
fulfillment for the new foreign mission movement developed since
Arthur Pierson had publicized the crisis of missions. Total contributions to foreign missions pyramided, and Student Volunteer
pledges reached an all-time high at the end of the decade. Every
auxiliary movement was expanding, spurred on by innovative
promotional techniques soon to be coordinated to test the
idealism of American Protestantism in the mammoth Interchurch
World Movement. Every index of success established by the
progressive generation promised the realization of their goal of
evangelizing the world within their lifetimes. Even abroad, there
were mass conversions, the triumphant evangelistic tour of the
Continuation Committee conferences in Asia, and peace based
permanently on interdependence. "The Church has been praying
for the day when heathenism should be supplanted and when
the nations should become brotherhoods," wrote Edward Capen
a few months before Sarajevo. "That day is upon us."[1]

The End of an Era
The war sounded the first stroke marking the end of an era
for the mission movement; the collapse of the Interchurch Movement the last. After the initial shock of the war's outbreak in
Europe had worn off, mission spokesmen divided into two uneven
segments. A majority tended to see the war as an opportunity and
enlisted wholeheartedly in the crusade. A minority composed of

173

both extreme evangelical conservatives and liberals were alienated and sought a divorce of secular and spiritual missions.

The search for positive meaning began with the assertion that the brutality and unscrupulous nationalism revealed by the European conflict provided a new incitement to continued evangelization.[2] It moved with American entry to the recognition that "so many beneficial results are clearly foreshadowed, some of them now actually being realized, that while men are not expressing gratitude for the war, they are uttering praise to a God who so rules the world that he can over-rule even this for good."[3] And by 1918 an editor of *Men and Missions* could state flatly that "the church is linking the world war with its mission to win the world for Christ."[4]

The Interchurch Movement then became a means of fighting "the world war to establish Christ's kingdom on earth," for mankind needed "a League of Churches to do for the cause of religion what the League of Nations proposes to do for politics."[5] In return, the sponsor of the political league gave his endorsement to the Interchurch Movement through which, "once more in the providence of God, America has opportunity to show the world that she was born to save mankind."[6] The hopes of the majority of mission leaders rose and fell with the Interchurch Movement. They took their losses philosophically and moved on to adapt their vision to the new conditions of the 1920s.

The fundamentalists who tried to cleanse the foreign mission boards of modernists during the decade after the armistice had shared a negative interpretation of the war with a minority of disillusioned liberals. Both groups became alienated from the easy confidence in an inevitably evolving world Christian community, but the fundamentalists substituted an eschatological emphasis for optimistic evolutionism. Thousands of them attended a Bible Conference on the Return of our Lord, organized in 1918 by the secretary-treasurer of the China Inland Mission and other Philadelphia laymen, to discuss "the personal return of the Lord Jesus." They listened to "eminently safe and sane pastors and Bible teachers,"[7] one of whom blamed the war and most American social ills on "that ripe, rank, rampant, rotten new theology made in Germany." The audience was adjured to return to the simple gospel, and to make "strenuous war, and fight to a finish, against foreign innovation or immigration into our religious world."[8]

Meanwhile liberals had discovered with Harry Emerson Fosdick that "war is unchristian—essentially, hideously unchristian." "After a look at Europe," he wrote in 1917, "let no man ever again speak of a Christian war!"[9] Even before the United States became directly involved, the new president of the American Board suspected that Protestants had "been too confident perhaps that his Kingdom was drawing near." "Words which we uttered but two years ago," wrote Edward Moore in 1915, "seem now like the speech of children, so profound is our disillusionment."[10] Out of such disenchantment developed the deeper alienation of a Sherwood Eddy: "Behind the grim Medusa's head of the carnage at the front in World War I, I began gradually to see the symptoms of a world which at heart is hostile."[11] What this awareness produced, however, was not a retreat to fundamentalism, but dedication to the cure "of a sick and envenomed social order."

The most immediate impact of the war, however, occurred in the mission fields. Personnel replacement was slow when it occurred at all. Some missionaries took leaves of absence to serve as chaplains or with the YMCA in Europe. Inflation and exchange problems devoured the advances in income experienced by many societies. The international nature of the war made it more thoroughly disruptive than any previous conflict, both in the areas it affected and in the staff of such cosmopolitan societies as the China Inland Mission. There was also the psychological handicap created when "discredit was thrown upon the Gospel message by the sight of 'Christian' nations engaged in such a conflict."[12] Indeed, Fletcher Brockman, a close friend and colleague of John R. Mott for forty years, expressed in its strongest form the postwar feelings of a number of missionaries in China. Referring to the reception accorded Mott's evangelistic tour in 1913, he expressed his conviction that but for the World War China might have become Christian within a generation. "Unfortunately the World War stopped that," recalled Brockman. "We were deceived ourselves and had deceived them in thinking that we had any Christian countries. The paganism of Christendom checked the whole Christian movement in Asia."[13] Whether a direct reaction to the war or not, nationalism and anti-Christian movements on the mission fields challenged most American societies after 1920. Both at home and abroad World War I thus marked the end of an era and the beginning of a period of reassessment, innovation, and eventual decline for the Protestant mission movement.

The optimism and confident activism with which the movement had entered the war was transformed as it became obvious that Western civilization was not coextensive with its professed religion. "The climate of the environment was one of defense," wrote Kenneth Latourette of the postwar decades, "of seeking to conserve what had been won in a previous age."[14] Initially, the line was held, for not even the collapse of the Interchurch Movement prevented slight increases in contributions to foreign missions during the early 1920s. The relative decline in support which the boards suffered, however, indicates that they were riding in part on the preceding decades' momentum. During the prosperous 1920s, with church membership increasing, per capita giving for benevolences steadily decreased while per capita congregational expenses rose every year.[15] Money was contributed generously, but it was available predominantly for the construction of new churches and service facilities for their membership, and foreign missions felt the sharpest reduction in the share available for benevolences.[16] After the shattering economic collapse of 1929 all types of church income dropped sharply.[17]

The Student Volunteer Movement also waned with enrollments declining throughout the 1920s. The editor of the 1928 convention report noted both smaller attendance and an unusually widespread criticism of the missionary program. "The missionary movement seems to be in precarious health," he admitted, "Some have accounted it as already numbered with the dead."[18] Meanwhile, in the foreign field, nationalism stirred by the war raised increasing problems and resulted in the mass missionary evacuation of China at the end of the decade. Worldwide, the high point of Christian missions up to the middle of the twentieth century was reached in 1929, with 30,000 Protestant and an equal number of Roman Catholic missionaries in the field.[19]

As important as the tangible signs of decline was a debilitating loss of confidence. In 1930 a liberal Methodist traced the alteration of missionary motivation from "the belief that for men who die without Christ the future is hopeless," to the conviction that for those so deprived "the present is hopeless." The pessimistic characterization of his own era's ideology was the conviction that "the West, no less than the East, needs to be brought under the influence of Christ."[20]

The subtle loss of confidence was revealed even in the name of the movement. Instead of foreign missions for aliens and heathen, the world mission of the church was stressed. "World" replaced "foreign" in the World Missionary Council, Interchurch World Movement, and the later Laymen's Movement for a Christian World. Instead of counting the native converts of a particular denomination, reference was made to the health of the younger churches, and a sense of brotherhood replaced possessive head counts. Instead of paternalistic missions that did something *for* the lesser peoples, there was a transition to partnership, sharing, and advice given by senior to junior with the expectation of reciprocal benefits. A growing sensitivity or self-consciousness is reflected in the fact that the 1928 Student Volunteer convention was the first at which nonsegregated housing was provided for the delegates.[21] The same conference adopted a revision of the pledge card signed by thousands since 1892, by replacing the intent "to become a foreign missionary" with a commitment "to give my life as a Christian witness abroad."[22]

As the churches recognized their isolation and existence in a hostile world after World War I, their mission came to be reinterpreted in two ways. One path was to emphasize the distinction between secular and spiritual kingdoms and to restrict mission work to the simple proclamation of Christ's gospel for mankind. Fundamentalists in most denominations during the 1920s pressed this alternative in its most extreme form. Frustrated in their efforts to win control of or alter the policies of the major denominational boards, secessionists formed several new sending agencies or shifted their support to orthodox evangelical societies like the China Inland Mission.[23]

The alternative approach was to redefine the participation of the church in secular affairs and modify the claim of Christianity's uniqueness in an effort to gather the brotherhood by de-emphasizing differences. "Today we think of the missionary process as the cooperative endeavor of idealists of all nations to produce, through the motives of a social religion, an ennobled and friendly human society of varied and mutually contributing cultures," read a post-depression expression of this theme. If the American Board's Cornelius Patton did not consider this definition of missions sufficiently Christian, it nevertheless indicated the direction in which even the most spiritual supporters of the main movement were traveling.[24]

A few months before Pearl Harbor, a group of men associated with the old Laymen's Movement met to discuss its reactivation but were unable to reconcile the traditional and modern conceptions of missions. Subsequently, the sons of several of the charter members of the Laymen's Movement were instrumental in founding the new Laymen's Movement for a Christian World, which became a friendly rival instead of an affiliate of the surviving Chicago branch of the old organization. "Our fathers lived in a dual world—'home' and 'foreign'," noted the secretary of the new movement. The mid-century generation, on the other hand, agreed that the need for this distinction had disappeared. "The Christian world mission has created the germ of a Christian world community," they maintained. "We recognize the necessity of expanding this community, and shall try intelligently to assume the responsibility of Christian living and Christian action which this vision demands."[25] The Laymen's Movement for a Christian World proposed to undertake its mission not necessarily through organized societies and commissioned missionaries, but by the example of their lives and through private consultation and prayer. This marked the reemphasis of an earlier concept of missions and a more self-consciously Christian one, yet incorporated a view of the world that was foreign to the progressive generation.

The Balance Sheet of One Generation's Mission

What then were the characteristics and accomplishments of the generation which surrendered its direction of the foreign mission movement during the third decade of the twentieth century? Although cast by contemporary promotional literature in the roles of political commentator, explorer, civilizer, salesman, and revivalist, the missionary's main dedication and the movement's primary objective remained the evangelization of the non-Christian world. In its pursuit of this timeless objective, the progressive generation was dedicated to the spirit of the Student Volunteer and Laymen's Movement watchword. John R. Mott, the foremost promoter and defender of the watchword in both movements, always insisted that "the evangelization of the world in this generation did not mean the conversion of the world in a generation, or its Christianization in a generation, nor was it ever regarded as a prophecy of what was likely to take place." But it could be read to mean all these things, as well as the intended reminder "that it is the duty of each generation of Christians to bring the knowledge of Christ to its own generation."[26]

The frequent criticism of the watchword in mission circles indicates that the movement's lay supporters often misunderstood the slogan and, since no limits were fixed to each generation's duty, even the proper interpretation supported an optimistic and expansive view. "If we could give the same energy and intelligence to the works of missions that we now give to our own private business affairs," wrote a Canadian Laymen's Association leader in this spirit, "then the proposition to evangelize the world in this generation would be accomplished."[27] It is also obvious from mission literature that even the new keynote's critics and traditionalists at the turn of the century expected an unprecedented advance for the mission cause within their lifetime. Confidence in Protestantism's ability to respond to the challenge of a conclusive campaign distinguished this generation from its predecessors, while its characteristic optimism marked it off from the mood of its successors.

The difference between traditional and progressive emerged in a discussion of the new Laymen's Missionary Movement at the Edinburgh World Missionary Conference. The Rev. C. R. Watson of the United Presbyterian Board objected to allegations that the new movement was unspiritual, pointing out that there were two equally legitimate but divergent schools in the missionary camp. "There are those who are anchored in history, who are temperamentally and because of circumstance inclined to view all things from the historic point of view, as so many spiritual forces, as great ideas unfolding themselves in the world." They will tend to move slowly, to seek counterforces and to develop contrary influences in a thorough and unhurried way. The opposing school tends to plan in numerical terms. "It speaks of the great areas, the thousands of millions, and because it measures the problems in terms of numbers, it is also inclined to give the answer to the question somewhat in terms of numbers, and this school perhaps prides itself on its aggressiveness."[28] Although Watson urged the conferees to avoid extremes in either attitude and described reconciliation between the two camps as the need of the hour, the missions of the English-speaking countries continued to be dominated by the ahistorical school which took pride in aggressiveness.

Within Protestantism, the most consistent criticism of the direction taken by Anglo-American missions at the turn of the century came from German spokesmen frustrated by the unwillingness of the Student Volunteer Movement to define its terms or abandon its watchword. "Religious eccentricity may momentarily prove more effective than religious prudence," Professor D. Warneck told a Continental mission conference in 1897, "but it is not a sign of a healthy Christianity, when the exciting is taken for piety, and a movement which it is hoped will conquer the world is based on untenable rhetorical slogans."[29] But it is pride in human devices and dedication to benevolent activism that provide the most legitimate basis for criticizing the movement, not semantic quibbles dictated by well-bred distaste for youthful enthusiasm. The new spirit consisted of more than the impractical and evanescent sloganeering that Warneck described. Ambitious but not other-worldly, the men inspired by the watchword were practical in their plans. In their hurry to accomplish something Christians had been unable to achieve during 1900 years, they created an impressive machinery. But in the process of speeding up progress, confusion between means and ends developed.

Neither innovations in American theology, nor the growth of Protestantism in the United States at the end of the nineteenth century account for the hope that this generation would outdo the hundreds that had passed since the great commission was given. The reasons presented for expecting success were not new infusions of God's power or restatements of the command in theological terms, but they were based on optimism and confidence in the power and means provided by industrialism. At the centennial celebration of American foreign missions in 1906, Arthur Judson Brown repeated the familiar argument that, although a century earlier the whole non-Christian world had been closed or inac-cessible, technological innovations had leveled these barriers and made it possible for the missionary to go everywhere. "And if he can go, he ought to go," Brown insisted. "Opportunity is obliga-tion."[30]

Wealth to pay the bills, business methods to organize the forces, steamships, telegraphy, and other means of making every corner of the world accessible to the missionary—these were the modern tokens of success, and they reflect faith in man's power. This new mission enthusiasm was part of the optimism of the age and also a calculated act of will based on the hope that the youthful spirit of the student volunteers would infect others, as Samuel Mills at the beginning of the nineteenth century had urged the Brethren to remain steadfast in their dedication to the unpopular foreign mission, in the hope that, if the children led, perhaps the worthy fathers of the church would follow.[31] In discussing new foreign mission opportunities before the centennial audience, as well as the more ambitious objective of replacing the present age of skepticism with the spirit of the days of Whitefield, Lyman Abbott suggested that "we may attempt to do it by academic discussion, or we may attempt to do it by a call to service." But since "the academic way is not the American way," he called for a national revival through missionary activism.[32]

Horace Bushnell, an earlier intellectual leader of Congregationalism, worried that piety had become too nearly synonymous with action during the pre-Civil War decades. He saw a reason for elation over increasing mission activity only if it was the product of true apostolic piety, for "if the work is begun by a mere sally of impulse and prosecuted only as a dull mechanical labor; apart from any real union to God . . . not only will it fall to nothing, but the churches engaged will either be prostrated or effectively revolutionized." To Bushnell, the world mission was merely the natural expansion of the church over its allotted domain, assimilating all men to their redeemer. Artificial means, or a "mere society engine fed by money" he considered external and irrelevant to the church.[33] Lyman Abbott's generation, however, saw the mission movement as a distinct entity or a utilitarian function of the churches. If properly activated it might revitalize the church and produce among the senders of the gospel that piety which had not developed naturally among them. This may have been a spiritual motive, but it was utilitarian rather than instinctive to the church at that time. Benevolent activism was put forward as an antidote for churches beset by materialism and skepticism. "If men or churches are doing good, they can carry a heavy load of heresy or dead orthodoxy and still live," wrote Abbott's liberal contemporary Theodore Munger. Describing missions as the best and most common way of exercising religious benevolence, he warned that "the churches should look well to their *charities* as a hiding-place against the common storm."[34]

Activism and expansion thus became the movement's objectives with little attention paid to the springs of progress. Since the expansion of the missionary outreach at the end of the century owed much to secular motives and opportunities, and because confidence in human means characterized the goals set by the new leaders, the standards of judgment of the movement became increasingly secularized. In the absence of a state church, theology had never been as authoritarian in its application as on the Continent. It was easier for enthusiasts and laymen to seize control of a movement in America and thus to increase the impact of contemporary culture on the church. It was not difficult for dedicated mission leaders to go along with the new emphasis, both because they welcomed the unprecedented attention for their cause, and because they half believed the frequent warnings that the liberal trend in theology would cut the nerve of missions by making obsolescent the traditional concern for eternally damned souls.

They were never confident that the modern interest in missions was permanent, however. "Its tentative nature should give concern to all leaders of thought and activity who are responsible for conserving it and affording it expression," wrote William Ellis of the unprecedented new interest reflected in the Laymen's Movement.[35] They were concerned and did their best to institutionalize both the expression and promotion of interest. The challenge these leaders presented to their generation, however, was not the emulation of apostolic piety, but a performance measured by the mundane standards congenial to the newly enrolled laymen. "One is made indignant, and almost disgusted," wrote Ellis in summation of this job-oriented outlook, "to behold the two-penny character of a work that is designed to transform nations."[36]

So mission boards resorted to advertising and marketing programs. Unified budgets and cooperative promotion in massive campaigns replaced individual appeals and annual collections. By the end of the second decade of this century, nearly every major denomination had its Forward Movement or New Era Movement effectively directed by professionals. "I would not be afraid to tackle any city in this country and guarantee that they will do twice as much as they have done before," J. Campbell White told an audience of missionaries in explaining Laymen's Movement methods.[37] A young secretary of the successor Interchurch Movement informed his superiors that "it is the greatest thing in the world to advertise," and that he intended to approach his work from the standpoint of merchandising. "Concretely," wrote Tyler Dennett, "I construe my job to be to sell, through advertising and publicity, Christianity and the church to the people."[38] This was both a new kind of ministry and a novel interpretation of stewardship and the missionary fervor produced by promotionalism of this type required perpetual care. It led mission societies to base their plans on considerations that had no direct relationship to either spontaneous interest or divine decree.

If Protestants were serious about embarking upon a campaign to win the world for Christ, Horace Bushnell had written, the church would do well to "inquire most carefully whether she is expecting to succeed by the vital power of her piety and by unfolding her own internal growth, or by the clumsy expedients of mechanisms and by instruments that are carnal."[39] In 1920, a *Christian Century* editorial characterized the Interchurch Movement as another example of "this impulse to organize, outside of the church, some promotional agency of Christian enlargement."[40] "Quit all formal charities and efforts that outreach your love," Bushnell had written.[41] "Probably the constituency had been pushed beyond its normal convictions," wrote Latourette in explanation of declining mission support after the collapse of the Interchurch Movement.[42] "In the mood of solemn humiliation which now possesses us we are able to see how far we have drifted from our appropriate and natural sources of power," concluded the *Century's* examination of the bankruptcy of the promoter's approach.[43]

The optimism engendered by the numbers game of increasing pledges, volunteers, and convention attendance at the turn of the century was novel only in its source. Millennial expectations may have lain under the optimism of an earlier generation, but the businessman president of the American Board was not counting on the second coming when he predicted in 1904 that "at the present rate the whole world will be converted before the end of this century." "The child is born now who will see it," wrote Samuel Capen. "The world will be practically Christian, as much as America is today, in fifty years, and if we should put out our money and give our men as we might, from the human standpoint it could be

done in twenty-five years."[44] Capen spoke for a generation that
set its sights high, worked and promoted harder than any of its
American predecessors, and confidently expected to reach its goals
or at least to have made it possible for the succeeding generation to
complete the work of evangelization. The disappointment of these
expectations had little immediate effect on the movement or on
Protestant church leaders since in the ultimate sense they could
not fail.

They could maintain with Robert E. Speer that the efforts of all
previous generations to capture the essence embodied in Christ had
been futile, but that theirs had come closest to capturing the same
spirit because "the missionary enterprise during this last half century has been the most powerful and the purest statement of the
essential nature of the Christian Gospel that we have known in the
modern world."[45] Or they could affirm, as Sherwood Eddy did at
the age of eighty-four despite repeated disappointments: "Never
in my life have I believed more firmly in missions than I do today."
The qualification was that foreign missions alone were no longer
enough, for "it has become crystal clear that the same love which
the missionary takes to the uttermost parts of the earth must be
the controlling power in the lives of men who profess Christianity
at home."[46] In either case the mission advocate could be expected
to return from his special errand back to the church that had sent
him. He must try to revive the spirit that had become ossified by
religious institutionalization and to combat the intellectual trends
of skepticism and easygoing liberalism that Latourette found
prevalent in the Protestant churches at the middle of this century.
"From such a Christianity no vigorous foreign mission enterprise
can be expected," wrote the leading American historian of missions.
"Unless new revivals reinvigorate it, it is doomed, even in its own
strongholds."[47]

For various reasons, then, the identification of missions as a
separate entity was rejected, and the place of the movement as an
integral part of the whole Christian Church was re-emphasized.[48]
At the beginning of this century the vigorous revival of the foreign
mission movement distinguished it from the complacent churches

of which it was a part and gave both the appearance and at least rhetorical existence to missions as a distinct religious configuration. The characteristic sense of crisis expressed by the young enthusiasts of the 1880s, however, was submerged in the subsequent process of institutionalization.[49] The artificial crises of unseized opportunities and well-publicized financial and personnel deficiencies replaced the simple religious ones.

The perpetual identification of a series of crises by mission leaders as a promotional device may have been unwise, but it was neither hypocritical nor unnatural. Crisis is a characteristic evangelical concept and a precondition to the experience of personal conversion. Similarly, if a church could be induced to recognize that the neglect of its missionary obligation was critical to its spiritual health—that "the cure of it all is the foreign missionary spirit"[50]—then a wholehearted commitment to that duty might well bring the promised general revival and salvation of that body. Thus, while there was an unquestionable connection between revivals and an increase in missionary zeal, the sequence in which they occurred was not the expected one. There was less evidence at the turn of this century of a general spiritual revival in American Protestantism, which expressed itself in an expanded mission movement, than of a conscious effort by mission leaders to instigate such a revival to aid the cause they held dearest. In this effort, as Samuel Capen said, every ally must be used.[51] In using such allies as the fear of colored races, or international war or materialism, and social revolution, secular crises became the utilitarian point of emphasis. Failure in meeting these, however, did not invalidate the basic Christian missionary motive.

The progressive generation made considerable gains in naturalizing the semi-independent movement it had inherited within the American churches. It succeeded in replacing the British as leaders of Protestant foreign missions on a world-wide basis. But, ironically, the least tangible accomplishment of the movement before 1920 was in the mission field itself. Large populations remained unevangelized, and the growth of national churches was painfully slow.[52]

The inevitable result was a loss of spirit. Both in the field and at home, too much had been promised. More consistently than ever before, missions had been popularized as a civilizing agency rather than a means of evangelization. World War I showed how little Christianized the West was. Nationalism, expressed through boycotts, riots, and revolutions, demonstrated that little progress had been made in the field either. It was one thing to inculcate ideas of humanitarian and fraternal responsibility for social welfare in an emerging nation, and another to promise to provide such services to hundreds of millions of people when resources were insufficient to accomplish the same goals in the United States. This is not to say that the mission of the Protestant churches should not have been undertaken, but it does indicate that a clearer distinction made among the missionaries' goals in the non-Christian world might have forestalled both the inflated optimism perpetrated by the movement's promoters in the United States, and reduced the violent reaction and disappointment when the grand adventure failed. The gap between actual accomplishments in the field and the professed civilizing task was increasingly obvious to the public as mission magazines and books became a minor part of the total available literature on foreign lands.[53] The boards could no longer edit accounts of the actual work to fit the plans announced in efforts to win home support, particularly when the fundamentalists publicized the difference between civilizing and evangelizing for postwar Protestants.

The divergence between hopes and accomplishments, increasingly noted by mission critics after 1920, rested in part on the basic relationship between the boards and their agents. The missionary was a relatively independent pastor whose ideas, methods, and support were not dependent upon his charges. Although he did owe an accounting to his board, he was separated from it by thousands of miles. Weeks if not months would pass before he could be disciplined or his policies reversed. Board policies incorporated intellectual and political changes at home, but he was relatively immune to these directions and tended to become parochial in dealing with *his* work and *his* converts. The churches at home might

profess to be engaged in a civilizing mission, but its agents supported by inadequate resources were preoccupied with their
district and its needs. It was grand to challenge Americans to seize
the opportunity presented by China's thirst for Western knowledge
or to shape new nations through Christian education. Yet this made
little impression on a man whose request for $100 to rent a school
building or $40 to buy new texts had been denied by a board
experiencing budget difficulties.

The American secretaries and trustees administered a totally
inadequate machine for effecting the transformation of nations or
conquering the East for the Christian West. Professions in the
United States and needs on the field were perpetually unbalanced
because the boards depended on the voluntary support of the
public. The constituency had to be wheedled, cajoled, and shown
great results or promised imminent success. Promotion was an
inherent necessity at the home base but ineffective in accomplish-
ing anything in the field. The board administrators had the thank-
less task of mediating between these two kinds of reality. As the
public became aware of this process, it tended to react with scorn
or disinterest rather than with the funds needed to redress the imbalance between hope and necessity.[54]

The secular failure of the Protestant foreign mission movement is related directly to this loss of credibility. Few, if any, non-
governmental organizations in nineteenth-century America dis-
bursed as many millions to thousands of agents as these voluntary
agencies who were totally dependent upon free-will offerings. In
the twentieth century, however, they moved rapidly into the
shadow of national philanthropic foundations while remaining outside the political system which increasingly allotted public funds
for similar purposes. Determined to rely on voluntary support, the
movement based its hopes on obtaining sufficient resources from a
fragment of the American population. Despite the valiant efforts
of fund raisers and the application of sophisticated promotional
techniques, they were not even able to persuade this small proportion to contribute a major share of its philanthropic giving to
foreign missions. The desire to identify Protestant foreign missions

with the mission of America failed because of the dubious assumption that America was a Christian nation which would realize its manifest destiny by offering to share her ideals and institutions with the less fortunate. The civilizing mission that a Beveridge or Burgess or Strong or Fiske attributed to America at the end of the nineteenth century was confidently assumed to be an American Protestant model. The model was neither that coherent, nor was America's role in international relations to be predominantly a Christian one. From the original position of the church as an almoner, secular agencies by the 1920s had taken over all but overseas philanthropy. After World War II, even this field of activity became dominated by governmental programs and agencies, with religious groups reduced to developing public support for Point Four and similar forms of foreign aid.[55]

Meanwhile, the older tradition lived on. "America's manifest destiny in the next chapter of her history is to help the indigent majority of mankind to struggle upwards toward a better life than it has ever dreamed of in the past," wrote Arnold Toynbee in 1962. "The spirit that is needed for embarking on this mission is the spirit of the nineteenth-century American Christian missionaries."[56] It was also, in part, the spirit which was preserved or had been rekindled in a new movement dominated by youth. "I think spiritual (not religious) reasons prompted many of us," wrote a Peace Corps recruit in explanation of his decision, "spiritual in the sense that we hoped for an experience so different, even alien, from what we were accustomed to that the total effect would be one of purification."[57]

Although no longer expressed as religious duty, this same idealism had been at the core of the earlier missionary spirit. The dominance of spiritual goals provided the best commentary for both the failure and lack of realism of the foreign mission movement. As the preoccupation of a minority of mission supporters among the over-all minority of evangelical Protestant church members in the United States, the movement's constituency was pitifully small. Even if the mission forces had succeeded in their efforts to enlist all church members in wholehearted support of world evangelization, they would have depended upon perhaps one third of the American population. Yet the propaganda and declarations of the movement reflected no recognition of this status. They planned great things: the evangelization of the world in this generation. They claimed to speak for America, or at least for all right-thinking Americans.

To support these plans vast resources were required. A more acute realism was reflected in the efforts to increase support at the turn of the century than in defining the objects to which the funds and personnel were to be applied. But ultimately the movement's leaders were engaged in an unrealistic task. They never answered the criticism raised when the movement was first organized in this country a century and a half ago—that the evangelization of the non-Christian world could not be achieved by men or human endeavor alone but required providential intervention. A precondition to a natural expansion of Christianity, it was argued, was loyalty and a spiritual reawakening at home. "God is the ultimate Home Base of Missions," declared W. H. T. Gairdner in 1910.[58] His generation acknowledged, but did not embody, this principle. Caught in the dilemma of letting God do it—waiting another 1900 years and letting unprecedented opportunities pass—or acting, promoting, and developing, a science of missions, they chose to act and made themselves subject to judgment by secular standards as scientists, teachers, and business administrators.[59]

"Therefore it *is* true that GOD is to-day the ultimate Home Base of Missions," insisted the Reverend Gairdner, "the available and sufficient source and resource."[60] He did not seem sufficient to the impatient generation. A sufficient and available resource would be reached only through a great and general awakening. But a revival of the sending churches required the Christianizing of the home base which had so long been the subject of a debate over priorities. In an important sense this was the most serious debilitating factor. America was not a Christian nation because too much promotionalism was required to make her assume her missionary duty. Perhaps more than World War I, rising nationalism, materialism, and the resistance of traditional religions, the weakness of the sending churches caused the failure of this mission. A generation only dimly aware of their minority status as Christians in a hostile world, and slow in adopting a corresponding humility, perhaps needed the lesson taught by failure. Mission leaders had always pointed to the fact that the majority of the world's population was not Christian. Before the 1920s this fact elicited pity and acted as a spur to action. After that decade it served as a reproach and led to introspection and a reassessment of the mission.

The generation that came to the fore during the 1880s made their unique contribution by organizing and expanding a movement. At the conclusion of their stewardship not all approved of either their methods or accomplishments. A dedicated minority had sought a sublime goal by worldly means.[61] But the evangelization of the world by the optimistic timetable of the promoter had proved an illusion. Although there were doubts, few of the succeeding generation admitted that the movement was ended. They could learn from the mistakes of the past but also found it necessary to innovate and adjust the old message to a new environment.

The basic missionary impulse will exist as long as Christianity remains vital, but each generation must re-interpret this mission in its own way. To point out that the job is incomplete and the Kingdom not yet achieved is merely to phrase a lasting incentive in negative terms. It is just as objective to recognize the continuing need of the churches to have an agency whose sole duty it is to adapt their message to the changing problems of the non-Christian world beyond our boundaries and to minister to the needs of those areas in the name of American Protestantism. The need for this interpretation and service is mutual. In this sense, missions have both a dynamic challenge and the assurance of a task that will last as long as the world remains peopled by imperfect men and women.

NOTES

List of Abbreviations

ABCFM	American Board of Commissioners for Foreign Missions
ABMU	American Baptist Missionary Union
ABP	Papers of the American Board of Commissioners for Foreign Missions, Houghton Library, Harvard University
ACMS	American Christian Missionary Society
CIM	China Inland Mission
FCMS	Foreign Christian Missionary Society (Disciples of Christ)
FMCNA	Foreign Missions Conference of North America
IMC	International Missionary Council
IMU	International Missionary Union
IWM	Interchurch World Movement
LMM	Laymen's Missionary Movement
MECMS	Methodist Episcopal Church Missionary Society
MRL	Missionary Research Library, Union Theological Seminary, New York
PBFM	Presbyterian Church in the U.S.A., Board of Foreign Missions
PCUSA	Presbyterian Church in the U.S.A.
PHS	Presbyterian Historical Society, Philadelphia
SVM	Student Volunteer Movement for Foreign Missions
WUMS	Woman's Union Missionary Society of America

Introduction

1. Statistics differ because of difficulty in distinguishing between purely
   foreign mission organizations and such groups as the American Bible
   Society or denominational joint home and foreign boards which also
   employed some of their resources outside the United States. Robert E.
   Speer counted 21 distinctly foreign mission organizations in this country at the beginning of the 1880s. Robert E. Speer, "A Few Comparisons of Then and Now," *The Missionary Review of the World* 51.1:5
   (January 1928). Since the United States remained classified as a mission
   area by the Roman Catholic Church until 1908, and the establishment
   of Maryknoll as a seminary for missionary priests and brothers in 1911
   marks the first official involvement by the American Church in overseas
   evangelization, the foreign mission movement remained a predominantly
   Protestant phenomenon during the period considered in this study. John
   Tracy Ellis, ed., *Documents of American Catholic History* (Milwaukee,
   1956), p. 592.

2. Despite Christ's Great Commission (Matthew 28:19–20, and Mark 16:15),
   and the validity of Ernest Hocking's conclusion that "To any one, man
   or church, possessed of religious certainty, the mission in some form is a
   matter not of choice but of obligation," Protestants found it possible to
   rationalize their lack of missionary zeal for centuries. *Re-Thinking
   Missions, A Laymen's Inquiry after One Hundred Years,* William E.
   Hocking, Chairman, Commission of Appraisal (New York, 1932), p. 6.
   Apart from work aimed at expanding membership in the established
   church, and desultory and largely individual efforts to Christianize the
   Indians during the colonial and early national periods, the missionary
   imperative received little attention in America before the nineteenth
   century. A generally accepted theology of missions, as distinct from
   social or political incentives for proselytizing efforts, was thus extremely
   slow to develop. As late as the 1952 Willingen World Missionary Conference, the chairman of a committee designated to report on mission
   theology had to declare the group's inability to fulfill their charge, and
   confessed that, properly speaking, there was as yet no such thing as a
   theology of missions. Wilhelm Andersen, *Auf Dem Wege zu einer
   Theologie der Mission,* vol. 6 of *Beiträge zur Missionswissenschaft und
   Evangelischen Religionskunde* (Gütersloh, 1957), pp. 7–8. The executive secretary and historian of America's oldest foreign mission board
   came to the same conclusion in his survey of 150 years of worldwide
   activity. Fred Field Goodsell, *You Shall Be My Witnesses* (Boston,
   1959), p. 290.

3. The board of the Methodist Episcopal Church, South, in 1854, for example, had 28 of a total of 34 missionaries serving with the American Indians. The older northern branch of the denomination, 29 of 56. The American Baptist Missionary Union sent 7 men to the Indians, and only 2 to all of Africa. The pioneer Burma mission, however, claimed most of 49 assigned to Asia and surpassed the combined total of all other fields in which the Baptist Missionary Union was active in 1854. Harvey Newcomb, ed., *A Cyclopedia of Missions* (New York, 1860), pp. 114, 547.

4. "In that access of denominational fervor," wrote a later advocate of ecumenicism, "the ecclesiastical politicians in all bodies were eager to possess and to exploit a work which was already successful, which they would hardly have touched had it failed." Edward C. Moore, "Bible Societies and Missions, Their Joint Contribution To Race Development," *Journal of Race Development* 7.1:69 (July 1916). The process is illustrated by the fate of the initially nondenominational American Board, which lost the support of the Dutch Reformed Church in 1857. Nine years later the German Reformed Church followed this example to form its own mission agency. In 1870 the New School Presbyterians, who had remained loyal supporters after the main Presbyterian body had established its own board, left the American Board no recourse but nearly total dependence upon the Congregational Churches. Goodsell, *Witnesses,* pp. 131, 134, 136.

5. Edward Beecher, "The Scriptural Philosophy of Congregationalism and of Councils," *Bibliotheca Sacra* 22.86:312 (April 1865).

6. *Fifty-Fifth Annual Report of the American Board of Commissioners for Foreign Missions* (Boston, 1865), p. 29.

7. Fred Field Goodsell, comp., "Receipts and Expenditures, 1810–1956," American Board Papers. Goodsell's figures are based on official board reports, which apparently make no distinction between contributions in greenbacks or gold currency.

8. *Sixty-Second Annual Report of the American Board of Commissioners for Foreign Missions* (Boston, 1872), p. xxi. The ABCFM's previous high point of 395 missionaries in the field in 1850, had decreased by 80 when the Civil War ended, and did not creep back to the prewar level for another decade. Goodsell, *Witnesses,* p. 290.

9. *Seventy-First Annual Report of the American Board of Commissioners for Foreign Missions* (Boston, 1881), p. xiv; Goodsell, *Witnesses,* p. 215.

10. The FCMS was organized because of the dissatisfaction of foreign mission advocates among the Disciples with the record of the joint home and foreign American Missionary Society. Since the AMS's formation in 1849, only three missionaries had been sent to the foreign field, and all had been recalled for lack of sufficient support. Despite the assumption of the new society's sponsors that the Disciples' foreign outreach had been handicapped by the ACMS's preoccupation with the new denomination's expansion in this country, the FCMS limped along during its first decade with average annual contributions of $15,000 from those of the half-million Disciples who cared. Archibald McLean, *The History of the Foreign Christian Missionary Society* (New York, 1919), pp. 22, 62.

11. Arthur T. Pierson, *The Crisis of Missions, or, The Voice Out of the Cloud* (New York, 1886), p. 273.

12. Ibid., p. 282.

13. The scale of support for missions was measured against such discoveries as the fact that the total number of communicants in the evangelical churches had increased 14.5-fold between 1800 and 1860, a rate two and one half times greater than that of the population of the United States in the same period. Jesse T. Peck, *The History of the Great Republic Considered From a Christian Stand-Point* (Boston, 1877), p. 550.

14. Pierson, pp. 304, 202, 281.

15. Ibid., p. 354.

16. Speer, "A Few Comparisons," p. 5.

17. *Handbook of the Christian Movement in China Under Protestant Auspices,* Charles L. Boynton and Charles D. Boynton, comps. (Shanghai, 1936), pp. 1–131. The numbers indicated do not include interdenominational service organizations in China, or such mission-supported institutions as the Christian colleges.

18. In addition to the well-known interest of American expansionists in

China at the turn of the century, and preoccupation with the potential of the China market, it is revealing that a study of periodical literature dealing with foreign missions disclosed that in the period 1810–1934 the editors of some 70 secular periodicals were far more willing to publish missionary articles if they dealt with China than with any other field. Ortha May Lane, *Missions in Magazines* (Shanghai, 1935), p. 34. Some indication of the proportional commitment is provided by the fact that, of a total of 8,140 Student Volunteers who sailed to the foreign field between 1888 and 1920, 2,524 were sent to China. Only 867 had been sent to the entire continent of Africa, 1,570 to the second-ranked field of India-Burma-Ceylon. *North American Students and World Advance,* Burton St. John, ed. (New York, 1920), p. 61.

SVM figures do not distinguish between United States and Canadian volunteers, and this fact provides the occasion for a warning concerning other data related to the foreign mission movement. All personnel and financial information given for American mission societies in this study must be considered approximations. Both denominational and collective reports published before the 1930s are notoriously incomplete, even for the boards normally responding. Some agencies, like the North American Branch of the China Inland Mission, did not report financial or personnel statistics as a matter of policy. Information relating to locally supported or individual "faith missionaries" is unavailable. Since the citizenship of missionaries was not reflected in any published reports, no adjustments can be made for this factor either despite known instances of the appointment of Canadians and Europeans by American boards.

In addition, personnel statistics in particular were often given for "North American" societies, including Canadian organizations who, by M. Searle Bates's estimate, may have contributed as much as 9% of the American missionary force in China in this century. M. Searle Bates, "The Theology of American Missionaries in China, 1900–1950," in John K. Fairbank, ed., *The Missionary Enterprise in China and America* (Cambridge, Mass., 1974), p. 136. Whenever the form in which statistics were published has allowed, information for Canadian societies has been subtracted from the totals cited in this study for American mission organizations. In other instances, the term North American is used.

19. President James B. Angell of the University of Michigan, also a member of the American Board, provided an example by comparing the Chinese with the Saxons in their staying power and determination. If they would only "give up their vanity and accept Christ," he concluded, "we may be assured they will wield a power which will be felt not only through-

out Asia, but throughout the world." James B. Angell, "China a Field
for Missions," *Missionary Herald* 79.12:478–479 (December 1883).
"These Oriental Yankees, once brought to Christ," agreed Arthur Pierson a few years later, "will become the aggressive missionary race of the
Orient." Pierson, p. 94. Another developing theme at the end of the
century is reflected in the Rev. William Durban's rhetorical question:
"Is China to be civilized before it is Christianized?" The answer, frequently restated on both sides of the Atlantic, implied un-Christian concern about the Yellow Peril: "The great Churches of the West have
decided that this must not be permitted. A Far Eastern national Renaissance without the grace of God is an appalling contingency." Foreword
to W. Remfry Hunt, *Heathenism under the Searchlight* (London, 1908),
p. 7.

20. *American Board Almanac of Missions, 1894* (Boston, n.d.), p. 19.

21. "In China it took thirty-five years to win the first six, and at the end of
    fifty years there were less than a thousand who professed evangelical
    Christianity . . ." wrote a contemporary student of missions, "but at the
    end of the second half-century there are a round quarter million in the
    Protestant community there, and the members have increased sevenfold
    in two decades." Alva W. Taylor, *The Social Work of Christian Missions*
    (Cincinnati, 1911), p. 41.

22. American Board of Commissioners for Foreign Missions, *General Report
    of the Deputation Sent By the American Board to China in 1907*
    (Boston, 1907), pp. 55–56.

23. *Missions of the American Baptist Missionary Union in East China, and
    Minutes of the Eastern Baptist Mission Conference* (Shanghai, 1907),
    p. 12.

24. W. H. T. Gairdner, *Echoes From Edinburgh, 1910* (New York, 1910),
    p. 133.

25. J. E. Williams, "The Present Situation in China, Its Causes, Elements
    and Possibilities," *Men and Missions* 3.8:12 (April 1912). "I am haunted
    with solicitude," wrote John R. Mott of the effort to influence the first
    generation of modern Chinese students, "lest we miss this absolutely
    unique opportunity." Basil Mathews, *John R. Mott, World Citizen* (New
    York, 1934), p. 416.

26. Harlan P. Beach, *Dawn on the Hills of T'ang* (New York, 1898), p. 104.

27. Harlan Beach and B. St. John, eds., *World Statistics of Christian Missions* (New York, 1916), p. 63. Total Protestant mission personnel in China in 1916 numbered 5,750 representatives of 108 societies. The second largest national contribution was made by Great Britain. Seventeen British societies maintained a foreign staff of 625 in 1898, which rose to 21 mission agencies supporting 1,252 in 1916. Ibid., p. 63.

28. Cornelius H. Patton, *The Business of Missions* (New York, 1924), p. 43. In his survey of 125 years of Protestant activity, Latourette singled out China as one of the primary mission fields throughout the era of expansion. Despite nationalistic reactions, Japanese incursions, and wholesale evacuation of several provinces by all foreign missionaries, more Protestant evangelists were at work in China as late as 1936 than in any other country in the world. Kenneth S. Latourette, *Missions Tomorrow* (New York, 1936), p. 27.

1. The Movement Organized

1. Francis Wayland (1796–1865), quoted in David McConaughy, "The Laymen, A Latent Force for the Evangelization of the World," in FMCNA, *Thirteenth Conference of the Foreign Mission Boards in the United States and Canada* (New York, 1906), p. 88.

2. William T. Ellis, *Men and Missions* (Philadelphia, 1909), p. 292.

3. Although this principle continued as the ideal of such Continental mission leaders as Gustav Warneck, others considered it unscriptural. J. H. Bavinck, *An Introduction to the Science of Missions* (Philadelphia, 1960), p. 59.

4. The negative counterpart of this ambition was the lasting fear of the morally corrosive concentration of power in the hands of board officers exercising authority in God's name; this fear persisted into the twentieth century among the Disciples and the smaller denominations clinging to an older Calvinism. Critics considered mission societies an impudent and useless effort by man to do God's work by proxy, for God alone was responsible for timing the evangelization of men, and had never intended that the church should maintain permanent instrumentalities for

the spread of the gospel beyond the apostolic era. James L. Batchelder, *Societyism and Its Evils* (Chicago, 1871), pp. 13, 24, 40.

5. Quoted in H. Richard Niebuhr, *The Kingdom of God in America* (Hamden, Conn., 1956), pp. 165–168. Anthony F. C. Wallace makes a similar assumption in asserting that "all organized religions are relics of old revitalization movements, surviving in routinized form in stabilized cultures." Anthony F. C. Wallace, "Revitalization Movements," *American Anthropologist* 58:268 (April 1936).

6. Hadley Cantril, *The Psychology of Social Movements* (New York, 1941), pp. 144–147.

7. Samuel B. Capen, *Disloyalty and Its Remedy* (Boston, 1904), p. 19.

8. J. Campbell White, *Methods of Enlisting Men in Missions* (New York, n.d.), p. 25.

9. Samuel B. Capen, *The Uprising of Men for World Conquest* (New York, 1909), p. 7. Emphasis in original.

10. Adoniram Judson Gordon, quoted in McConaughy, "The Laymen," p. 88.

11. Horace Bushnell, "The Kingdom of Heaven as a Grain of Mustard Seed," *The New Englander* 2.8:605–606 (October 1844).

12. Charles E. Merriam, *American Political Ideas* (New York, 1920; 1969 rep.), p. 450.

13. Frank B. Copley, *Frederick W. Taylor, Father of Scientific Management* (New York, 1923), I, 104.

14. Samuel Haber, *Efficiency and Uplift; Scientific Management in the Progressive Era, 1890–1920* (Chicago, 1964), pp. ix, 64; Frederic C. Howe, *The Confessions of a Reformer* (New York, 1925), pp. 76–77.

15. John D. Rockefeller, *Random Reminiscences of Men and Events* (Garden City, New York, 1933), p. 172. Before appointing Frederick T. Gates as his philanthropic adviser, Rockefeller tested the former Baptist minister's mettle by sending him on several trips to investigate and administer new investments.

16. Patton, *The Business of Missions*, pp. viii–ix.

17. Twelve Protestant foreign mission societies had been formed during the
    150 years between 1649 and 1800, 22 were added during the next
    three decades, then 116 distinctly foreign mission groups were organized
    during the 40 years before the post-1870 outburst. James S. Dennis,
    "Abstract of Centennial Statistics," in *Ecumenical Missionary Conference,
    New York, 1900* (New York, 1900), I, 429–430.

18. When a former missionary and secretary of the Southern Presbyterian
    Foreign Mission Board suggested that the appointment and support of
    missionaries be transferred to local bodies of ministers and elders, his
    colleagues at the first North American conference of board secretaries
    uniformly rejected his plan. Without reference to their vested interests
    in the status quo, they dismissed the idea as chimerical. M. H. Houston,
    "Mission Work in the New Testament as Related to Mission Work Today,"
    in FMCNA, *Interdenominational Conference of Foreign Missionary
    Boards and Societies in the United States and Canada* (New York, 1893),
    pp. 11–12.

19. In 1844 the General Conference appointed a General Missionary Com-
    mittee representing the various Annual Conferences, to determine allo-
    cations with the independent Board of Managers of the Mission Society.
    The Society's Board, which was unusual in assuming responsibility for
    both home and foreign missions, retained considerable autonomy until
    the General Conference obtained the right to elect the Board of Managers
    in 1872. Wade Crawford Barclay, *The Methodist Episcopal Church,
    1845–1939, Widening Horizons, 1845–1895*, vol. 3 of *History of
    Methodist Missions* (New York, 1957), pp. 115–118.

20. The American Baptist Missionary Union was the offspring of a conven-
    tion held in 1814 to discuss support for two of the first American Board
    missionaries to be sent abroad, who had been converted to Baptism
    after their departure from the United States. The secession of the
    southern churches led to a change of name and the incorporation of the
    American Baptist Missionary Union in 1845. Edmund F. Merriam, *A
    History of American Baptist Missions* (Philadelphia, 1900), p. 70. Tied
    closely to the Northern Baptist Convention by 1910, the name changed
    again to American Baptist Foreign Mission Society.

21. The Methodist Board of Managers was advised by regional and functional

standing committees, but retained the right to conduct the entire "management and disposition of the affairs and property" of the society for half a century. Barclay, p. 121. The only significant restriction on the Baptist society's executive committee was the provision requiring a supporting vote of three-fifths of the Board of Managers' membership in any case involving the dismissal of a missionary. *A Handbook of the Northern Baptist Convention, And Its Cooperating and Affiliating Organizations, 1919–1920* (Philadelphia, 1919), pp. 60–61.

22. This was especially true of denominations like the Methodists and Disciples, who combined home and foreign missions in single societies. For a warning that denominational policies were promoting a breakoff of foreign mission supporters, see James M. Thoburn, "The Gospel of 'Benevolences,'" *The Christian Advocate* 76.36:8 (New York, Sept. 5, 1901).

23. The resistance of most Disciples to any form of unbiblical ecclesiastical system was reflected in the ACMS's name-change to the General Christian Missionary Convention. In effect from 1869 to 1895, the change was an effort to get rid of the onus attached to the word "Society." McLean, pp. 16, 22, 25, 35, 419.

24. The charter set no limits on membership and listed no denominational affiliation, but did provide that not less than one-third of the membership must at all times be composed of respectable laymen, "that another third shall be composed of respectable clergymen, and the remaining third to be composed of characters of the same description, whether clergymen or laymen." Quoted in William E. Strong, *The Story of the American Board* (Boston, 1910), p. 305.

25. Goodsell, *Witnesses,* p. 142.

26. William J. Tucker, *My Generation* (Boston, 1919), p. 152.

27. Goodsell, *Witnesses,* pp. 146–147.

28. The original corporate membership of 24 expanded as the supporting churches grew, to 348 in 1902, 876 in 1932, and 1,377 in 1952. After 1913, members of the National Council of Congregational Churches and veteran missionaries were accorded automatic membership. Thousands of honorary members were also elected, at first on the basis of financial contributions, later according to their interest or other

contributions to the cause of missions. Goodsell, *Witnesses,* pp. 198–199.

29. The Prudential Committee was expanded to 12 members in 1894, and the president and vice-president of the board allowed to participate in an *ex officio* capacity. *Eighty-Fourth Annual Report of the American Board of Commissioners for Foreign Missions* (Boston, 1894), p. vi. President Samuel Capen (1899–1914) utilized this provision to greatly increase the powers and effective leadership of the presidency. He attended weekly meetings regularly, spent nearly as much time at the work as the professional secretaries, and generally refused to play the traditional role of venerable figurehead in his effort to introduce business methods into the administration of the Board. Chauncy J. Hawkins, *Samuel Billings Capen: His Life and Work* (Boston, 1914), p. 129.

30. The natural elitism of mission board governance was reinforced by the search for businesslike efficiency, as exemplified by the veteran American Board corporate member who advised President Capen against holding a referendum to determine the nature of the society's reorganization. "Perhaps I am not very much enamoured of the spirit of the times," admitted Yale historian Williston Walker, "but I have yet to be convinced that a sufficient amount of ignorance added together makes wisdom. That may be undemocratic but it is business." Williston Walker to Samuel Capen, March 26, 1913, "Samuel B. Capen Material, Letters," ABP.

31. With a membership approaching 200,000 in over 1,100 churches, the present leadership still prefers not to be called a denomination. Instead they constitute a missionary movement welcoming anyone who subscribes to their fourfold gospel and enthusiasm for evangelization. A. E. Thompson, *A. B. Simpson: His Life and Work* (Harrisburg, Pa., 1960), pp. 128–129, 134–135. Other fundamentalist sects, such as the Missionary Church Association formed in Indiana in 1898, also use the Christian and Missionary Alliance as a foreign mission work outlet. Frank S. Mead, *Handbook of Denominations in the United States* (New York, 1961), pp. 63, 105.

32. The Missionary Bands of the World, for example, organized as young people's societies by a Free Methodist minister in 1885, became self-conscious and dissatisfied as Methodists, and eventually declared their independence as the Pentecost Bands of the World. At mid-century, the sect still claimed several hundred members in five active societies in

three midwestern states. Elmer T. Clark, *The Small Sects in America*
(New York, 1949), p. 77.

33. One of the most exotic was the "Holy Ghost and Us" sect, founded in
    1893 by the Rev. Frank W. Sandford, an ordained Free Baptist minister
    who left his New Hampshire pulpit to evangelize the world with a capital
    of three cents. Most of the stern New Englanders who surrendered their
    property upon entering his communist community near Lisbon Falls,
    Maine, had been Methodists and Baptists before encountering the self-
    styled missionary "Prophet Elijah." Sandford's dictatorial direction of
    the sect's missionary fleet led to his conviction of manslaughter on the
    high seas, and the community's reported dissolution during his incarceration
    in Atlanta federal penitentiary. "Nineteen Years of 'Shiloh,' " *Literary
    Digest* 44.4:164-165 (Jan. 27, 1912). See also William Hiss, "Frank W. Stan-
    ford and the Kingdom, 1893-1948" (Ph.D. Dissertation, Tufts University,
    1978).

34. Lettie B. Cowman, *Charles E. Cowman, Missionary::Warrior* (Los
    Angeles, 1928), pp. 41, 107-113, 416.

35. Howard and Geraldine Taylor, *"By Faith . . .";* Henry W. Frost and the
    China Inland Mission (Philadelphia, 1938), pp. 59, 66, 90.

36. CIM income in North America increased steadily from $40,694 in 1900
    to $146,121 in 1916. It never fell below $100,000 again, and reached
    its peak with $502,017 contributed in 1929. Ibid., pp. 292-293. Using
    income as an index of the number of supporters is questionable in view
    of wide differences in per capita giving among various denominations.
    But, as a rough indication of the importance of the CIM to the Ameri-
    can mission effort, a comparison suggests a constituency about equivalent
    to that supporting the Christian and Missionary Alliance, or either of the
    two Reformed Church bodies. All three generally exceeded CIM receipts
    slightly before World War I, but were outstripped by the North American
    branch during the third decade of this century.

37. One of the founders of the Methodist Episcopal Woman's Foreign Mis-
    sion Society listed twenty similar denominational woman's groups
    which were established between 1868 and 1880. Apart from local organi-
    zations, only the Woman's Union Missionary Society, incorporated in
    1861, was founded before the war. Mrs. L. H. Daggett, ed., *Historical
    Sketches of Woman's Missionary Societies in America and England*
    (Boston, 1883), passim.

38. At the end of its first two decades, the WUMS had employed 92 missionaries and an additional 165 "native Bible readers." The $561,000 it had collected was secured strictly through individual solicitation, to avoid denominational jealousy and criticism. Ibid., pp. 198–199.

39. Three regional women's boards were cooperating with the American Board by 1873. Strong, p. 311. The Methodist Episcopal Woman's Foreign Mission Society was established in 1869, but fought until 1884 before being recognized as an official organ of the church. Barclay, p. 139.

40. The same year, 24 British women's societies maintained 494 missionaries, while 10 Canadian groups had sent only 48. *American Board Almanac of Missions for 1891*, p. 32.

41. The report to the conference was satisfactory, and Barclay found that the administrative expenditures of the Methodist Missionary Society "were maintained throughout the period at a remarkably low level." The Society's C. C. McCabe reported in 1887 that, of every dollar contributed to missions, .927 went into direct missionary appropriations, .023 to an emergency fund, .0274 to incidental missionary expenses, .0091 to the publication and distribution of missionary literature, and only .0135 to board salaries and office expenses. Barclay, p. 134.

    In 1909, Samuel Capen refuted charges that it took two dollars to get one dollar to the field, by stating that "the total expenses of administration, collecting funds, correspondence, agencies, rents in Boston, New York, Chicago, and Berkeley, publications and miscellaneous charges is 9.45%." From this the American Board deducted the interest from a special fund established for that purpose, "leaving the net expense account 9.18%." Samuel B. Capen, *Facing the Facts* (Boston, 1909), p. 23.

42. Charles H. Daniels, "Home Department Finances," in FMCNA, *Ninth Conference of the Officers and Representatives of the Foreign Mission Boards and Societies in the United States and Canada* (New York, 1902), p. 27.

43. Patton, *The Business of Missions*, p. 207.

44. Arthur Judson Brown, *Memoirs of a Centenarian*, W. N. Wysham, ed. (New York, 1957), p. 31.

45. John R. Mott, "The Vision of the Haystack Realized," in *The One Hundredth Anniversary of the Haystack Prayer Meeting* (Boston, 1907), p. 197.

46. Samuel B. Capen, "The Necessity of Making the Financial Plans of the Church Commensurate with the Magnitude of the Task of the World's Evangelization," in *World-Wide Evangelization, The Urgent Business of the Church* (New York, 1902), p. 177.

47. Samuel B. Capen, "The Responsibility of Laymen for the Promotion of the Foreign Missionary Enterprise," in *Students and the Present Missionary Crisis* (New York, 1910), p. 475.

48. John R. Mott, *Five Decades and a Forward View* (New York, 1939), p. 8.

49. Ibid., p. 18; Kenneth S. Latourette, *World Service* (New York, 1957), p. 57.

50. E. Clark Worman, *The Silver Bay Story* (Silver Bay, New York, 1952), pp. 26–27.

51. "Report of the Educational Committee," in "Minutes of Various Committees 1911," LMM Papers, MRL.

52. Worman, p. 26.

53. Quoted in *Men and Missions* 10.5:136 (January 1919).

54. Samuel B. Capen, "Laymen's Share in Advocacy" (address delivered at Edinburgh Synod Hall, June, 1910), "Samuel B. Capen Material. Addresses, Documents," ABP.

55. *Report of Commission VI, The Home Base of Missions*, vol. 6 of *World Missionary Conference, 1910* (Edinburgh and New York, 1910), p. 196. Three decades later, John R. Mott made the more moderate assessment that the LMM "was the most significant development in the world mission during the first decade of the present century." Mott, *Five Decades*, p. 30.

56. Members were defined as laymen of the Protestant churches of North America who signed and filed a copy of the following declaration of

purpose with the New York office: "Believing it to be the duty of the Church of Christ to preach the Gospel to every creature, it is my purpose to pray, to give, to study and to work as God may give me the opportunity that the church of this generation may obey this command." In the absence of dues or means of uniting these members, membership constituted little more than a gesture of sympathy. "Plan of Organization and Work of the Laymen's Missionary Movement," undated typescript in "LMM Birth (1906), History and Minutes of First Meetings of Executive Committee, Nov.-Dec. 1906," LMM Papers. Subsequent organizational information is based on this document, unless otherwise indicated.

A self-perpetuating General Committee selected without participation by the national membership met twice a year to make policy. It in turn elected an executive committee that could meet at will, and that consisted predominantly of New York area laymen able to attend such meetings. Until his death in 1914, Samuel Capen was chairman of this select group which supervised the employment of staff, prepared the budget, established subcommittees, and otherwise effectively directed the movement. Laymen known to the public were sought from all professions and denominations for the showcase General Committee, either on the basis of prominence like Alfred Thayer Mahan, or on the basis of financial ability since the movement never made a public appeal for funds for its own work. Minutes of the Executive Committee, Dec. 18, 1908; Minutes of the General Committee, Nov. 1, 1907, LMM Papers. A Maryland businessman, for example, found himself unanimously elected to the Executive Committee shortly after pledging $10,000 toward the expenses of a national LMM campaign. This is not to say that the Laymen's Movement was ever so crude as to sell positions on its governing board, but surely it was easier for a rich man to enter this particular corner of the Kingdom, than for an eager poor man to aspire to the same.

57. The founders were content to make policy in the background while continuing their professional careers. Even the offer of "employing a first rate man to look after your business interests for you" did not succeed in luring Capen into giving his full time to the direction of the LMM. J. Campbell White to Samuel Capen, January 9, 1912, "Samuel B. Capen Material. Letters," ABP.

58. The same criteria were prescribed by headquarters for the executive secretaries of more than a dozen denominational Laymen's Movements. Minutes of the Executive Committee, June 26, 1907, LMM Papers.

59. "Address of Dr. William Jay Schieffelin, President of the American Church Missionary Society at the Reception Given by the United Board of Missions, May 29th, 1907," uncatalogued typescript in LMM Papers.

60. If anywhere in the twentieth-century foreign mission movement one would expect to find evidence of a connection between overseas missions and expansionism, it would be in a national men's organization directed by a businessman, incorporating elements of the Eastern establishment in the executive structure, and served by a politically astute public relations conscious professional staff. Yet, despite a careful biographical study of the men associated with the Laymen's Movement, and a diligent search for such motives throughout the course of this study, none of the men identified were found to have any commercial or political interests that could be served through an expanded foreign mission movement. Even the grand strategist of expansionism, Alfred Thayer Mahan, viewed his brief official connection with a businessmen's organization for the promotion of American religious expansion in a purely apolitical fashion. "The impression chiefly carried away by me from the meeting," he wrote after attending a General Committee session in 1911, "was that of moral and spiritual refreshment and encouragement from the general tone evidently pervading the little assembly, and the unanimity of devotion to our Lord Jesus Christ which transparently underlay all the utterances." Undated letter from Alfred Thayer Mahan read into Minutes of the General Committee, February 22, 1911, LMM Papers. Clarion calls to the civilizing mission of the Christian nations, and testimonials to the commercial value of the missionary were obviously reserved for popular consumption and did not invade the quiet atmosphere of committee meetings which were invariably opened with scripture readings and prayer.

61. The vigorously self-sufficient Chicago office of the Central Division began to challenge New York over program control in its area soon after its establishment, and finally refused to abide by the decision to disband the movement in 1919. The national Executive Committee had retained the right to appoint or approve all regional committees, and demanded copies of their minutes for a central file. Furthermore, no election to any local or state committee formed during national campaigns was valid until approved by both the regional division officers and the national Executive Committee, and similar permission was required for the publication of all literature bearing the movement's name in the United States. Excerpts from Executive Committee Minutes, "National Missionary Campaign, 1915-1916," LMM Papers.

62. While the Executive Committee was willing to provide advice and even personnel to the denominational affiliates, it also declared that "the Laymen's Missionary Movement, being a Movement and not an organization, has no organic relation to these Movements or Organizations." Minutes of the Executive Committee, September 20, 1907, LMM Papers. Much energy was subsequently expended in developing denominational movements which the LMM could not control, while their members, as Cornelius Patton complained, had their horizons restricted rather than broadened by being able to visualize their missionary obligation strictly in terms of denominational propaganda. Cornelius Patton, "Twenty-Five Years After," *The Congregationalist* 116.41:1361 (Oct. 8, 1931).

63. S. B. Capen, typescript of untitled LMM convention address, 1908; "Samuel B. Capen Material, Addresses, Documents," ABP. With exclusivity threatening the movement's effectiveness, the leadership allowed the promotion of home missions for the first time in the form of a concerted effort to spread the adoption of the every member canvass through the Protestant denominations during the national campaign of 1913–1914. "Comments and Suggestions Made at the Organizing Conference of the Field Work of the United Missionary Campaign, New York, April 17, 1913," typescript, pp. 2–4. LMM Papers. The compelling reason for the belated policy shift was awareness that the movement had "lost business men because business men say it is not businesslike to divide Home and Foreign interests." F. B. Haggard, "How to Unify the Forces Within a Denomination," typescript attached to Minutes of the Secretarial Council of the Laymen's Missionary Movement and Allied Movements, Boston, Mass., May 2, 1911, LMM Papers.

64. The Presbyterian Board's Robert E. Speer scarcely succeeded in preventing the Congregational board's Samuel Capen from resigning as LMM chairman for this reason. Robert E. Speer to Samuel B. Capen, January 6, 1913, "Samuel B. Capen Material. Letters," ABP. Capen probably expressed the reason for both denominations' lack of enthusiasm when he replied to General Secretary Millar's importuning that "the Congregational churches as a whole and the laymen in particular are weary of so much machinery." Samuel B. Capen to William B. Millar, December 5, 1912, "Samuel B. Capen Material. Letters," ABP.

65. J. Campbell White, *The Genesis and Significance of the Laymen's Missionary Movement* (New York, 1909), p. 5.

66. J. Campbell White, *The Origin and Work of the Laymen's Missionary*

Movement (New York, 1913), pp. 4–5. The Canadian Committee of the
LMM anticipated the parent body with a campaign during 1907–1908,
capped by the Toronto Missionary Congress in April 1909, which
attracted over 4,000 registered commissioners. What delighted the
sponsors even more than the fact that paid attendance at some of the
campaign dinner meetings exceeded 2,000 was that these were not the
old ladies and men who traditionally attended missionary meetings, but
men of affairs in numbers often exceeding the total of male church
members in the towns visited by LMM teams. S. B. Capen, "The Nation's
Response to the National Campaign," typescript of address delivered at
Chicago congress May 4, 1910, "Samuel B. Capen Material, Addresses,
Documents," ABP. The even more successful United Missionary Campaign of 1913–1914 created mixed feelings in New York, since the price
for having the boards and FMCNA launch the first nationwide cooperative appeal for missions under LMM direction, was the inclusion of home
missions. Samuel B. Capen to Edward D. Eaton, April 10, 1913,
"Samuel B. Capen Material, Letters," ABP. Despite friendly warnings,
dinners and conventions continued to be scheduled during the war,
with attendance uniformly higher in 1918 by as much as 100 percent.
Men and Missions 9.10:303 (June 1918).

67. The 1914 Minister's Convention in Rochester, N.Y., attracted 700
pastors representing 2,000 western New York churches, and was imitated
on a small scale in other areas. Despite its resounding success, however,
headquarters considered it somewhat anomolous for laymen to arrange
such meetings for the clergy. "Annual Report, Laymen's Missionary
Movement, February 12, 1915," typescript, p. 12, LMM Papers. Working without the major components of what was later called the mass
media, the LMM's secretaries reached remarkable numbers with their
publicity. During a five-month period ending in February 1914, for
example, teams including 200 LMM speakers addressed 425 separate
interdenominational conferences. In the process, coaching conferences
for canvassers had also been held and over 300,000 books and pamphlets
sold. Minutes of the General Committee, February 23, 1914, LMM
Papers.

68. A 1910 convention in Boise City, for example, must have been the
biggest community event since the last national election. All local
businesses were closed for the day to allow clerks and workers to
attend, and the governor of Idaho joined the mayor of Boise City in
leading a two-mile-long procession to the convention site. In the morn-
ing Bible study groups searched for spiritual guidance, then separated

into small prayer groups. With the stage set in this manner, it was no surprise that Governor James Brady eventually marched to the lectern to declare: "I have never made a personal sacrifice before for missions and I will begin by giving this watch as an offering to missions now." Quoted in Capen, "Nation's Response to the National Campaign."

69. Minutes of the Executive Committee, June 12, 1914, LMM Papers. The Southern Baptists had a particularly vigorous denominational movement, which outlasted the parent body by at least a decade. Beyond this, however, the movement was not firmly established in the rural South.

An outline of the movement's future in 1916 focused on three areas for expanded activity. Rural sections, which had hitherto been largely ignored, were to be reached through conventions at selected county seats. Additional ministers' conferences were planned after the success of the experimental session in Rochester, New York. It was also pointed out that the "colored laymen in this country have been almost entirely unreached by the Movement and earnest appeals are coming for the extension of the work among them." William B. Millar, *The Advance of a Decade* (New York, 1916), pp. 32–33. The employment of Adolphus Lewis as the first and only black LMM secretary in 1916 was at best a belated token response to these appeals, despite his personal vigor and effectiveness in organizing numerous conventions for black men in southern cities during the next two years.

70. "The Future of Laymen's Movements," *Men and Missions* 9.5:131–132 (January 1918).

71. Patton, "Twenty-Five Years After," p. 1360.

72. White, *Methods of Enlisting Men,* pp. 21, 24.

73. Mott, *Five Decades,* p. 40.

74. George H. Trull, "The Abiding Impressions of the Organization Meeting of the Laymen's Missionary Movement Made Upon the Only Minister Present," undated typescript, John R. Mott Collection, VII, 15, Day Missions Library. Even the formerly skeptical Arthur Henderson Smith admitted after closer examination that "the great sweep of the Laymen's movement gives promise that our members are to awake from the dead." "Surely," mused the veteran missionary to China, "if the Kindom of God is ever to come it must be in some such way as this." Arthur Henderson Smith, London, to Mrs. George W. Hinman, August 3, 1910,

"Smith, Arthur Henderson, North China Mission 1872–1925," ABP.

75. Quoted in Samuel B. Capen, "The Responsibility of Laymen," p. 475.

76. Bushnell, "Kingdom of Heaven," p. 607.

77. The YMCAs were the primary beneficiaries of this movement, but temperance, abolitionist, and missionary societies in this period also found they received the most generous responses to their appeals when approaching churches or communities in the full tide of religious revival. Timothy L. Smith, *Revivalism and Social Reform in Mid-Nineteenth-Century America* (New York, 1957), pp. 46, 48, 143, 146.

78. Niebuhr, *Kingdom of God,* p. 185.

79. "Summary of the Discussions at the Conference of Laymen's Missionary Movement Secretaries," Dec. 23, 1914, LMM Papers.

80. *The History and Program of the Laymen's Missionary Movement* (New York, 1912), p. 9.

81. "The Laymen's Missionary Movement has sought for six years to awaken the American and Canadian Churches to their missionary duty," observed a wistful member of the Executive Committee in 1912, "and its experience has convinced it that the greatest need of the present hour is *not* organization or education or agitation, but prayer and the depth of life in God which flows from prayer and from which prayer flows." Minutes of the Executive Committee, June 5, 1912, LMM Papers. Emphasis supplied.

82. Samuel B. Capen, "Nation's Response."

83. D. Brewer Eddy, "Raising Money for the American Board," typescript, Dec. 6, 1942, p. 47, ABP.

84. *Men and Missions* 9.8:242–243 (April 1918).

85. "Coffee of Old Leaders of L.M.M.," Union League Club, NYC, June 6, 1924; ms. notes of John R. Mott, file XII. a.2, John R. Mott Collection, Day Missions Library.

86. Minutes of the Executive Committee, Sept. 21, 1910, LMM Papers. Thirty years later Mott declared that "it was never the intention of the

pioneers of the Movement to let it develop into a fixed and permanent organization," while at the same time agreeing with the sentiments of others of the old leaders that "it might have been better had the parent Movement continued in existence as a coordinating body." Mott, *Five Decades,* pp. 43–45.

87. Mott, "The Vision of the Haystack," p. 193.

88. Frederick D. Leete, *Christian Brotherhoods* (Cincinnati, 1912), p. 386.

89. Samuel M. Zwemer, "A Pull All Together," *Men and Missions* 10.6:172 (February 1919).

90. Mott, *Five Decades,* pp. 64–65; *Report of the Winding Up of the Interchurch World Movement of North America, Inc. Submitted by the Business Men's Committee* (New York, 1923), p. 3.

91. "Records of the Prudential Committee" (Meetings of January 6, 1920, February 17, 1920), xxxiii, 704, 732, ABP; Eddy, pp. 48–49.

92. John E. Lankford, "Protestant Stewardship and Benevolence, 1900–1941" (Ph.D. dissertation, University of Wisconsin, 1962), pp. 62–69; "Conference on Financial Campaign" (December 3, 1919), "History of Interchurch World Movement," vol. 2, chap. 6, p. 9. (Bound remnants of IWM Papers, New York Public Library).

93. Report of the Committee of '20, January 12, 1919, in ibid., vol. 1, ch. 1, p. 7; Mott, *Five Decades,* p. 64.

94. "Minutes of the Joint Meeting of the Home Base Committee and the Committee on Efficiency," New York, February 26, 1913; "Minutes of the Conference of the Representatives of the Home and Foreign Boards," New York, March 19, 1913, LMM Papers.

95. The result of relying on "friendly citizens" and "unchurched people friendly to the Christian spirit" for promotional expenses was bankruptcy and indebtedness to the Rockefeller family for over one-third of the money raised. Raymond B. Fosdick, *John D. Rockefeller, Jr., A Portrait* (New York, 1956), p. 210.

96. "History of the IWM," vol. 2, ch. 5, p. 134; Fosdick, *Rockefeller,* p. 209; Lyman L. Pierce's Report, "History of the IWM," vol. 2,

ch. 6, p. 27. "History of the IWM," vol. 2, ch. 5, p. 128.

97. William Hiram Foulkes, "Like a Tide of God," *Men and Missions* 10.6:171 (February 1919).

98. J. Campbell White, "A World Program," *Men and Missions* 10.6:175 (February 1919).

99. Report to the Committee of 20, January 12, 1919, "History of the IWM," vol. 1, ch. 1, p. 7.

100. "History of the IWM," vol. 1, ch. 1, pp. 48–49.

101. Mott, *Five Decades,* pp. 64–65.

102. Charles H. Pratt, "The Mind and the Spirit," *Men and Missions* 10.6:173 (February 1919).

103. "Discussing the 'Collapse' of the Interchurch Movement," *Current Opinion* 69.2:221–222 (August 1920).

104. Mott, *Five Decades,* p. 65.

105. FMCNA *Report, 1893*, p. 13.

106. The Foreign Missions Conference of North America was organized in 1893, the Federal Council of Churches of Christ (expanded into the National Council of Churches in 1950), not until 1908. The International Missionary Council was officially organized in 1921, the World Council of Churches not until 1948.

107. Samuel B. Capen, "Christian Unity and Missions," typescript of address delivered May 23, 1913, Cambridge, Mass., "Samuel B. Capen Material. Addresses, Documents," ABP. Similar reluctance was shown in the rejection by Capen's own board of a suggestion for an interdenominational committee of all North American mission boards to supervise the collection and distribution of funds when major disasters or national calamity should strike anywhere in the world. It appeared to be an uncontroversial project which could easily have been assumed by the existing Foreign Missions Conference, but the Prudential Committee and presumably the other boards "did not deem it expedient to endorse the

plan." "Records of Prudential Committee, 1897 to 1900" (Meeting of March 20, 1900), XXV, 649, ABP.

108. William R. Hogg, *Ecumenical Foundations* (New York, 1952), p. 78.

109. Patton, *The Business of Missions*, pp. 169–170. Since women were excluded from the FMCNA, they formed their own Federation of the Woman's Boards of Foreign Missions of the United States in 1906. Less elaborately organized, they consulted for purposes similar to those of the male organization. Only women's boards and such groups as the YMCAs were eligible for membership. Delegates to the conferences were apportioned according to the income of their respective societies, thus assuring control by the larger denominations. *Annual Report of the Federation of Woman's Boards of Foreign Missions of North America* (New York, 1926), pp. 70–73.

110. *Twenty-fifth Annual Conference of the International Missionary Union* (Clifton Springs, New York, 1908), pp. 21, 24.

111. *The International Missionary Union, Nineteenth Annual Conference* (Clifton Springs, New York, 1902), p. 60.

112. *Men and Missions* 9.8:248 (April 1918).

113. The delegates received a "most sympathetic and appreciative message from the King," as well as letters from the German Colonial Office and former President Roosevelt. *The History and Records of the Conferences,* vol. 9 of *World Missionary Conferences, 1910* (Edinburgh and New York, 1910), pp. 18–20.

114. Hogg, p. 142.

115. Ibid., p. 16.

116. Gairdner, p. 53.

117. *World Missionary Conference, 1910*, IX, 7–8. The London conference brought together a significant representation from the English-speaking nations, and raised hopes for a continuation of the exchanges initiated there. "It is not impossible, and it would be in many ways desirable," ventured J. S. Johnston with one eye on the denominations that had

withheld delegations, "that a future Conference of a similar kind should not only arrive at such complete unanimity of opinion, but at such an intimate knowledge of one another's character and habits as to enable it to pass rules and form an executive body for carrying them out." *Report of the Centenary Conference of the Protestant Missions of the World*, James Johnston, ed. (New York, 1888), I, ix.

118. The Ecumenical Missionary Conference was held to discuss the missions of a new century, and combined serious business sessions dealing with comity agreements, financing, medical work, and other professional topics, with open meetings addressed by such prominent public figures as William McKinley, Theodore Roosevelt and Benjamin Harrison. An exhibit of mission field exotica supervised by imported natives and missionaries in native dress, drew over 60,000 visitors to a small church hall in a week's time. Press tickets were exhausted well before the Conference, and "probably no religious convention was ever so fully reported" in the major national dailies. *Ecumenical Missionary Conference*, I, 12–17.

119. Mathews, p. 224.

120. Quoted in Hogg, p. 109.

121. *World Missionary Conference*, IX, 7–8.

122. Andersen, pp. 15–16.

123. Mott, *Five Decades*, p. 48.

124. Although many missionary statesmen, notably Dr. J. H. Oldham, shared equal credit with the 45-year-old American, Edinburgh marked a new stage in Mott's career. "It not only gave him a central, responsible, representative place in the leadership of missionary expansion," wrote his official biographer, "but it harnessed his energies, hitherto concentrated for the most part upon the recruiting and training of youth for that purpose, to the major strategy and executive tasks of missions as a whole." Mathews, p. 226.

125. *The Continuation Committee Conferences in Asia, 1912–1913* (New York, 1913), p. 9.

126. Ibid., pp. 10–11; Mathews, p. 123.

127. Hogg, p. 161.

128. *Foreign Missions Yearbook of North America, 1919,* B. St. John ed. (New York, 1919), pp. 11-12.

129. Hogg, p. 197.

130. Mathews, p. 234.

131. Hogg, pp. ix–x.

132. William R. Hogg considers the events culminating in the formation of the IMC as part of a "metamorphosis from 'ecclesiastical colonialism' to a global fellowship," and the Edinburgh Conference as the "root-symbol" of the twentieth-century ecumenical movement. "In large measure Edinburgh and its radiating impulses helped to shape the new Christian world community with its growing recognition of inner unity and outer hostility," he concluded. (Ibid., pp. 101, 130, 139.) In view of the explicit prohibition on discussion of matters of doctrine or polity at Edinburgh, it would seem that relatively little progress toward union, as opposed to functional cooperation, could be made. The Faith and Order movement as one path to Christian unity is thus declared insignificant by definition, and only the Life and Work aspect, which other historians of religion have found more directly served by cooperation in the implementation of the social gospel, is left as the narrow road to ecumenicism. Paul A. Carter, *The Decline and Revival of the Social Gospel* (Ithaca, N.Y., 1956), pp. 101, 104.

One also wonders if an assembly of Western sending agencies plotting a campaign of final conquest was ready to accept a subordinate position in the "global fellowship" that might develop. Or were they still thinking in terms of imposing their order or perpetuating their "ecclesiastical colonialism" only to have the few farsighted leaders who persevered to establish a permanent international council accept the partnership of the younger churches when it seemed wise to do so, and after their original proxies had expired? "The most immediate practical thinking growing out of Edinburgh," wrote Henry Leiper, "had to do with the next steps in the technical process of developing functional cooperation." There was at the same time no movement for church, as distinguished from Christian cooperation at the beginning of this century. And whereas interdenominational cooperation which does not commit the churches involved might be helpful and lead in the right direction, Leiper argued that no one at mid-century was willing to call this ecumenicism in any genuine sense. Henry S. Leiper, "Reunion and the Ecumenical Movement," in Arnold S. Nash, ed., *Protestant Thought in the Twentieth Century* (New York, 1951), pp. 249, 257, 267.

2. Supporters and Staff

1. *American Board Almanac of Missions, 1916,* p. 3.

2. Theodore T. Munger, *Essays for the Day* (Boston, 1904), pp. 29–30.

3. Isaac T. Headland, *Some By-Products of Missions* (Cincinnati, 1912), p. 198.

4. George W. Perkins's generosity to the International Committee of the YMCAs, for example, continued a family tradition of support for the association's work. John A. Garraty, *Right-Hand Man, The Life of George W. Perkins* (New York, 1960), p. 379. New York businessman William E. Dodge Jr. helped to organize and finance the Ecumenical Missionary Conference in 1900. William E. Dodge Sr. had signed the call for the first Union Missionary Meeting in 1854. *Ecumenical Missionary Conference, New York 1900,* I, 11.

5. John D. Rockefeller, Jr., "The Christian Church: What of Its Future?" *Saturday Evening Post* 190.32:16 (Feb. 9, 1918).

6. Raymond B. Fosdick, pp. 202 ff.

7. Sunday school superintendent Benjamin Harrison, for example, served both as a Presbyterian elder, and as honorary chairman of the Ecumenical Conference on Foreign Missions in 1900. President William Howard Taft, although not an evangelical Protestant, addressed the Washington Convention of the National Missionary Campaign in 1911, and had his speech selected for mass distribution in pamphlet form by the Laymen's Missionary Movement. Kenneth S. Latourette, *The Great Century, A.D. 1800–A.D. 1914: Europe and the United States of America,* vol. 4 of *A History of the Expansion of Christianity* (New York, 1941); p. 412 has a sketch of presidential religious affiliations and activities.

8. *Men and Missions* 10.6:164 (February 1919).

9. Howe, p. 130. If this wish was only a conversational pleasantry, there is at least Mary Baird Bryan's assessment that "in his zeal for souls, he was like an evangelist." William J. and Mary Baird Bryan, *The Memoirs of William Jennings Bryan* (n.p., 1925), p. 454.

10. Theodore Roosevelt, *The Strenuous Life; Essays and Addresses* (New York, 1911), p. 25.

11. "The clergyman is no longer held in awe," observed the innovative businessman president of the American Board and chairman of the Laymen's Movement, because "he is not, as formerly, the only educated man in the community." Samuel Capen quoted in Hawkins, p. 164.

12. Philadelphia department store magnate John Wanamaker, for example, had sufficient additional energy to play an active role in national and state Republican politics, as well as in the YMCA, Moody's revival campaigns, the Salvation Army and the International Sunday School Union. Born to a Methodist father and Reformed Church mother, he attended a Lutheran Sunday school in his youth, joined the Presbyterian Church, and for half a century taught in the nondenominational Philadelphia mission he founded, which grew into what he proudly referred to as the largest Sunday school in the world. Joseph H. Appel, *The Business Biography of John Wanamaker* (New York, 1930), pp. 22, 36.

13. David P. Jones to Samuel Capen, October 2, 1906, "Samuel B. Capen Material," ABP.

14. Daniel Aaron, *Men of Good Hope* (New York, 1951), p. 287.

15. Samuel B. Capen, "Ought the Church to Lead or to Follow in Questions of Moral Reform" (address before the Congregational Club, Boston, October 3, 1881), typescript in "Samuel B. Capen Material, Addresses, Documents," ABP.

16. Hawkins, pp. 2–3.

17. Howe, p. 17.

18. Ibid., p. 1.

19. Ibid., p. 279.

20. Quoted in Howard and Geraldine Taylor, pp. 28, 32.

21. Ibid., p. 39.

22. Richard Hofstadter, "Manifest Destiny and the Philippines," in D. Aaron, ed., *America in Crisis* (New York, 1952), p. 183.

23. Samuel B. Capen, "The Laymen and Missions," February, 1912, "Samuel B. Capen Material; Addresses, Documents," ABP.

24. William T. Ellis, "America's World Leadership," *Men and Missions* 4.9:18 (May 1913).

25. *Men and Missions* 9.4:127 (December 1917).

26. John Hay to Samuel Capen, October 6, 1904, "Samuel B. Capen Material," ABP. Biographical material from Hawkins, passim. "If doubts ever visited me as to the validity of the role I played in charity work," Frederic Howe wrote of his impoverished Cleveland days, "I paid no attention to them. I enjoyed the monthly meetings with men and women whose names appeared in the papers and who were known as the best people in the city." Howe, pp. 76–77.

27. Son of a small-town Massachusetts factory worker killed in the Civil War, Brown nevertheless managed to obtain the training necessary to become a Presbyterian minister whose reputation within the denomination was sufficient to make him a candidate, though unsuccessful, for moderator of the General Assembly at age 40. In 1895 he accepted a completely unexpected and unsolicited call to the Foreign Mission Board, despite his previous rejection of positions in other churches and seminaries. During this entirely new career, the Holliston orphan met and was consulted by every President from Cleveland to Hoover. He was received by the heads of state of China, Siam, Korea, Japan, Hungary, Sweden, Greece, Holland, and Germany, and received a drawerful of honorary degrees and foreign decorations. Brown, pp. 1–20, 89 ff., 163.

28. George R. Grose, *James W. Bashford, Pastor, Educator, Bishop* (New York, 1922), p. 112.

29. Clifford S. Griffin, *Their Brothers' Keepers, Moral Stewardship in the United States, 1800–1865* (New Brunswick, N.J., 1960), p. x.

30. R. S. Storrs to James L. Barton, September 2, 1899. Series 2, vol. 11, no. 404, ABP.

31. A typical statement in Arthur L. Gillett to Samuel B. Capen, Oct. 1, 1906. Entire correspondence in uncatalogued letter file marked "Samuel B. Capen Material," ABP.

32. Albert J. Lyman to Samuel B. Capen, Oct. 1, 1906, "Samuel B. Capen Material," ABP.

33. "From the Records of the Meeting of the Prudential Committee of the American Board, March 10, 1914," typescript in "Samuel B. Capen Material," ABP.

34. Mornay Williams, "The Ideal Business Man," *Men and Missions* 5.7:15 (March 1914).

35. Francis G. Peabody, *Jesus Christ and the Social Question* (New York, 1902), p. 224.

36. George Mowry found the typical California progressive to be an extremely religious man. "His mind was freighted with problems of morality, his talk shot through with biblical allusions. He often thought of the political movement he had started as part of the 'Religion Forward Movement.'" George E. Mowry, *The California Progressives* (Berkeley, 1951), p. 97. At the beginning of the present study a fairly significant interrelationship between the humanitarian and reform motives of progressivism and similar trends away from simple evangelism in foreign missions was anticipated in the form of individuals active in both movements. Yet comparing a file of over 900 leaders and prominent contributors to denominational mission societies and the nondenominational Laymen's Missionary Movement with a list of some 400 contemporary progressive leaders disclosed only two individuals identified with both fields of interest. Neither of these men had more than a marginal connection with missions as an occasional financial contributor. Additional information of the comparison in Valentin H. Rabe, "The American Protestant Foreign Mission Movement, 1880–1920," app. 2 (Ph.D. dissertation, Harvard University, 1965).

37. Samuel B. Capen, untitled election eve address, n.p., n.d. (ca. 1899), "Samuel B. Capen Material, Addresses, Documents," ABP.

38. Hawkins, p. 69.

39. Quoted in ibid., p. 191.

40. "In Memoriam, Samuel B. Capen" (transcript of memorial service at Old South Church, Boston, March 7, 1914), p. 8, ABP.

41. Samuel B. Capen, *Uprising,* p. 19.

42. Quoted in Hawkins, p. 118.

43. Samuel B. Capen, *Save the World to Save America* (Boston, 1905), p. 27.

44. Samuel B. Capen, *Uprising,* p. 20.

45. Edward Lincoln Smith, "Dr. Capen and the Peace Movement," *Men and Missions* 5.7:7 (March 1914). Unity through conformity spelled security in home missions also. The appeal of another Congregational businessman with mission interests illustrates the parallel preconceptions. After an inspection of Chicago's Bohemian quarter, Caleb F. Gates was astonished to find "one district almost entirely without English Protestant efforts of any kind." "From that quarter dangers to state and city thickens"; he warned, "from those godless homes issue streams full of deadly poison, fatal not only to themselves but to us all." There was a mutually beneficial solution to this problem which scarcely differed from the foreign missionary's offer to civilize the future leaders of resurgent China and provide better customers for American goods. "You can well afford to give largely to me to help permeate their home with the gospel of Christ, because it will make them better citizens and render your property more secure." Quoted in Caleb F. Gates, *A Christian Business Man, Biography of Deacon C. F. Gates* (Boston, 1892), pp. 137, 162-163.

46. For a summary of these distinctions see David E. Swift, "Conservative Versus Progressive Orthodoxy in Latter 19th Century Congregationalism," *Church History* 16.1:23 (March 1947).

47. For details of this survey, see Rabe, app. 1.

48. Constituting at least half the population, and a greater proportion of active church members, women were an obvious answer to the movement's domestic personnel problems. Traditional male prejudice and determina-

tion to change the public's association of foreign missions with ladies' circles and mite societies made this solution impractical. After 1900 women received both broader opportunities and equal status as missionaries. In the United States they continued to bear much of the burden of local fund raising and publicity, but occupied positions of authority only in auxiliaries and the more than 50 subordinate women's boards.

49. Mathews, pp. 27, 61.

50. John R. Mott, "The Commitment of Life and How God Leads Men," in *Christian Students and World Problems,* Milton T. Stauffer, ed. (New York, 1924), p. 63.

51. G. Sherwood Eddy, *Eighty Adventurous Years* (New York, 1955), p. 35.

52. W. Reginald Wheeler, *A Man Sent From God* (Westwood, N.J., 1956), p. 49. The curious youthful predilection for law of mission leaders extended also to such clergymen as Bishop James Bashford, who still toyed with the idea while in theological school (George R. Grose, p. 28). The most plausible explanation of this pattern is that the law provided wider career opportunity and required less extensive preparation than other professions. For Mott, Bashford, and Speer, however, early religious convictions and the stubborn imperative of being of wider service eventually overcame professional ambitions.

53. Brown, p. 173.

54. See testimonials in Wheeler, pp. 268 ff.

55. Robert E. Speer to Courtenay H. Fenn, May 5, 1904 (copy), Speer Papers, Doc. S742 A2, vol. 4, Speer Library, Princeton Theological Seminary.

56. Batchelder, p. 21.

57. "Position Description; Executive Secretary, Laymen's Missionary Movement of North America, Inc.," undated transcript, MRL.

58. *Home Base and Missionary Personnel,* ed. Orville A. Petty, vol. 7 of Laymen's Foreign Missions Inquiry, Fact Finders' Reports, Supplementary Series, Part Two (New York, 1933), pp. 51, 59.

59. *Who's Who in America,* vol. 8 (1916–1917), vol. 25 (1948–1949).

60. His initial annual salary as general secretary of the LMM in 1907 was
    $4,000 plus $1,000 travel expenses. (Minutes of the Executive Comit-
    tee, Nov. 1, 1907, LMM Papers, MRL.) In 1920, only 1 percent of
    American ministers received a salary of $4,000 or more, while 80 per-
    cent earned less than $1,000. Roger W. Babson, *Religion and Business*
    (New York, 1922), p. 131.

61. J. Campbell White to Executive Committee, LMM, July 16, 1915,
    "L.M.M. Minutes: Meetings of Executive and General Committees,
    Jan.–Dec., 1915," MRL.

62. Batchelder, p. 23.

63. Samuel B. Capen, "The Supreme Opportunity," *The Missionary Herald*
    96.1:13 (January 1899).

3. The Missionaries

 1. George F. Pentecost, "The Enduement of Power and Foreign Missions,"
    The Independent 50.2601:975 (Oct. 6, 1898); *Ninety-third Annual
    Report of the American Baptist Missionary Union* (Boston, 1907), p.
    22. A Congregational secretary provided indirect corroboration the same
    year when he declared that the myth of too many applicants posed a
    serious problem to the American Board which found the supply of quali-
    fied personnel quite inadequate. "Extracts from the Report of the Home
    Secretary, Rev. Cornelius H. Patton, D. D.," in *The One Hundredth Anni-
    versary of the Haystack Prayer Meeting* (Boston, 1907), p. 15.

 2. John Gillespie to the Ningpo Station, Oct. 25, 1890; Reel 233, vol. 71,
    no. 89, PBFM Correspondence, PHS.

 3. Robert E. Speer to J. N. Hayes, Feb. 10, 1892; Reel 233, vol. 71, no.
    158, PBFM Correspondence, PHS.

 4. *Tenth Conference of the Officers and Representatives of the Foreign
    Mission Boards and Societies in the United States and Canada* (New
    York, 1903), pp. 60–63. "When there has been a supply of missionaries
    ready to go, that has called forth the funds to send them," an ABCFM
    secretary concluded from a survey of thirty years' experience, "and

when ample funds have been furnished by the churches, that has multiplied the number of missionaries offering themselves to be sent." *Report of the American Board of Commissioners for Foreign Missions Presented at the Thirty-third Annual Meeting* (Boston, 1842), pp. 66. A prudent application of this experience in informing a board's constituency of current deficiencies in one or the other area could thus produce a perpetual escalation of requirements and prevent an adequate supply of either men or money from being reached before the millennium.

5. Samuel B. Capen, *A Million Dollars For Foreign Missions* (Boston, 1901), p. 21.

6. This conclusion is based on official reports, not promotional pronouncements nor the sort of visionary schemes which were periodically put forward as plans for instant world conquest. "We constantly get letters from people who evangelize the world on paper," complained Robert Speer in 1900. Robert E. Speer to Charles G. Trumbull, March 21, 1900 (copy); Robert E. Speer Collection, doc. S 742 A2, vol. 1, no. 353, Speer Library, Princeton Theological Seminary. A few years later, a fellow Presbyterian produced an example from a more reputable source, setting a goal of one missionary for every 25,000 people remaining to be reached. At a time when slightly over 13,000 missionaries of all denominations and nations were in the field, J. Campbell White's program for the Laymen's Movement proposed a total of 40,000. J. Campbell White, *Our Share of the World* (New York, n.d.), pp. 5–6.

7. *Men and Missions* 10.4:100 (December 1918).

8. H. E. B. Case, "Number of Missionaries of the American Board of Commissioners for Foreign Missions, 1900–1929," typescript in File AB12Z9, ABP.

9. Charles H. Fahs, "Recruiting and Selecting New Missionaries," in *Home Base and Missionary Personnel*, p. 17.

10. Of 6,633 missionaries supported by North American societies in 1909, 2,086 were ordained men, 2,169 were missionary wives, 1,754 unmarried women, 624 laymen. White, *Our Share*, p. 7.

11. A survey of some 1,400 missionaries and administrators taken in 1916 found a majority responding that the boards' "principal need is for

evangelistic missionaries who must be of an all-around type." Board of
Missionary Preparation, *The Preparation of Missionaries Appointed to
Educational Service* (New York, 1916), p. 3.

12. FMCNA, *Foreign Missions Conference of North America, Being the
Report of the Twenty-first Conference of Foreign Mission Boards in the
United States and Canada* (New York, 1914), p. 75.

13. ABCFM, *The One Hundred and Sixth Annual Report of the American
Board of Commissioners for Foreign Missions* (Boston, 1916), p. 15.

14. These objections must have been valid, for only 76 short-term workers
were listed among the 7,663 foreign staff members of all Protestant
mission societies active in China in 1925. Ordained men that year were
outnumbered by 2,357 wives and 2,538 unmarried women or widows,
followed by 1,293 unordained men. Harlan P. Beach and C. H. Fahs, eds.,
World Missionary Atlas (New York, 1925), p. 76. Another adjustment,
which had the effect of lowering standards, was the occasional acceptance of volunteers from denominations with lower qualifications for
ordination, or the employment of transfer or independent missionaries
in the field who would not have qualified for commissioning in the
United States. In such cases, the temptation to secure immediate reinforcements for an understaffed station overcame scruples about applying even minimal standards. See Committee on Missions in China, Sept.
15, 1908, in "Sub-Committee Reports, 1907 through 1909," ABP.

15. R. Pierce Beaver, "Pioneer Single Women Missionaries," *Missionary
Research Library Occasional Bulletin* 4.12:1–2 (Sept. 30, 1953).

16. Both single women and ordained men's wives were generally designated
as missionaries. Wives, however, were compensated only indirectly
through adjustments in their husband's subsistence allowance, and
single women were long restricted to the types of activity considered
appropriate by male secretaries and other superiors. Personality differences and variant methods of decision-making at individual mission
stations make generalizations difficult, but before the 1920s women
seem generally to have been given an equal voice only in matters relating to their own responsibilities. The American Board, for example,
which seems to have been ahead of general practice when it decided in
1894 that women should henceforth have an equal voice and vote with
men at meetings in the field, restricted this privilege to the "consideration of questions touching their own work." ABCFM *Eighty-Fourth*

Annual Report of the American Board of Commissioners for Foreign Missions (Boston, 1894), p. 5.

17. The American Board, for example, supported 1,269 "Indigenous Workers" in 1880, 3,472 by 1900, 4,941 in 1920. A far more significant increase in this area followed World War II. Goodsell, *Witnesses,* p. 291. The American Baptist Foreign Mission Society increased the total of its native workers from 1,200 in 1884, to nearly 6,200 in 1914, while its missionary force barely doubled. H. B. Grose and F. P. Haggard, eds., *The Judson Centennial, 1814-1914* (Philadelphia, 1914), p. 300.

18. Harlan P. Beach, *A Geography and Atlas of Protestant Missions* (New York, 1903), II, p. 23.

19. Board administrators at the 1893 Foreign Mission Conference unanimously rejected a suggestion that they reinstitute the early nineteenth-century experiments of training natives of mission fields in the United States for return as co-workers with American missionaries. They objected to the greater expense of an American education when ample facilities existed in most mission fields, and feared the personal and political complications of commissioning non-Caucasian foreigners. FMCNA, *Interdenominational Conference of Foreign Missionary Boards and Societies in the United States of America and Canada* (New York, 1893), p. 20.

20. ABCFM, *The Seventieth Annual Report of the American Board of Commissioners for Foreign Missions* (Boston, 1880), p. xxi.

21. Some parents seem to have promoted their reading as a moral tonic. Caleb F. Gates, a Chicago businessman and home mission leader, recalled being required to read each monthly issue of *The Missionary Herald* from cover to cover, "not even the notices of contributions being omitted." Caleb F. Gates, p. 18.

22. *World Missionary Conference,* VI, 304.

23. Ibid.

24. Ibid., pp. 310-311. Hicks's statement was corroborated by students of the new "science of conversion," according to which "conversion is in general a fact of adolescence." James Strachan, "Conversion," in *Encyclopedia of Religion and Ethics,* J. Hastings, ed. (Edinburgh, 1911), IV, 108.

25. *Men and Missions* 10.4:124 (December 1918). The Young People's Missionary Movement was organized in 1902 to reach non-students not being cultivated by the SVM. Mott, *Five Decades,* p. 18. It enlarged its field as the Missionary Education Movement, an interdenominational organization closely supervised by the sending agencies. Its function was to prepare and syndicate mission literature, lesson plans, and training manuals. Supervision of summer training and interdenominational mission conferences were also MEM responsibilities before its fusion with the Interchurch World Movement in 1919.

26. "The authorities in the Sunday-school movement," observed Speer with satisfaction, "are coming more and more to recognize their obligations to connect their movement with the work of the world's evangelization." FMCNA, *Fourteenth Conference of the Foreign Mission Boards in the United States and Canada* (New York, 1907), p. 99.

27. *Yearbook of the Churches,* Clyde F. Armitage, ed. (New York, 1918), p. 145. Francis E. Clark to E. K. Alden, August 24, 1893, ser. 10, vol. 84, no. 318, ABP.

28. John F. Goucher, "The Strategic Importance of the Student Volunteer Movement in the World's Evangelization," in *Students and the Modern Missionary Crusade* (New York, 1906), p. 175.

29. Hawkins, p. 187. Fahs, "Recruiting and Enlisting New Missionaries," pp. 22–24. Between 1906 and 1930, thirty major colleges and universities, including most of the Ivy League and Big Ten, never produced more than 12.5 percent of the volunteers who had sailed, with the contribution dipping to 6.7 percent in the postwar decade. Ibid., pp. 19–21.

30. The American Board, for example, consistently received far more candidates from Beloit, Grinnell, and Oberlin, than from any of the Ivy League or large state universities. ABCFM, *Annual Report for 1880,* p. xxi; *Annual Report for 1916,* p. 16.

31. A study undertaken by a Baptist medical missionary uncovered a more direct correlation between the number of female applicants from particular colleges and the "missionary spirit" of their founders than with any objective factor such as Student Volunteer activity or board promotion on those campuses. Grace M. Kimball, "Development of Missionary Spirit in Women's Colleges in America," in FMCNA, *Report of the Seventh Conference of Officers and Representatives of the Foreign*

Mission Boards and Societies in the United States and Canada (New York, 1899), pp. 163–164. One of J. Campbell White's reasons for resigning from the Laymen's Missionary Movement to accept an Ohio denominational college presidency was his conviction that he could rally lay support for missions in an area where it had been notably lacking. He intended to influence the students by introducing a new approach to the study of the Bible in the curriculum which would stress the missionary imperative. J. Campbell White to Executive Committee, LMM, July 8, 1915, "LMM Minutes: Meetings of the Executive Committee and General Committee, January–December 1915," LMM papers, MRL.

32. Personnel also moved in the opposite direction. The Rev. Judson Smith, for example, came to the attention of the American Board by teaching a standard church history course in terms of the expansion of Christianity, and doing it so enthusiastically that he not only induced a series of applications to the board, but also the formation of a Student Volunteer Band pledged to go to China in its entirety. When the Volunteers asked Smith to lead them to China, however, he announced that he felt he could make a more significant contribution to the movement by becoming a board secretary. Edward P. Eaton, "Address in Memory of Rev. Judson Smith, D.D.," in ABCFM, *One Hundredth Anniversary*, p. 317.

33. Edmund David Soper, "The Study of Missions," Ohio Wesleyan University *Bulletin* 12.6:1–2, 4 (Nov. 1, 1913).

34. Henry C. King, "The Reasonableness of Expecting the Co-operation of a College or University Faculty in Arousing or Fostering the Missionary Spirit," in *Students and the Modern Missionary Crusade*, p. 561.

35. *The Duty of the Present Generation to Evangelize the World* (Buffalo, 1847), p. 42.

36. James Findlay, "Moody, 'Gapmen,' and the Gospel: The Early Days of the Moody Bible Institute," *Church History* 31.3:326 (Sept. 1962). For the revivalist's objectives in establishing three educational institutions, and the motives of the Chicago Evangelization Society which supervised the development of the Bible Institute, see James F. Findlay, Jr., *Dwight L. Moody, American Evangelist, 1837–1899* (Chicago, 1969), ch. 9 passim.

37. Lucy Rider Meyer, *Deaconesses, Biblical, Early Church, European, American* (Cincinnati, 1889), pp. 92, 140.

38. Pierson, pp. 340–341. "It is a sacrilege of Christianity," agreed Baptist Rev. Adoniram J. Gordon, "that the church has so often undertaken to manufacture missionaries by priestly ordination or by literary training." Cowman, p. 87.

39. F. F. Ellinwood to J. W. Lowrie, Aug. 12, 1889, reel 233, vol. 70, no. 141, PBFM Correspondence, PHS.

40. *Foreign Mission Policies* (Boston, 1917), pp. 21, 71.

41. FMCNA, *Report of the Fourth Conference of Officers and Representatives of the Foreign Mission Boards and Societies of the United States and Canada* (New York, 1896), p. 13.

42. *The Student Missionary Enterprise: Addresses and Discussions of the Second International Convention of Student Volunteers,* ed. Max W. Moorhead (New York, 1894), pp. 65–66.

43. *Students and the Modern Missionary Crusade,* p. 55.

44. The first dean of this pioneering venture was Dr. Edward Capen, son of the American Board's president. After earning his degree in sociology with honors at Columbia University, Capen conducted research for the ABCFM on a two-year tour of mission fields, and returned convinced of the need for far more adequate missionary training. Elmer E. S. Johnson, "Memorial Address for Edward Warren Capen, 1870–1947," uncatalogued typescript, ABP.

45. Goodsell, *Witnesses,* p. 185.

46. Fahs, "Recruiting and Selecting New Missionaries," p. 18.

47. Pierson's address at the Mount Hermon, Massachusetts, conference was the first reference to foreign missions, yet resulted in 40 percent of the delegates pledging themselves to missionary service. The desire to preserve the "Mount Hermon spirit" they brought back to their campuses led the YMCA to designate twenty-two-year-old John R. Mott, one of their new secretaries who had attended the conference, as a traveling organizer. His efforts were central to both the creation of the new international organization, and through his forty-year service on the SVM Executive Committee, to its future operations. John R. Mott, *The Student Volunteer Movement for Foreign Missions,* vol. 1 of *The*

Addresses and Papers of John R. Mott (New York, 1946), pp. 277–278; Mott, *Five Decades,* pp. 5-6.

48. "Whenever it has let the work and control pass too much into the hands of graduates and executive officers of an older generation, it has suffered loss," wrote John Mott. Mott, *Five Decades,* p. 21. His retrospective warning overlooks the fact that it was not until he retired from the executive committee after 40 years that its membership was enlarged and a rule adopted to ensure that at least half its members consist of undergraduate Student Volunteers. *Christian Students and World Problems: Report of the Ninth International Convention of the Student Volunteer Movement For Foreign Missions,* ed. Milton T. Stauffer (New York, 1924), p. 69.

49. Mott resisted efforts to change the wording of the pledge, and considered it the keystone of the entire movement which transformed lives even if the signer never left home. Mott, *Five Decades,* p. 22.

50. G. Sherwood Eddy, *Eighty Adventurous Years* (New York, 1955), p. 29. Writing at the end of his career, Eddy despaired of being able to translate the dynamic appeal and effect of the Volunteer Movement for another generation. Signing the pledge provided not only individual reorientation and revitalization, but was usually transferred to other areas of college life in which members of the Volunteer Band were almost inevitably the leaders.

51. The SVM initiated its formal educational program in 1894 when 30 mission study groups, including perhaps 200 students, were known to exist in North America. In 1914, the SVM alone sponsored 2,700 such study circles enrolling 40,400 students, 90 percent of whom were not volunteers. *Students and the World-Wide Expansion of Christianity: Addresses Delivered Before the Seventh International Convention of the Student Volunteer Movement,* ed. Fennell P. Turner (New York, 1914), p. 22.

52. The conventions were designed to mark the high point of the college careers of those who attended. As student gatherings they were unique for the period in the number of delegates attracted and institutions represented. Several conventions before 1920 attracted as many as 5,000 delegates. At Des Moines in 1920, "a student reaction against the old tradition of a regimented program in control of older leaders," produced greater student direction and participation in future programs, but numerically smaller assemblies than during the adult-

dominated heyday of the movement. *Students and the Future of Christian Missions: Report of the Tenth Quadrennial Convention of the Student Volunteer Movement,* ed. Gordon Poteat (New York, 1928), p. v.

53. Hogg, p. 95; Charles H. Hopkins, *The Rise of the Social Gospel in American Protestantism, 1865–1915* (New Haven, 1940), p. 298. The characteristic disregard for theological distinctions of the average volunteer inclined many of them to select mission boards which offered them the broadest opportunity, or access to the particular field in which they were most interested. Denominational agencies which were forced to apply creedal tests thus tended to get fewer benefits from SVM recruiting than societies like the American Board, which despite having become an official organ of the Congregational Churches, included only 35 Congregationalists among the 52 missionaries they sent to the field in 1916. ABCFM, *Annual Report for 1916,* p. 15. The American Board's tradition is reflected in Goodsell's estimate that, both during its early interdenominational career and after World War II, "approximately 50% of the missionary personnel were of non-Congregational connections." Goodsell, *Witnesses,* p. 288.

54. Quoted in Mathews, p. 95. Although the young organizer made a favorable impression in his appearance before the 1898 meeting, a sympathetic board secretary summed up the general impression that it was "a great mistake to have a watchword which we as a Conference are to endorse and which requires to have such an elaborate explanation as Mr. Mott has made today." FMCNA, *Report of the Sixth Conference of Officers and Representatives of the Foreign Missionary Boards and Societies in the United States and Canada* (New York, 1898), pp. 35–37.

55. John R. Mott, "The Tasks of Tomorrow," in *Students and the Christian World Mission: Report of the Twelfth Quadrennial Convention of the Student Volunteer Movement for Foreign Missions,* ed. Jesse R. Wilson (New York, 1936), p. 204.

56. FMCNA, *The Second Conference of the Officers and Representatives of Foreign Mission Boards and Societies in the United States and Canada* (New York, 1894), pp. 37–38. "The Volunteer Movement is quite as much concerned," explained Mott, "with making every young man who is to be a minister at home, and every young man and young woman who is to be a lay-worker at home, a true missionary in spirit as it is con-

cerned in getting recruits for the foreign field." ABCFM, *One Hundredth Anniversary*, p. 193. Despite this quite defensible position, the SVM stopped publishing figures allowing a comparison of total pledges signed with actual appointments the same year the FMCNA heard this criticism. After a vigorous search, only 3,200 of the far greater number of volunteers enrolled since the movement's beginning had been traced and were considered active members, including 686 who had actually been sent abroad by various boards. *The Student Missionary Enterprise*, pp. 69, 73. In 1891, the movement had reported that, of 6,200 Volunteers listed on its rolls since 1886, 2,600 were still attending educational institutions, about 760 had dropped out of college or died, and slightly over 1,000 had renounced their pledge or were untraceable. The tangible contribution to missions derived from 6,200 signed pledges was 320 men and women serving abroad, 20 more who had received appointments, and 100 "ready to go." Mott, *Student Volunteer Movement*, pp. 25, 28, 31.

57. *Students and the Christian World Mission*, p. 175.

58. *North American Students and World Advance*, ed. Burton St. John (New York, 1920), p. 62. Mott cited the same optimistic proportions in 1939. *Five Decades*, p. 12. A study of the proportion of volunteers among missionaries leaving the United States between 1917 and 1930 disclosed a high point of 58 percent of those sailing in 1918, and a low point of 31.8 percent in 1929. Fahs, "Recruiting and Selecting New Missionaries," p. 17. Since the peak of SVM enrollment and departures for the field occurred during the four years after 1919, it is most unlikely that a proportion over 58 percent was reached in the preceding decades or during the Depression years after 1929.

59. Niebuhr, *Kingdom of God*, p. 197.

60. *Re-Thinking Missions*, Commission of Appraisal, William E. Hocking, chmn. (New York, 1932), p. 10.

61. *FMCNA Report, 1893*, p. 13.

62. Not only were there few volunteers from the cities and coastal towns before the Civil War, but the American Board, at least, seems to have been suspicious of city-bred candidates as a matter of policy. Clifton J. Phillips, *Protestant America and the Pagan World* (Cambridge, Mass., 1969), p. 30. As late as 1880, only 19 percent of the American Board's

missionaries had been recruited from the interior states. ABCFM, *Annual Report for 1880*, p. xxi. The bulk of the Northern Presbyterian Board's force in the same decade, on the other hand, had been drawn from the trans-Allegheny West. F. F. Ellinwood to the Shantung Mission, Nov. 9, 1888, reel 233, vol. 70, no. 59, PBFM Correspondence, PHS.

63. *Student Missionary Enterprise,* pp. 71, 77. The following regional distribution was reported for 7500 volunteers carried on the SVM rolls in 1892:

Central States–2,345	New England–650
Western States–1,680	Canada–480
Middle Atlantic–1,440	Pacific States–60
Southern States–845	

The Western States included none further west than South Dakota. Ohio, Illinois, Indiana, and Michigan formed the predominant Central States region. Illinois led the nation with 809, thus producing more volunteers than either New England or Canada. Mott, *Student Volunteer Movement,* p. 16.

64. A general reluctance by southern denominations to participate in the national and interdenominational organizations of the mission movement was only slowly overcome by 1920. The fundamentalist issue of the later 1920s provided new cause for remaining aloof and working through independent or southern organizations.

65. See, for example, Courtenay H. Fenn, *Over Against the Treasury* (New York, 1910), pp. 12–13.

66. See, for example, Herbert H. Smith, "Millionaire Borden's Decision," reprinted from *The Continent* in *Men and Missions,* 4.4:25 f. (December 1912). William W. Borden was celebrated as a recently-ordained Chicago multi-millionaire who surrendered all to serve Christ and China. His tragic death en route to his post made him an even more effective symbol to later generations. See Mrs. Howard Taylor, *Borden of Yale '09: "The Life that Counts"* (Philadelphia, 1951).

67. The American Board, for example, was informed by one of its most promising candidates that he would pay his own salary and expenses, but would be forced to apply to another society if not sent to the North China mission he had selected. Horace T. Pitkin to the Secretaries of the American Board, Aug. 12, 1894, ser. 6, vol. 45, no. 258, ABP.

68. The following breakdown of 6,200 volunteers reported by the SVM in 1891 (Mott, *Student Volunteer Movement*, p. 31) is supplemented with the bracketed total number of communicants of each denomination according to the 1890 census. Henry K. Carroll, *The Religious Forces of the United States* (New York, 1893), p. xlvi. Multiplying the total number of communicants by 3½ provides the total adherents or part of the religious population represented.

Presbyterians	27%	(1,278,332)	Lutherans	3%	(1,231,072)
Methodists	24%	(4,589,284)	Episcopalians	2%	(540,509)
Congrega-			Friends	1½%	(85,216)
tionalists	17%	(512,771)	Other evangelical		
Baptists	17%	(3,717,969)	denominations	8½%	(1,914,330)

69. Nellie M. Chaney to Charles H. Daniels, Feb. 6, 1894, ser. 6, vol. 41, N. M. Chaney file, ABP.

70. Character Reference Form signed by G. J. Voss, March 26, 1915, ser. 6, vol. 116, J. E. Horn file, ABP. The same reluctance is reflected in an Oberlin professor's reference for a male applicant: "The only objection I have to your sending George to the foreign field is the need of our own country in this time of great need, when Romanism and Anarchy and Infidelity, not to mention other devices of the devil, are 'coming in as a flood'." "But then," concluded C. H. Churchill with an almost perceptible shrug, "the Lord needs them everywhere and you must take those who are willing to go." C. H. Churchill to C. H. Daniels, Dec. 26, 1893, ser. 6, vol. 47, no. 144, ABP.

71. Arthur H. Smith to Kate Hinman, Jan. 8, 1919, "North China Mission, 1872–1925" letter file, ABP.

72. "His motive was not a congerie of reasons and considerations," wrote Isaac Taylor of the ideal represented by George Whitefield, "it was an impulse, spontaneous, bright and fraught with love, hope, and a sure anticipation of abundant success . . . he so commingled himself with the Omnipotence on which he relied, that the thought of his own insufficiency passed out of his view." Quoted in ABCFM, *Report of the American Board of Commissioners for Foreign Missions Presented at the Forty-third Annual Meeting* (Boston, 1852), p. 25.

73. R. P. Mackay, "Qualifications of Missionary Candidates," in *FMCNA Report, 1899,* p. 27.

74. Henry N. Cobb, "Means of Securing Missionary Candidates of the Highest Qualifications," in *FMCNA Report, 1894,* p. 35.

75. John L. Mateer to Judson Smith, Apr. 8, 1892, ser. 6, vol. 44, no. 243, ABP.

76. Frank A. Waples to James L. Barton, July 3, 1892, ser. 6, vol. 47, no. 63, ABP. Emphasis in original.

77. Brewer Eddy to Earle Ballou, May 12, 1915, ser. 6, vol. 79, ABP.

78. George D. Wilder to C. H. Daniels, Dec. 16, 1893, ser. 6, vol. 47, no. 137, ABP.

79. Howe, p. 16.

80. Eddy, *Eighty Years,* pp. 26–27.

81. Quoted in George R. Grose, pp. 55–56.

82. George A. Gates, "Annual Sermon," in ABCFM, *One Hundredth Anniversary,* p. 54.

83. G. T. Manley, "Professional Opportunities for Exerting a Christian and Missionary Influence," in *Students and the Modern Missionary Crusade,* p. 578.

84. Horace T. Pitkin to the Secretaries of the American Board, Aug. 12, 1894, ser. 6, vol. 45, no. 258, ABP.

85. Life Sketch of Bertha Harding Allen, enclosed in B. Allen to D. Brewer Eddy, Jan. 29, 1916, ser. 6, vol. 75, B. H. Allen File, no. 14, ABP.

86. Life Sketch of Earle Hoit Ballou, enclosed in Ballou to the Prudential Committee of the ABCFM, May 6, 1915, ser. 6, vol. 79, E. H. Ballou File, no. 6, ABP. A 1932 inquiry into missionary motives answered by 704 men and women who had left the field found 48 percent had chosen their career because of the "greater foreign need," followed by only 21 percent who had acted in response to a "divine command." T. P. Bowen, "Causes for Withdrawal of Missionaries," in Laymen's Foreign Missions Inquiry, *Home Base and Missionary Personnel,* p. 55. Of 151 active missionaries polled at the same time, 100 percent of those

serving their third term and 86.6 percent of those on their first appointment had acted because of the "relatively greater need of the foreign field." Fahs, "Recruiting and Selecting," p. 38.

87. Paul A. Varg, *Missionaries, Chinese and Diplomats* (Princeton, 1958), p. 323.

88. Harlan P. Beach, "The Missionary Challenge to the Students of this Generation," in ABCFM, *One Hundredth Anniversary*, p. 202.

89. Quoted by S. Capen, "Closing Address," in ABCFM, *One Hundredth Anniversary*, p. 354.

90. Howard and Geraldine Taylor, p. 50.

91. The total foreign staff of all North American societies in China in 1916 was 2,862, followed by India, to which Canadians had a larger commitment, with 2,105. Beach and St. John, pp. 62–77. Of 8,140 student volunteers in the field by 1920, 2,524 had sailed to China. In comparison, 867 had gone to Africa, 216 to our own Philippines, 1,570 to the next most popular area of India-Burma-Ceylon. *North American Students and World Advance*, p. 61. "China was the goal, the lodestar, the great magnet that drew us all in those days," wrote Sherwood Eddy of his seminary experience with Horace Pitkin and Henry Luce. Even their athletic activities were justified by the prediction that "this will carry us another mile in China." G. Sherwood Eddy, *Pathfinders of the World Missionary Crusade* (New York, 1945), p. 50.

92. Quoted in George R. Grose, pp. 202–203.

93. Charles L. Storrs, Jr. to James L. Barton, Oct. 19, 1903, ser. 6, vol. 163, ABP.

94. Life Sketch of Douglas M. Beers, enclosed in letter to D. Brewer Eddy, Feb. 16, 1915, ser. 6, vol. 79, D. M. Beers File, no. 3, ABP. "So many more men think of China for romantic reasons," complained an ABCFM secretary to this candidate's father, "but for actual service and opportunities Turkey equals it." Brewer Eddy to Robert W. Beers, December 19, 1914, ser. 6, vol. 79, ABP.

95. Life Sketch of Bertha Allen, enclosed in letter to D. Brewer Eddy, January 29, 1916, ser. 6, vol. 75, B. H. Allen File, no. 14, ABP.

96. Personal interview with Mrs. C. M. L. Sites, Union Theological Seminary, New York City, December 21, 1961.

4. Financial Supporters

1. Samuel B. Capen, *The Next Ten Years* (Boston, 1910), p. 25.

2. *The History and Program of the Laymen's Missionary Movement,* p. 15.

3. *World Missionary Conference 1910,* VI, 322.

4. *History and Program of LMM,* p. 17.

5. Typical of numerous similar subjective estimates was the American Board president's claim that less than one-fourth of American Protestants contributed an offering to foreign missions worthy of the name. Samuel B. Capen, *Uprising,* p. 3.

6. Over 40 percent of the United Presbyterian Church's total contributions in 1916 were dedicated to work in the foreign field, compared to 28 percent for the Northern Presbyterian and 27 percent for the Southern Presbyterian branches. Compare this to other major denominations: Northern Baptist: 16 percent; Southern Baptist: 13 percent; Protestant Episcopal: 19 percent. Only two other bodies exceeded the 40 percent mark in 1916: the Congregational Churches (47.5 percent) and the Seventh Day Adventists (47.1 percent). Bureau of the Census, *Religious Bodies, 1916* (Washington, 1919), II, 99–100.

7. *American Board Almanac of Missions, 1914,* p. 30.

8. This obvious fact provided no immunity from the promoters, however. In 1917, the LMM hired a special secretary for colored laymen, and began to cultivate this group "naturally endowed with capacity for strong religious feeling." "It could hardly be expected that their offerings would compare with those of their white brethren," the editor of the LMM journal admitted, "but that these offerings could be largely increased on the basis of information, training and wise leadership has long been held by able men among them." *Men and Missions* 9.3:68 (November 1917).

9. The American Board, which despite the spread of Congregational churches and colleges to the Pacific had been unable to free itself of

predominant reliance on New England's support before the Civil War, made little progress in broadening its base before the end of the century despite a policy of assiduously cultivating Western Congregationalists. Phillips, pp. 239–240; ABCFM, *Fifty-Fifth Annual Report of the American Board of Commissioners for Foreign Missions* (Boston, 1865), p. 38; ABCFM, *Seventy-First Annual Report of the American Board of Commissioners for Foreign Missions* (Boston, 1881), p. xvii. Meeting of Sept. 17, 1865, "Records of Prudential Committee, 1894 to 1897," XXIV, 238. American Board Papers.

10. White, *Our Share*, p. 11.

11. Samuel B. Capen, *Million Dollars*, p. 6.

12. Over 40 percent of the American Board's income in 1899 came directly from the Women's Boards, a figure not including their contributions and promotion through regular church channels. From 1810 to 1918, out of total ABCFM receipts of $49,853,847, the Women's Boards formed during the late 1860s contributed $10,403,236, plus paying their own administrative and promotional expenses. Goodsell, *Witnesses*, pp. 165, 167. The Free Methodist Church of America provides a more dramatic demonstration. Between 1882 and 1914 its General Missionary Board received $188,845. Although a distinct Women's Foreign Missionary Society only formed in 1894, it collected $516,815 by 1914. In the 4-year period before 1914, the Women's Society collected more money than the General Board had during its entire 32-year existence. Wilson T. Hogue, *History of the Free Methodist Church of North America* (Chicago, 1915), II, 257–259. American women's societies also contributed more than twice as much as their British counterparts as early as 1891, while total foreign mission contributions in Great Britain normally exceeded those raised in the United States until shortly before World War I. *American Board Almanac of Missions, 1891*, p. 32.

13. "Report by the Committee on the Report of the Home Department," in ABCFM, *One Hundredth Anniversary*, p. 251.

14. Samuel B. Capen, *Million Dollars*, p. 14. Capen compared the ABCFM's reliance on legacies for 20 percent of its income to the lower figure of 9 percent for the Presbyterian Board, 12.5 percent for the Baptists, and 4.5 percent for the Methodists. His proposal to the board, however, was not to compensate for the decline by pressing for an increase from living donors, but to "strengthen ourselves at the weakest point."

15. "Report of the Standing Committee on Foreign Missions," in PCUSA, *Minutes of the General Assembly of the Presbyterian Church in the United States of America* (Philadelphia, 1902), pp. 69–70. Legacy receipts had soared to an annual average of $120,956 in the decade before 1892, but dropped to $101,619 per year during the next ten years. PBFM, *The Sixty-Fifth Annual Report of the Board of Foreign Missions of the Presbyterian Church in the United States of America* (New York, 1902), p. 4.

16. A twenty-year survey of legacy receipts of the five largest mission societies found the ABCFM leading, with a total nearly equaling the sum of the receipts of the next two agencies. ABCFM, *The One Hundred and Fourth Annual Report of the American Board of Commissioners for Foreign Missions* (Boston, 1914), p. 18.

17. Samuel B. Capen, *Million Dollars,* p. 6. Some idea of the magnitude of the "great gifts" can be gained by comparing the $700,000 in unlisted private contributions the board transmitted directly to the field for new buildings during the two years before 1912, with published receipts of $712,693 and $756,624 for 1910 and 1911 respectively. Samuel B. Capen to William B. Millar, Dec. 5, 1912. "Samuel B. Capen Material, Letters," ABP.

18. A special American Board committee analyzed lagging contributions in 1897 and concluded "that a large number of the constituency of the Board among its liberal supporters believe that too large a portion of the appropriation is given to the educational work." J. M. W. Hall, *A Special Business Paper from the Prudential Committee* (Boston, 1897), p. 7.

19. The former executive vice-president and late historian of the American Board estimated that during the 1930s 60 percent of the board's income came from the Congregational Churches, as much as 35 percent from investments, and the remainder from individual donors. Personal interview with Fred Field Goodsell, American Board Offices, Boston, March 9, 1961. Total receipts from donors not contributing through their own congregations thus varied from about 10 percent during the peak years of the 1920s to 5 percent during the depression decade. A secretary of the same board in 1920, however, estimated that not less than one-third of the annual receipts of the major boards came in the form of donations apart from church offerings. Cornelius H. Patton, *Business of Missions,* p. 200. An accurate determination of the significance of private gifts is virtually impossible. The American Board's chief fund raiser reported at

the end of three decades of activity that no record had been kept of conditional gifts and legacies from the individual donors' list, and very few public announcements made of special gifts. D. Brewer Eddy, pp. 1-2. In 1899, of forty-eight foreign mission societies reporting that an average of 25 percent of their work was supported by gifts for special objects, only fourteen entered such contributions in their official accounts. Arthur Judson Brown, "Report of the Committee on Special Objects," in FMCNA, *Report of the Seventh Conference of Officers and Representatives of the Foreign Mission Boards and Societies in the United States and Canada* (New York, 1899), pp. 55-56.

20. A diverse but related category of contributors consisted of wealthy individuals who could be induced to make occasional gifts for special purposes, or to satisfy a whim or preoccupation. Cultivating them was an art developed to a high degree by John R. Mott, who combined psychological insights and ego manipulation with businesslike cost accounting. John R. Mott, *Five Decades,* p. 79. Whether used to elicit thousands in matching contributions for general purposes, or expense accounts for world-traveling mission leaders, they produced unreported funds from sources outside the normal mission constituency. Mathews, pp. 138, 414-415; John R. Mott to Elizabeth Billings, July 14, 1914, in "Methods Used By Dr. Mott in Raising Money," John R. Mott Collection, Day Mission Library, Yale Divinity School. The successful practitioner was less a manipulator than someone who provided his prospect with an avenue for satisfying some personal objective. This could mean the motive that induced a Cleveland realtor to provide funds for the construction of mission stations "so located that the sun would never set on his work." Archibald McLean, *The History of the Foreign Christian Missionary Society* (New York, 1919), p. 110. Or it could provide the full support of several missionaries and special projects in China on the condition of anonymity, D. Brewer Eddy, p. 31, and a bequest of $3,000,000 to foreign missions with the proviso that the businessman donor's name not be memorialized in any institution or fund established with the money; Patton, *Business of Missions,* p. 271. It could also induce a New Hampshire manufacturer with a single-minded interest in simple evangelical preaching to live on $3,000 a year during the 1920s, while fully supporting 262 native evangelists in various fields; D. Brewer Eddy, p. 8. The millions contributed to foreign missions in these examples were not accessible through regular channels or available for the normal functions of mission boards.

21. FMCNA, *Ninth Conference of Officers and Representatives of the*

Foreign Mission Boards and Societies in the United States and Canada (New York, 1902), p. 32.

22. David McConaughy, *Money the Acid Test* (New York, 1918), p. 3.

23. There have been attempts to describe the spectacular increase in benevolent giving and enterprises during the past 150 years purely in terms of the development of a general stewardship movement within Protestantism, as a result of which men strove to live according to the principle: "To have is to owe, not to own." Luther P. Powell, "The Growth and Development of the Motives and Methods of Church Support With Special Emphasis Upon the American Churches" (Ph.D. dissertation, Drew Theological Seminary of Drew University, 1951), II, 383. Both as an explanation of philanthropy, and as evidence of the proximity of the Kingdom of God, this thesis requires too much qualification to be useful. (See Ibid., I, 3, II, 385, 393, 416.)

   Far more convincing is John Lankford's conclusion that, despite increased emphasis on stewardship by American writers and clergymen in the early decades of this century, the traditional principle was only one facet of a much broader Protestant "theology of giving." He found that stewardship lent itself to so many interpretations, was so difficult to put into practice, and so radically contrary to fundamental American values and the principle of private property, that it was neither an effective promotional theme nor accepted by more than a handful of American Protestants. Lankford, "Protestant Stewardship," pp. 19, 426–428.

24. Samuel B. Capen, *Disloyalty,* pp. 11–14.

25. Ibid., p. 25.

26. Samuel B. Capen, *The Next Ten Years,* p. 24.

27. Edwin M. Poteat, "Christian Stewardship," *Men and Missions* 10.1:26 (September 1918). Emphasis in original.

28. F. F. Ellinwood to J. L. Nevius, June 10, 1889, reel 233, vol. 70, no. 124, PBFM Correspondence, PHS.

29. McConaughy, *Money,* pp. x, 95.

30. D. Riesman, N. Glazer, R. Denny, *The Lonely Crowd* (New York, 1953), p. 139.

31. McConaughy, *Money*, pp. 7–8, 12.

32. The Seventh-Day Adventists, counting 79,355 members, contributed $736,046 for foreign mission work in 1916. A mere 9,625 members of the Christian and Missionary Alliance gave $140,003 for the same purpose, and 32,259 communicants of the Pentacostal Church of the Nazarene, $50,300. To these figures for denominations largely recruited from lower income Americans, compare the $822,402 contribution of 1,092,821 communicants of the Protestant Episcopal Church, or even the $3,925,728 offering of 5,823,264 members of the major branches of the Methodist Episcopal Church. Bureau of the Census, *Religious Bodies, 1916*, II, 99–100.

33. Quoted in Raymond B. Fosdick, pp. 414, 432.

34. Quoted in John Lankford, "Methodism 'Over the Top': The Joint Centenary Movement, 1917–1925," *Methodist History* 2.1:32 (October 1963).

35. Le Tourneau eventually inverted the standard 10 percent tithe and income relationship and established a foundation to administer these funds for religious work. He personally supervised his own two mission stations in Liberia and Peru, went on extensive evangelical speaking tours, and hired industrial chaplains to conduct services in his plants during working hours. Robert G. Le Tourneau, *Mover of Men and Mountains* (Englewood Cliffs, N.J., 1960), pp. 204–210.

36. Powell, p. 427.

37. Quoted in Lankford, "Methodism 'Over the Top,' " p. 28.

38. Quoted in Appel, p. 39. Emphasis supplied.

39. Hawkins, p. 95.

40. H. A. Etheridge, "Stewardship and Partnership," *Men and Missions* 5.7:19–20 (March 1914).

41. Samuel B. Capen to William B. Millar, Dec. 5, 1912, "Samuel B. Capen Material, Letters," ABP.

42. Millar, p. 4.

43. *Men and Missions* 10.1:interior cover (September 1918).

44. Millar, p. 16. Emphasis supplied.

45. Samuel B. Capen, "Men and Missions," typescript of Oct. 15, 1908 address, "Samuel B. Capen Material, Documents," ABP.

46. The great philanthropists at the turn of the century rarely made more than a small part of their contributions to religious objects. Despite persistent appeals, despite even John D. Rockefeller's personal piety and reliance on a former Baptist minister as his philanthropic advisor and executive secretary for giving, secular schemes for general improvement received more of his money than religious ones. Edward Kirkland saw this as inevitable, since both the ideology that justified the creation of these fortunes, and the programs for their dispensation, were expressed in terms of natural law. Churchmen might try to christianize philanthropy by justifying the accumulation of great fortunes as Christian duty, but "charity was usually associated with Christian stewardship; philanthropy was secular." Edward C. Kirkland, *Dream and Thought in the Business Community* (Ithaca, N.Y., 1956), pp. 148–149.

47. Report of George Innes, "Minutes of the Secretarial Council of the Laymen's Missionary Movement and Allied Movements," May 2, 1911, "Minutes of Various Committees, 1911," LMM Papers, MRL. The 1910 aggregate was $141,604,000 of which $61,000,000 went to education, $56,000,000 to charities, $12,000,000 to religious institutions, and $9,000,000 for art.

48. Samuel B. Capen, untitled typescript of 1908 Boston address, "Samuel B. Capen Material, Addresses, Documents," ABP.

49. Judson Smith, "The Cry of the Pagan World," in ABCFM, *Eighty-First Annual Report of the American Board of Commissioners for Foreign Missions* (Boston, 1891), p. xxix.

50. Samuel B. Capen to John R. Mott, June 13, 1908. Capen file, John R. Mott Collection Day Mission Library.

51. John Mott's list of fund-raising hints included advice to "lay stress on the urgency of the situation." While warning against employing this merely as subterfuge, he clearly recognized the efficacy of the tradi-

tional utilization of the "element of urgency." Mott, *Five Decades,* p. 80.

52. Charles H. Case to Judson Smith, Feb. 17, 1896, ser. 10, vol. 84, no. 116, ABP.

53. Samuel B. Capen, "Laymen's Missionary Movement Why and How," typescript of address delivered Apr. 23, 1908, Chattanooga, Tenn., "Samuel B. Capen Material, Addresses, Documents," ABP.

54. James Thoburn, "The Gospel of 'Benevolences,' " *Christian Advocate* 76.36:8 (New York, Sept. 5, 1901).

55. F. F. Ellinwood to the Shantung Mission, Nov. 9, 1888, reel 233, vol. 70, no. 59, PBFM Correspondence, PHS.

56. Frederick T. Gates to John D. Rockefeller, Jr., Oct. 19, 1911, in Raymond B. Fosdick, p. 204.

57. *History and Program of the LMM,* p. 16.

58. Samuel B. Capen, "Laymen's Share in Advocacy," typescript of address delivered at Edinburgh Synod Hall, June, 1910, "Samuel B. Capen Material, Addresses, Documents," ABP.

59. Quoted in Samuel B. Capen, " 'Together' Campaign," typescript of address delivered Mar. 2, 1909, New York City, "Samuel B. Capen Material. Addresses, Documents," ABP. " 'Every dollar given to foreign missions develops ten dollars' worth of energy for dealing effectively with the tasks at our own doors,' " promised Jacob Riis in another gratefully quoted testimonial. Mott, *Five Decades,* p. 16.

60. PCUSA, *Minutes of the General Assembly, 1902,* p. 72.

61. Samuel B. Capen, "Wanted, More Denominational Fidelity and Enthusiasm," typescript of address delivered Dec. 3, 1888, "Samuel B. Capen Material. Addresses, Documents," ABP.

62. Lyman Abbott, "Discussions as to the Future Policy of the Board at Home," in ABCFM, *One Hundredth Anniversary,* p. 263.

63. Samuel B. Capen, *The Next Ten Years,* p. 9.

64. Samuel B. Capen, *Uprising,* p. 20.

65. *The Laymen's Missionary Movement* (New York, n.d.), pp. 2–3.

66. Samuel B. Capen, *Next Ten Years,* p. 22.

67. *Laymen's Missionary Movement,* p. 4.

68. Etheridge, "Stewardship and Partnership," p. 20.

69. Quoted in G. Sherwood Eddy, *The Kingdom of God and the American Dream* (New York, 1941), p. 7.

70. W. J. Tucker, "A Missionary Century," in ABCFM, *One Hundredth Anniversary,* p. 73.

71. Kirkland, p. 164.

72. Samuel B. Capen, untitled typescript of LMM convention address, 1908, "Samuel B. Capen Material. Addresses, Documents," ABP.

73. Samuel B. Capen, "The Supreme Opportunity," p. 18.

74. Etheridge, "Stewardship and Partnership," p. 21.

75. Quoted in Hopkins, p. 227.

76. W. X. Ninde, "Christ's Measure of Giving," in *The Student Missionary Appeal* (New York, 1898), p. 112.

77. For a discussion of this trend in postwar nonmission circles, see William T. Doherty, "The Impact of Business on Protestantism, 1920–29," *The Business History Review* 28.2:141–153 (June 1954).

78. Samuel B. Capen, *Save the World,* p. 2.

79. William Strachey, *The Historie of Travell Into Virginia Britania (1612),* L. B. Wright and V. Freund, eds. (London, 1953), p. 21. "International trade was conceived in the bed of religion," wrote Perry Miller of the seventeenth-century promotional literature, and its pursuit was sanctified because salvation followed on the heels of commerce. Perry Miller, *Errand Into the Wilderness* (Cambridge, Mass., 1956), pp. 116–117.

80. Batchelder, p. 24.

81. Quoted in Hawkins, p. 149.

82. Quoted in Kirkland, pp. 163–165. Businessmen clung to the benign view of their civilizing function longer than mission spokesmen. The life insurance industry in particular borrowed much of the movement's terminology, several insurance executives referring to their business as "missionary work." New York Life's Darwin P. Kingsley identified life insurance as "the very spirit of the Anglo-Saxon race," and aspired beyond dividends to the creation of a worldwide "community of interest with all men." Morton B. Keller, *The Life Insurance Enterprise, 1885–1910* (Cambridge, Mass., 1963), pp. 28, 30.

83. Capen, *Uprising,* pp. 5–6.

84. Headland, p. 34.

85. Chester Holcombe, *The Real Chinese Question* (New York, 1908), p. 155.

86. W. A. P. Martin, *A Cycle of Cathay* (New York, 1896), p. 456.

87. J. S. Powell, "Missionaries as Drummers," *Men and Missions* 10.7:209 (March 1919). A U.S. Army officer during the Boxer uprising also knocked ideals when he asserted that American trade in China would increase tenfold if an end was put to the futile effort of forcing Christianity down the Chinamen's throats. Bascom W. Williams, *The Joke of Christianizing China* (New York, 1927), p. 56.

88. *American Board Almanac of Missions, 1887*, p. 3.

89. Samuel B. Capen, *The Next Ten Years,* p. 14.

90. Samuel B. Capen, *Save the World,* p. 5.

91. Frederick Simpich, "How Missionaries Help Foreign Trade," *Saturday Evening Post* 196.7:119 (Sept. 8, 1923).

92. Paul A. Varg, *The Making of a Myth: The United States and China, 1897–1912* (East Lansing, Mich., 1968), pp. 51, 53.

93. Even the canny founder and owner of the Dollar Steamship Line, who reportedly "gave liberally to missions, not only from Christian motives, but because he thought that such gifts would pay economically," made offerings also to other gods. Walter W. Jennings, *20 Giants of American Business* (New York, 1953), p. 381. In 1910, Dollar provided and transported free of charge 78 of the largest timbers to be found in the United States for the reconstruction of a Chinese temple in Hangchow. Robert Dollar, *Memoirs of Robert Dollar* (San Francisco, 1917), p. 149. A careful scrutiny of the business interests of hundreds of major contributors to foreign missions failed to reveal another individual whose largesse might be interpreted as a means of directly advancing his particular enterprise. See Rabe, p. 335 and app. 1.

94. Patton, *The Business of Missions,* p. 250.

95. PCUSA, *Minutes of the General Assembly, 1902,* p. 70.

96. Quoted in Appel, p. xv.

97. *Laymen's Missionary Movement,* p. 3. A decade earlier Rhodes was used as a symbol of a different attitude by Dartmouth President William Tucker in the context of an attack on "the unendurable and unpardonable arrogance of our western civilization." An empire and God's kingdom could not be sought in the same spirit, he told the Haystack Centennial assembly. "If you are not able or do not care to see Africa as David Livingstone saw it, you can see it as Cecil Rhodes saw it." Tucker, "A Missionary Century," in ABCFM, *One Hundredth Anniversary,* pp. 74, 76.

98. "Minutes of the Secretarial Council of the LMM and Allied Movements," May 2–3, 1911, LMM Papers, MRL.

99. Samuel B. Capen, *Uprising,* p. 8.

100. Hawkins, p. 139.

101. *Laymen's Missionary Movement,* p. 3.

102. Patton, *The Business of Missions,* p. vii.

103. The Rev. Washington Gladden coined this phrase in a disquisition on the symbolic character of money a decade before the imbroglio with

which it is normally identified. "The question of tainted money," he predicted, "is a question which this generation must face." Washington Gladden, "Tainted Money," *The Outlook* 52.22:886 (Nov. 30, 1895). Ironically, when Mark Twain used the famous phrase in attacking the unseemly haste and efficiency with which some missionaries had collected compensation in the aftermath of the Boxer uprising, Gladden was among those criticized. Twain argued that Gladden had identified himself with a revision of the eighth commandment which now read: "Thou shalt not steal—except when it is the custom of the country." Mark Twain, "To My Missionary Critics," *North American Review* 172.533:528–529 (April 1901).

104. Etheridge, "Stewardship and Partnership," p. 19.

105. William Lawrence, "The Relation of Wealth to Morals," *World's Work* 1.2:287 (December 1900).

106. *Report of the Centenary Conference on the Protestant Missions of the World* (New York, 1888), I, 97.

107. Peabody, *Jesus Christ,* p. 223.

108. *Men and Missions* 3.9:21 (May 1912).

109. Gladden, who used his position as moderator of the National Council of Congregational Churches to launch an attack on the American Board for accepting conscience money from the "arch-enemy" of honest working people, later wrote that the whole controversy could have been avoided had the board admitted its initiative in soliciting the donation at the time of the initial announcement of its receipt. Washington Gladden, "The Church and the Reward of Iniquity," *The Independent* 58.2942:870 (Apr. 20, 1905). Washington Gladden, *Recollections* (Boston, 1909), p. 406.

110. Frederick T. Gates to John D. Rockefeller, Feb. 1905 (copy), p. 4: "Samuel B. Capen Material, Letters," ABP.

111. Gladden, *Recollections,* p. 408.

112. Gates later noted that representatives of other denominations, who had been willing enough to request and accept Standard Oil money before the 1905 controversy broke, sanctimoniously joined in the attack on

Rockefeller and the ABCFM. Frederick T. Gates, "The Memoirs of Frederick T. Gates," *American Heritage* 6.3:78–79 (April 1955).

113. Of 245 corporate members who replied to a private poll taken by the board, only 24 disapproved of the Prudential Committee's handling of the whole situation. "Autobiographical Notes of James L. Barton," typescript, 1936, ABP. Small wonder, wrote one of the few dissenters, since the board's "voting membership is composed almost exclusively of three classes—rich men, rich men's pastors, and educators who depend on rich men." John L. Sewall to Samuel B. Capen, Apr. 13, 1905, Rockefeller Gift Letter File, ABP.

114. John L. Barry to Samuel B. Capen, Mar. 24, 1905; Rockefeller Gift Letter File, ABP.

115. Samuel B. Capen to Lyman Abbott, May 26, 1905; Rockefeller Gift Letter File, ABP.

116. Samuel B. Capen to John D. Rockefeller, May 6, 1905 (copy), Rockefeller Gift Letter File, ABP.

5. Fund Raising and Financial Policies

1. ABCFM, *Report of the American Board of Commissioners for Foreign Missions Presented at the Forty-Third Annual Meeting* (Boston, 1852), p. 21.

2. Samuel B. Capen, "The Supreme Opportunity," *The Missionary Herald* 96.1:3 (January 1899).

3. ABCFM, *One Hundredth Anniversary*, p. 273.

4. PBFM, *The Sixty-Fifth Annual Report of the Board of Foreign Missions of the Presbyterian Church in the United States of America* (New York, 1902), p. 10.

5. Charles H. Daniels, "Home Department Finances," in FMCNA, *Ninth Conference of Officers and Representatives of the Foreign Mission Boards and Societies of the United States and Canada* (New York, 1902), p. 27.

6. Samuel B. Capen, *The King's Business Requires Haste* (Boston, 1903), p. 13.

7. J. E. Crowther, "Survey Charts," *Men and Missions* 3.9:11 (May 1912).

8. Oliver Elsbree, *The Rise of the Missionary Spirit in America, 1790–1815* (Williamsport, Pa., 1928), p. 63.

9. Samuel B. Capen, "Woman's Influence: What it has Been and What it May Be," p. 2, typescript of address to W.B.M.I., Apr. 20, 1900, Samuel B. Capen Material. Addresses, Documents, ABP.

10. Samuel B. Capen, *Disloyalty,* pp. 19–20.

11. See n. 5 above.

12. Ibid., p. 27.

13. *Ecumenical Missionary Conference,* I, 197.

14. Arthur Brown, "Report of the Committee on Special Objects," in FMCNA, *Report of the Seventh Conference of Officers and Representatives of the Foreign Mission Boards and Societies in the United States and Canada* (New York, 1899), p. 161.

15. Of 45 boards surveyed, 36 either discouraged or prohibited their missionaries from making direct appeals for gifts to their friends at home. Ibid., pp. 57, 67.

16. McLean, pp. 365–366. The Methodist Episcopal Missionary Society supplemented its income during the 1890s by selling life memberships for $20, asking $150 for a lifetime position as honorary manager, and $500 to be an honorary patron. MECMS, *Seventy-Ninth Annual Report of the Missionary Society of the Methodist Episcopal Church for the Year 1897* (New York, 1898), p. 399.

17. "Sub-Committee Reports, 1904 through 1906," Cabinet Meeting of Feb. 21, 1905, ABP.

18. Patton, *The Business of Missions,* p. 199.

19. A rare example of political activity by foreign mission boards was

provided by a petition to Congress in 1900, which sought legislation reducing the tax burden on legacies made for religious or educational purposes. "Records of Prudential Committee, 1897 to 1900" (Meeting of Jan. 16, 1900), pp. xxv, 590, ABP.

20. Within twelve years of initiating such a plan, the Foreign Christian Missionary Society realized from this source alone three times the income received from regular bequests during the entire forty years since the Society's organization; McLean, pp. 369–370. The American Board adopted a similar system in cooperation with several other denominations but consistently refused to approve a plan adopted by other societies for soliciting insurance from Congregationalists who were to name the ABCFM as beneficiary. "Records of Prudential Committee, 1897–1900" (Meeting of Sept. 20, 1898), pp. xxv, 225, ABP.

21. The income derived from such restricted funds matched receipts from legacies during the second 75 years of the American Board's existence. During the earlier period, bequests had been the largest single supplement to annual contributions by living donors. Goodsell, p. 218.

22. The director and founder of its North American Branch held rigidly to the biblical injunction to "owe no man anything." In either individual or collective life, maintained Henry W. Frost, God had strictly forbidden man to incur any debt. He qualified this prohibition somewhat by pointing out that a debt is not a debt if one has funds to cover it, and that the injunction only forbade owing for something which it would be impossible to pay for. Howard and G. Taylor, pp. 73–74. Frost prayed for specific sums of money for particular projects as the need arose, reflecting an almost fanatical belief in the superiority of prayer to business management.

   To avert criticism from other boards that it was diverting funds from their coffers, the CIM avoided public appeals and campaigns. Dwight L. Moody received an unaccustomed shock when the CIM's British founder held a Chicago mass meeting Moody had arranged spellbound, and then resolutely refused to allow a collection to be taken. Hudson Taylor did not wish to hinder the work of older denominational societies. "If any one wishes, over and above their accustomed gifts, to have fellowship with the China Inland Mission," he explained, "they can communicate with us through the mail." Quoted in ibid., p. 93.

23. McLean, pp. 64–65. If this principle was utilized by ABCFM fund

raisers, they were careful not to acknowledge it publicly. The Prudential Committee proclaimed in 1889 "that it resolutely adheres to the principle it has adopted for several years . . . never, if it can possibly be avoided, to report a debt." ABCFM, *Seventy-Ninth Annual Report of the American Board of Commissioners for Foreign Missions* (Boston, 1889), p. 21. The principle had been adopted in a resolution at the 1860 jubilee when the membership reacted to a report that the ABCFM had reported a debt in 30 of its 50 years. Strong, pp. 312-313.

24. Hall, p. 5.

25. D. Brewer Eddy, pp. 16-18. Beginning with the depression year of 1893, the ABCFM incurred a serious deficit during all but one of the next eight years. The employment of the Twentieth Century Fund after 1908 reduced the number of debit years to only three more before 1920, but then the after-effects of the war and over-commitment on the field caused further debts before the depression made deficit financing a way of life. Every year from 1920 to 1940 closed with either an operating or accumulated deficit showing on the board's books. Goodsell, *Witnesses,* pp. 220, 228. Although other factors contributed to this gloomy financial picture, the American Board was obviously making its commitments in anticipation of future income.

26. "Report of the Standing Committee on Foreign Missions," in PCUSA, *Minutes of the General Assembly, 1902,* p. 70.

27. FMCNA, *A Study of Foreign Mission Financing, 1919-1948* (New York, 1949, mimeo), pp. 1-2.

28. Goodsell, *Witnesses,* p. 232.

29. Although some fund raisers came to look upon their work as an exciting game, rivalry was usually subordinated to a strong sense of ethics and fair play. In an unusual letter to his American Board counterpart, for example, Robert E. Speer told of receiving a substantial check from a young lady who had received no response to an earlier letter addressed to the ABCFM. Speer knew that the rush of preparing for the annual meeting had delayed a reply. Since he was unwilling to take advantage of the pressure of work on the secretary, he had written the donor that he would "hold her checks until we hear again from her, inasmuch as she might have heard or soon hear from you, presenting to her some object to which her gift might be devoted in connection with the work of her

own church." Speer knew the young lady well, vouched for her piety, and pointed out that this was her first large gift and that she was therefore more concerned over it than older people might be. Robert E. Speer to Judson Smith, Oct. 8, 1895, ABP, ser. 10, vol. 92, no. 309. With a sizable check in hand from a prospective lifetime contributor he knew personally, and about whom the rival board knew nothing, the Presbyterian secretary still felt compelled to write his Congregational counterpart confidentially to offer him another opportunity to capture this prize.

30. Patton, *The Business of Missions,* p. 200.

31. Walter Rauschenbusch, *Christianizing the Social Order* (New York, 1913), p. 298.

32. ABCFM, *The One Hundred and First Annual Meeting of the American Board of Commissioners for Foreign Missions* (Boston, 1911), p. 18.

33. PBFM, *Annual Report for 1902,* p. 10.

34. D. Brewer Eddy, pp. 34–40. More often than not, Eddy managed to solve such mysteries. He was particularly adept at bargaining for large contributions to reduce the board's debt, usually conditional on its elimination by the time of the annual meeting. He was also not above exploiting human foibles if other appeals failed to produce results. In one case he secured $70,000 from a previously uninterested Chicago businessman's wife, after informing her that her sister-in-law had given half that amount to construct a mission building which would bear her name. Ibid., p. 27.

35. Ibid., pp. 11–12.

36. Mott, *Five Decades*, pp. 75–82.

37. D. Brewer Eddy, p. 5.

38. Mathews, p. 426.

39. Quoted in ibid., p. 409.

40. Mott, *Five Decades,* p. 75.

41. Quoted in Mathews, p. 416.

42. A witty, widely published veteran of the China field like Arthur Henderson Smith might be praised for commending "missionary work to men and women of intelligence who have not heretofore been interested in it," but still make little difference in enlarging his board's normal basis of support. "Records of Prudential Committee, 1905–1907," Meeting of May 15, 1906, pp. xxviii, 283, ABP.

43. Robert E. Speer to James L. Barton, Nov. 23, 1899, ser. 10, vol. 92, ABP; "Records of Prudential Committee," Meeting of Dec. 17, 1918, XXXIII, 452.

44. National Council of Congregational Churches, *Report of the Committee of Fifteen on Mission Work* (Boston, 1901), p. 24.

45. Samuel B. Capen, *The Next Ten Years*, p. 10.

46. Samuel B. Capen, "Wanted, More Denominational Fidelity and Enthusiasm," typescript of address delivered Dec. 3, 1888, "Samuel B. Capen Material. Addresses, Documents," ABP.

47. Quoted in Allan Nevins, "Frederick T. Gates and John D. Rockefeller," *American Heritage* 6.3:68 (April 1955).

48. Samuel B. Capen to John R. Mott, June 13, 1908. Capen letter file, John R. Mott Collection, Day Mission Library.

49. Samuel B. Capen to John B. Clark, May 1, 1905, Rockefeller Gift Letter File, ABP.

50. F. F. Ellinwood to the Chefoo Station, Oct. 30, 1883, Correspondence of the Presbyterian Board of Foreign Missions, reel 233, vol. 67, no. 57, PHS.

51. W. X. Ninde, "Christ's Measure of Giving," pp. 110–111.

52. Scattered evidence supports this assumption. When a Disciples missionary returned from China in 1911 to raise $500,000 for maintenance and enlargement of the work in the entire field, for example, "he found that moneyed men were not interested in an attempt to raise half a million; the amount was too small. He found it necessary to ask for a million." When the amount was unexpectedly raised, Disciples leaders had learned their lesson and immediately launched a new $6,000,000

campaign for the whole denomination. McLean, p. 369.

53. Hall, p. 6.

54. Samuel B. Capen, " 'Together' Campaign," typescript of address
    delivered March 2, 1909, New York City, "Samuel B. Capen Material.
    Addresses, Documents," ABP.

55. Samuel B. Capen, *The King's Business,* p. 26.

56. Samuel B. Capen, *A Million Dollars,* p. 7. Although this was basically
    the installment buying system successfully being adopted in the busi-
    ness world, credit for its discovery was claimed for an earlier missionary.
    Citing text and verse in an exposition of St. Paul's "rule of three" for
    Christian giving to an assembly of board officers, Luther Wishard main-
    tained that only the terminology had changed, for "the installment
    plan is the thing that commended itself to Paul." "Discussion on Home
    Department Finances," in *Report of the FMCNA, 1902,* pp. 33–34.

57. Samuel B. Capen, *The King's Business,* pp. 20–22.

58. J. Campbell White, "What Number of Missionaries Ought We Aim to
    Send Out?", in FMCNA, *Thirteenth Conference of the Foreign Mission
    Boards in the United States and Canada* (New York, 1906), p. 46.

59. David McConaughy, "The Laymen, A Latent Force For the Evangeliza-
    tion of the World," in *Report of the FMCNA, 1906,* pp. 85, 88.

60. The American Board hired its first press relations man in 1903 and
    vigorously "studied the art of getting its name and news into the papers."
    Editorial Department to Messrs. Potter and Olcott, Special Committee
    on Joint Publicity, Feb. 3, 1928, ser. 5.4, vol. 3, no. 562, ABP. Another
    major board maintained a full-time press agent who succeeded in making
    a monopoly arrangement with 80 newspapers to provide "live" mis-
    sionary news. *World Missionary Conference 1910,* VI, 45. Others pooled
    their resources, like the southern societies that organized a cooperative
    missionary news bureau which by 1914 syndicated material to nearly
    450 newspapers with a claimed readership of six million. *Men and
    Missions* 5.7:3 (March 1914). The smaller denominations were forced
    to buy advertising space, sometimes as the result of initiatives by lay-
    men. The United Presbyterian Church adopted periodical advertising as
    a permanent fund-raising method after a trial newspaper campaign

suggested by a Philadelphia layman brought a traceable return of 600 percent to the mission board. *Men and Missions* 3.7:14 (March 1912). An Illinois layman even personally employed a traveling salesman to conduct a missionary education campaign in that state's Presbyterian churches. Report of W. S. Marquis, Minutes of the Executive Committee, May 7, 1909, LMM Papers, MRL.

61. *Handbook and Guide of the World in Boston* (Boston, 1911), passim.

62. Charles Rowland, "Presentation and Discussion of the Report," in *World Missionary Conference, 1910,* VI, 324.

63. This coincidence throws doubt on the well-publicized official version of the movement's origin in which it arose spontaneously from a New York City prayer meeting for businessmen, to which John B. Sleman had brought the spark caught at a Student Volunteer convention in the spring of 1906. Mott, *Five Decades,* pp. 30–32; William T. Ellis, p. 72. Sleman, a young Washington bank executive who gave up his business career to serve the LMM and died four years later at the age of 37, did meet the criteria set by the movement's future chairman in 1901 when Samuel Capen suggested that the mission cause "needed a leader among our laymen to do for the businessmen a work similar to that of Drummond and Mott for the students of Great Britain and America." He hoped for "a man of great consecration, perhaps of social standing and culture, who by his own sacrifices and enthusiasm will set the pace for the many who are still living almost wholly for themselves." Samuel B. Capen, *Million Dollars,* p. 28.

64. "Presentation and Discussion of the Report," *World Missionary Conference, 1910,* VI, 320.

65. A revealing contrast is provided between the presentation of the respective programs of the American and Australian Laymen's Movements at the Edinburgh Conference. The Americans stressed the productive promotional aspects of their work and relegated prayer and spiritual ends to the conclusion of their reports. Ibid., pp. 320, 325. The Australian LMM, which had been formed in response to American initiatives, had deliberately avoided an early financial campaign in favor of more "than a year of prayer and work directly for the consecration of lives to the cause," producing not only increased interest in foreign missions, but also "the deepest spiritual movement that has ever come to Victoria." Ibid., p. 199.

66. Samuel B. Capen, *Uprising,* p. 8.

67. Millar, p. 20.

68. White, *Origin and Work,* p. 7.

69. Samuel B. Capen, *Uprising,* p. 9.

70. Minutes of the General Committee, Feb. 27, 1911, LMM Papers, MRL.

71. W. Lloyd Warner, M. Meeker, and K. Eels, *Social Class in America* (Gloucester, Mass., 1957), pp. 21-23.

72. Since "Christian stewardship demands that an individual must desire to give regardless of the needs that beckon for his gift," (Powell, I, 437, 519), the LMMs claim that its admittedly effective every member canvass techniques constituted a system rooted in the principles of Christian stewardship is open to question.

     The long-run use of subtle pressures may also have been self-defeating. Bishop William Lawrence, who considered fund raising an invigorating avocation more exciting than trout fishing or gambling, would never allow a person to sign a pledge in his presence. "If I should get it by personal pressure," the highly successful practitioner explained, "I should never succeed with that man a second time." Quoted in Cleveland Amory, *The Proper Bostonians* (New York, 1947), p. 176. In reaching this only recently tested conclusion, as well as in acting on the assumption "that much charitable behavior is motivated by guilt and shame," Lawrence and other religious fund raisers were at least a half-century ahead of modern psychological theory. See Dennis Krebs and Phillip Whitten, "Guilt-Edged Giving, The Shame of it All," *Psychology Today* 5.8:50, 52 (January 1972).

73. White, *Our Share,* pp. 15, 18.

74. White, *Origin and Work,* p. 8.

75. Millar, p. 20.

76. Minutes of the Executive Committee, May 13, 1910, LMM Papers, MRL.

77. A 22-city campaign in 1907-1908, for example, produced pledges that nine Southwestern cities would raise their $181,300 gift to foreign mis-

sions to $705,000 a year thereafter. Seven Canadian cities voted an increase from $344,537 to $977,000; 6 Pacific Coast conventions pledged $470,000 instead of $116,150. Minutes of the General Committee, April 21, 1908, LMM Papers, MRL.

78. Headland, p. 206.

79. D. Brewer Eddy, p. 46.

80. LMM, *Annual Report of the Central Division of the Laymen's Missionary Movement* (Chicago, 1912), p. 8.

81. Samuel B. Capen, *Uprising,* p. 12. Often the number for which a particular church assumed responsibility was derived merely by listing the total population of areas in which they were already engaged in mission work. Even so, the National Plan required a denomination to take specific notice of its foreign mission work and sometimes led to resolutions to expand their "parish abroad."

82. Patton, *The Business of Missions,* p. 195. "In every point of our investigation the Commission has been confronted by the one stupendous fact, that there is not a Missionary Society in any one of the countries named that is properly supported to-day for the conduct of its work," reported the American chairman of Commission VI at the Edinburgh World Missionary Conference in 1910. "All of the Societies are organized for a far larger work than they are able to conduct because of the lack of support." James L. Barton in *World Missionary Conference, 1910,* VI, 294.

83. Later students of religious financing often expressed dissatisfaction with the official figures available to them. G. H. Fahs, *Trends in Protestant Giving* (New York, 1929), p. 5. But even contemporary participants like Samuel Capen referred to statistics available in yearbooks and annual reports as "almost valueless for accurate work." Capen, " 'Together' Campaign." An indication of the magnitude of unreported income is provided by a 1912 summary of the total receipts of North American foreign mission societies during the Laymen's Movement's first five years, which included the note that some $5,000,000 in special funds collected only during the preceding two years were not included in the official figures. *The History and Program of the Laymen's Missionary Movement,* p. 8.

84. William W. Sweet, *Religion in the Development of American Culture, 1795–1840* (New York, 1952), p. 275.

85. Kenneth S. Latourette, *History of Christian Missions in China* (New York, 1929), p. 392; Abdel R. Wentz, *A Basic History of Lutheranism in America* (Philadelphia, 1955), p. 192; H. Kamphausen, *Geschichte des Religiösen Lebens in der Deutschen Evangelischen Synode von Nord-Amerika* (St. Louis, 1924), p. 203.

86. For a classic exposition of these themes, see Rufus Anderson's "Instructions of the Prudential Committee to the Reverend Ira Tracy, and Mr. Samuel Williams," ser. 8.1, vol. 2, pp. 31-32, ABP.

87. Nearly $88 million was contributed to this cause between 1915 and 1927, most of it from the United States. Fahs, *Trends*, p. 54.

88. F. F. Ellinwood to J. W. Lowrie, Aug. 12, 1889, reel 233, vol. 70, no. 141, PBFM Correspondence, PHS.

89. Herbert W. Schneider, *Religion in 20th Century America* (Cambridge, Mass., 1952), p. 44. John E. Lankford, "Protestant Stewardship," pp. 3, 410.
    Of some relevance in this connection is Lord Bryce's celebration of America's unsurpassed concern for benevolence, with contributions larger relative to the wealth of the United States than in any European country. James Bryce, *The American Commonwealth* (New York, 1927), II, 790. The encomium was not deserved in the area of foreign missions where about half as many Englishmen long surpassed, and up to 1908 nearly matched, the contributions of American Protestants. White, *Our Share*, p. 5.

90. Samuel B. Capen, "Supreme Opportunity," p. 7.

91. FMCNA, *Report, 1902*, p. 28. A later study of the share of gifts from living donors to the benevolent work of eleven denominations showed foreign mission boards receiving 31.6 percent of the total in 1913, then dropping to 28.9 percent in 1920, which was the peak year for total benevolences before the depression. Fahs, *Trends*, p. 53.

92. Ibid., pp. 27-28.

93. Lankford, "Protestant Stewardship," p. 420.

94. Ibid., p. 71; Samuel B. Capen, *Facing the Facts*, p. 8.

95. Average gifts per member of $14.77 for local church expenses, however, continued the established pattern, despite an increase in total giving over the preceding decade which was nearly three times the rate of the national denominations represented by the California churches surveyed. *Men and Missions* 9.8:246 (April 1918).

96. Pierson, p. 308.

97. Lankford, "Protestant Stewardship," p. 409.

98. Samuel B. Capen, *Uprising,* p. 18.

99. Samuel B. Capen, *Next Ten Years,* p. 21. By 1908 the United States had replaced Great Britain as the largest single source of foreign mission funds and as leader of the English-speaking nations who were said to have contributed about 85 percent of the total given for the spreading of the Protestant gospel in the non-Christian world. White, *Our Share,* p. 5. Of a total income of $38,922,822 received by 412 Protestant foreign mission societies during 1915, $18,055,836 represented the income of 128 United States agencies, $13,819,340 the receipts of 92 societies in Great Britain and Ireland. Beach and St. John, p. 54.

100. Samuel B. Capen to William B. Millar, Dec. 5, 1912, "Samuel B. Capen Material, Letters," ABP.

101. Total receipts in 1901 of $5,300,100 rose to $7,617,987 in 1906, the year before the LMM began its activities. By 1917 they had nearly doubled to $14,752,854. American entry into the war produced a sharp increase to $21,288,749 in 1919, followed the next year by another jump to $29,671,076, largely the product of several major fund drives and the Interchurch World Movement. An insignificant increase of $162,651 set a highpoint in 1921 which was not reached again before the depression. Fahs, *Trends,* pp. 6, 46.

102. John R. Mott, *Liberating the Lay Forces of Christianity* (New York, 1932), p. 21; Mott, *Five Decades,* p. 63.

103. Samuel B. Capen, *Uprising,* p. 15.

104. *History and Program of the LMM,* p. 7.

105. Millar, p. 25.

106. D. Brewer Eddy, pp. 47, 15.

107. FMCNA, *Tenth Conference of the Officers and Representatives of the Foreign Mission Boards and Societies in the United States and Canada* (New York, 1903), p. 59.

108. Millar, p. 25.

109. Lankford, "Protestant Stewardship," p. 410.

Epilogue

1. Edward W. Capen, *Sociological Progress in Mission Lands* (New York, 1914), p. 277.

2. Edward C. Moore, *The World Crisis and Missionary Work* (Boston, 1915), pp. 5, 10, 15.

3. *Men and Missions* 9.3:67 (November 1917).

4. *Men and Missions* 10.1:15 (September 1918).

5. *Men and Missions* 10.6:163–164 (February 1919).

6. Woodrow Wilson quoted in "History of Interchurch World Movement," vol. 1, chap. 1, p. 52.

7. *Light on Prophecy* (New York, 1918), pp. 7, 12.

8. Cortland Myers, "War on German Theology," in ibid., pp. 176–177. When the first World's Bible Conference met in Philadelphia the next year it was not to discuss participation in the postwar mission of Christian America, but to condemn modernism and establish the vigorous and reactionary World's Christian Fundamentals Association. Steward C. Cole, *The History of Fundamentalism* (New York, 1931), pp. 230–233.

9. Harry Emerson Fosdick, *The Challenge of the Present Crisis* (New York, 1917), p. 42.

10. Moore, *World Crisis*, pp. 23–24.

11. G. Sherwood Eddy, *Eighty Adventurous Years*, p. 117.

12. Howard and Geraldine Taylor, p. 285.

13. Quoted in Mathews, p. 181.

14. Kenneth S. Latourette, *Advance Through Storm*, p. 15. A few years later a confidential study made for the Foreign Missions Conference concluded that the prewar "years of creative interest and activity . . . largely account for the steady progress up to 1918." In contrast, "the next twenty years were marked rather by studies of policy, some quite critical, and problems of the growing churches overseas which did not arouse enthusiasm at home but rather tended to alienate many former supporters, especially in the depression years." The mission movement had not yet recovered from the negative effects of the years between the world wars, the report concluded. FMCNA, *A Study of Foreign Missions Financing, 1919–1948*, concluding section, pp. 1–2. Extended denominational surveys showed that only 25 percent of Protestant church members actually contributed to foreign missions during the decade before World War II. Benevolent giving, particularly to foreign missions, had failed to keep pace with increases in national income after 1920. Mott, *Five Decades*, p. 71.

15. Fahs, *Trends*, p. 6.

16. John Lankford, "The Impact of the Religious Depression Upon Protestant Benevolence, 1925–1935," *Journal of Presbyterian History* 42.2:105, 121 (June 1964).

17. The religious depression which began in the mid-1920s was most obvious in its effect on foreign missions. Using mission support as a sensitive indicator of religious vitality, Roberty Handy documented a sharp reduction in interest, contributions, and the total missionary force in the years prior to the economic depression of 1929. Robert T. Handy, *The American Religious Depression, 1925–1935* (Philadelphia, 1968), pp. 4–5. After the crash, even those able to continue their support seem to have shared the views of a long-time contributor to the American Board who had anonymously channeled his thousands through secretary D. Brewer Eddy. "Not another penny goes out of the country while this thing is on," wrote Sidney Shepherd. And Eddy obligingly administered local relief work with Shepherd's funds while the American Board struggled along on a severely restricted budget. D. Brewer Eddy, p. 36.

18. *Students and the Future of Christian Missions,* pp. vii–viii.

19. Vergilius Ferm, ed., *An Encyclopedia of Religion* (New York, 1945), p. 496. The subsequent depression imposed a general policy of allowing the missionary contingent to dwindle by not recruiting replacements. By 1948, the missionary staffs of 19 major societies still stood 34.4 percent below the high point experienced during the 1920s. FMCNA, *A Study of Foreign Mission Financing,* opening section, p. 4.

20. Quoted in Lankford, "Impact," p. 108. It was a combination of this attitude and John R. Mott's growing awareness on his 1929 world tour that much of traditional mission work was no longer relevant that led Mott to enlist a group of former Laymen's Movement members to undertake a thorough study of the foreign mission movement. John D. Rockefeller, Jr., who had been concerned about the waning interest of the younger generation, financed the disturbing and unorthodox Laymen's Foreign Missions Inquiry. Raymond B. Fosdick, *John D. Rockefeller, Jr.,* p. 214. While the conclusions of the inquiry were generally met with hostility by the major denominations which had not been directly involved in the survey, their agencies confirmed many of the study's conclusions in the directions they took after the second decade of the century.

21. *Students and the Future,* p. vii.

22. Jesse R. Wilson, "Shall We Change Our Declaration Card?" *The Student Volunteer Movement Bulletin* 8.2:55–56 (November 1927).

23. As developed in the writings of Roland Allen, this evangelical focus became the basis of a new mission strategy adopted after World War II by many faith missions working in previously untouched mission fields. R. Pierce Beaver, "The History of Mission Strategy," *Southwestern Journal of Theology* 12.2:27 (Spring 1970).

24. Quoted in Cornelius Patton, "Twenty-Five Years After," p. 1362.

25. Weyman C. Huckabee, "Laymen's Missionary Movement; Summary of Chicago Conference of Messrs. Compton, Wheeler, and Taylor representing the Central Committee, and Messrs. Gwinn, Speers, and Capron representing the Eastern Area Committee," mimeo, LMM Papers, MRL.

26. John R. Mott, "The Tasks of Tomorrow," in *Students and the Christian World Mission*, p. 126.

27. Joseph N. Shenstone, *The Laymen's Missionary Movement* (n.p., n.d.), p. 6. Some experts supported laymen in such expectations. A professor of missions, whose text was filled with warnings concerning the tedious difficulties involved in all efforts to effect cultural change from the outside, was less cautious in predicting results. "The first million converts of the modern missionary era were won in one hundred years," he wrote in 1911; "the second million were added in twelve years, and the next million will be gained in six years." Alva W. Taylor, pp. 41, 56.

28. C. R. Watson in "Presentation and Discussion of the Report in the Conference," *World Missionary Conference, 1910,* VI, 298.

29. D. Warneck, "Die Moderne Weltevangelisations-Theorie," in *Verhandlungen der neunten Kontinentalen Missionskonferenz zu Bremen* (Berlin, 1897), pp. 37, 40, 56.

30. Arthur Judson Brown, "The Future of Missionary Work," in ABCFM, *One Hundredth Anniversary,* p. 111.

31. Gardiner Spring, ed., *Memoirs of the Rev. Samuel J. Mills* (New York, 1820), p. 40. The Brethren were a *sub rosa* fraternity founded by Samuel J. Mills at Williams College in 1808 which accepted only prospective foreign missionaries as members. The very existence of the group remained a secret until 1854, despite the transfer of the society's constitution and records with Mills to Andover Seminary in 1810, while others established chapters at additional divinity schools. Richard D. Pierce, "A History of the Society of Inquiry in the Andover Theological Seminary, 1811-1920." B. D. dissertation, Andover-Newton Theological School, 1938, p. 16. Some 300 Brethren went into the foreign field before the group's demise in 1872, while hundreds of others became home missionaries or entered the regular ministry and helped to win support for their overseas colleagues. C. M. Clark, "The Brethren, A Chapter in the History of the American Board," typescript, 1893, pp. 3, 15, 26, 28. Box AB 12 29, ABP.

32. Lyman Abbott, "Discussion As to the Future Policy of the Board at Home," in ABCFM, *One Hundredth Anniversary,* pp. 264-265.

33. Horace Bushnell, "The Kingdom of Heaven," pp. 605–606.

34. Munger, p. 32. Emphasis in original.

35. William T. Ellis, p. 81.

36. Ibid., p. 45.

37. J. Campbell White, "The Laymen's Missionary Movement," in IMU, *Twenty-Fifth Annual Conference of the International Missionary Union* (Clifton Springs, N.Y., 1908), p. 82. White guaranteed doubled income and predicted a fourfold increase in national foreign mission contributions, not because of the inherent appeal of the cause but because he and the other secretaries had developed a system.

38. "Advertising Budget," typescript, Nov. 25, 1919, Interchurch World Movement File, VII, 12, John R. Mott Collection, Day Mission Library.

39. Bushnell, "Kingdom of Heaven," pp. 600–602.

40. "Discussing the 'Collapse'," p. 221.

41. Bushnell, "Kingdom of Heaven," p. 605.

42. Latourette, *Advance through Storm,* p. 61.

43. Quoted in "Discussing the 'Collapse'," p. 222.

44. Samuel B. Capen, *Disloyalty,* p. 32. The history of Christianity reveals, wrote a Presbyterian clergyman many years earlier, "that among its sincere and sanguine disciples, there has always been prevalent an expectation that its grand and ultimate triumphs were about to dawn upon the world." "Our principal objection," the Rev. Colton concluded in his critique of the early mission boards, "is to the want of frankness in reporting things as they are, and to a disposition to raise unwarrantable expectations, as a basis of support." Calvin Colton, *Protestant Jesuitism* (New York, 1836), pp. 119, 121.

45. Robert E. Speer, "The Achievements of Yesterday," in *Students and the Christian World Mission,* p. 179.

46. G. Sherwood Eddy, *Eighty Adventurous Years,* pp. 79–81.

47. Kenneth S. Latourette, *The Christian World Mission in Our Day* (New York, 1954), p. 128.

48. The identification of the work of missions as an integral part of the problems of the church at home was a turning point in the modern history of missions of which William Hocking could find no evidence before 1921. Even in 1952, he only described an impression that "the mission enterprise appears to the church less autonomous, less separable than before." William E. Hocking, *Evangelism* (Elgin, Ill., 1952), p. 20.

49. The most serious obstacle to preserving the vision and dynamism of a spiritual enterprise, wrote Niebuhr, is the inevitable loss of the sense of crisis which had permeated the original movement. Niebuhr, *Kingdom of God*, p. 167.

50. Newell Dwight Hillis, "The Significance of this Anniversary," in ABCFM, *One Hundredth Anniversary*, p. 81.

51. "We are fighting indifference, ignorance, and lying at home, and heathenism and false religions abroad," the American Board's president had advised the 1901 annual meeting. "We must use every ally." Samuel B. Capen, *A Million Dollars*, p. 18.

52. In 1910 John R. Mott served as chairman of the Edinburgh Conference Commission which listed and investigated unoccupied mission fields. "I am pained to state tonight that not a few of these fields, after this lapse of twenty-five years, are still unoccupied," he told one of the last Student Volunteer conventions. Mott, "Tasks of Tomorrow," p. 203. In a mid-century survey, Latourette praised the phenomenal success of mission agencies in translating and broadcasting the gospel, adapting and innovating in methods—indeed, in all phases of the work except the building of the Christian Church. "In none of the major areas to which missionaries have gone do the younger churches include more than one per cent of the population," he reported. "In most lands it is smaller." Latourette, *The Christian World Mission*, p. 95.

53. Competition from world travelers, correspondents, and academicians after the turn of the century combined with the role assumed by various groups which distributed books written by missionaries as official texts in mission courses, to make it increasingly difficult to secure publication through established commercial presses. Robert E. Speer, *The World's Debt to the Missionary* (New York, 1909), p. 4. Although the space

given to articles written by missionaries in secular magazines increased markedly after 1890, it never formed a significant proportion of the total content. In religious periodicals missionary contributors usually exceeded any other single group of writers, although the proportion of their predominance decreased during the early decades of this century. Lane, pp. 21, 29.

54. Latourette described a similar reaction when impatient Chinese charged that Christianity had neither saved the Occident from war, moral corruption, and industrial injustice, nor made significant progress in solving any of the new Eastern republic's problems. Latourette, *A History of Christian Missions,* p. 622. Only a few contemporaries, like Methodist bishop Francis McConnell, called attention to the basic divergence caused by board policies. He worried about a "temper of mind begotten under a western environment, which, when intrusted with large financial sums to be expended in missionary enterprises, casts about for some results which will be instantaneously intelligible to the contributors of the money, regardless of whether those results are secured at the cost of the spiritual spontaneity of the peoples aided." Francis J. McConnell, *Church Finance and Social Ethics* (New York, 1920), pp. 113-114.

55. Robert H. Bremner, *American Philanthropy* (Chicago, 1960), p. 183. It is dubious, however, that the relative deterioration of the mission movement's position during this century can be traced to the changes in which individual initiative and creativity were replaced by governmental control and direction. Kenneth S. Latourette, *The Great Century,* p. 12. The state, at least in its American form, does not restrict voluntary philanthropic or humanitarian activities, nor does it usurp the missionary's duty. Even the post-World War II foreign aid and Peace Corps programs interfere only with the peripheral aspects of Christian missions which have no direct relation to saving souls. If voluntary efforts to extend Christianity were not as vigorously made as before, then the fault lies in the convictions of American Protestants and their failure to live up to nineteenth-century standards, not in the state or a collectivist spirit hostile to individual effort.

56. Arnold Toynbee, "Has America Neglected Her Creative Minority?", *The St. Olaf Alumnus* 10.1:8 (January 1962).

57. Robert Pearson, "Report from Afghanistan," *Cranbrook Alumni News* 27.3:3 (February 1963).

58. Gairdner, p. 259.

59. Eventually such standards were even openly applied by the Chinese. "Do not stop sending missionaries," wrote Dean Timothy Lew of Peking University's Theological Seminary in 1923, "but send us better ones." Quoted in Milton T. Stauffer, "Shall We Send Fewer Missionaries to China?" *The Missionary Review of the World* 46:624 (August 1923). A decade later, another Chinese critic voiced his fears "that missionaries are not selected with the same care as are the managers of the Oil and Tobacco Companies." Quoted in Charles G. Trumbull, *Foreign Missionary Betrayals of the Faith* (Philadelphia, n.d.), p. 3.

60. Gairdner, p. 259. Emphasis in original.

61. "Mission-minded people have always been in the minority down through Christian history," a member of the SVM General Council reminded the introspective 1936 convention, "in every church, in every Christian Association, in every student group, in every group of any kind of which I have ever heard." E. Fay Campbell, "The Student Volunteer Movement," in *Students and the Christian World Mission,* pp. 226–227.

BIBLIOGRAPHY

Manuscript Sources

Archives of the American Board of Commissioners for Foreign Missions, Houghton Library, Harvard University, Cambridge, Massachusetts.

"History of Interchurch World Movement," two volumes of correspondence copies, New York Public Library.

Laymen's Missionary Movement Papers, Missionary Research Library, Union Theological Seminary, New York City.

John R. Mott Collection, Day Missions Library, Yale Divinity School, New Haven, Connecticut.

Presbyterian Church in the U.S.A., Board of Foreign Missions Archives, microfilm copies, Presbyterian Historical Society, Philadelphia, Pennsylvania.

Robert E. Speer Papers, Speer Library, Princeton Theological Seminary, Princeton, New Jersey.

Articles, Books and Other Works Consulted

Aaron, Daniel. *Men of Good Hope: A Story of American Progressives.* New York, Oxford University Press, 1951.
American Board of Commissioners for Foreign Missions, Annual Reports, 1810–1920, various titles and Boston publishers.
—— *General Report of the Deputation Sent by the American Board to China in 1907.* Boston, American Board of Commissioners for Foreign Missions, 1907.

—— *The One Hundredth Anniversary of the Haystack Prayer Meeting: Celebrated at the Ninety-Seventh Annual Meeting of the*

271

272

American Board in North Adams, and By the Haystack Centennial Meetings at Williamstown, Mass., October 9–12, 1906. Boston, American Board of Commissioners for Foreign Missions, 1907.

American Board Almanac of Missions. Boston, American Board of Commissioners for Foreign Missions, 1886–1916.

Amory, Cleveland. *The Proper Bostonians.* New York, E. P. Dutton, 1947.

Andersen, Wilhelm. *Auf Dem Wege zu einer Theologie der Mission.* Vol. 6 of *Beiträge Zur Missionswissenschaft und Evangelischen Religionskunde.* Gütersloh, Carl Bertelsmann, 1957.

Angell, James B. "China a Field for Missions," *Missionary Herald* 79.12:475–479 (December 1883).

Appel, Joseph H. *The Business Biography of John Wanamaker; Founder and Builder.* New York, Macmillan, 1930.

"Are Foreign Missions Worth the Cost?," *Current Literature* 48.5: 522–525 (May 1910).

Babson, Roger W. *Religion and Business.* New York, Macmillan, 1922.

Barclay, Wade Crawford. *The Methodist Episcopal Church, 1845–1939; Widening Horizons, 1845–95,* vol. 3 of *History of Methodist Missions.* New York, Methodist Church Board of Missions, 1957.

Barton, James L. "Autobiographical Notes of James L. Barton." Typescript, 1936.

Batchelder, James L. (A Chicagoan, *pseud.*). *Societyism and Its Evils: The Instrumentality of Individuals and Churches in the World's Evangelization.* Chicago, Western News, 1871.

Bates, M. Searle. "The Theology of American Missionaries in China, 1900–1950," in John K. Fairbank, ed., *The Missionary Enterprise in China and America.* Cambridge, Mass., Harvard University Press, 1974.

Bavinck, J. H. *An Introduction to the Science of Missions,* tr. D. H. Freeman. Philadelphia, Presbyterian and Reformed Publishing Company, 1960.

Beach, Harlan P. *Dawn on the Hills of T'ang.* New York, Student Volunteer Movement for Foreign Missions, 1898.

—— *A Geography and Atlas of Protestant Missions.* New York, Student Volunteer Movement for Foreign Missions, 1903.

—— and Burton St. John, eds. *World Statistics of Christian Missions.* New York, Committee of Reference and Counsel of the Foreign Missions Conference of North America, 1916.

—— and Charles H. Fahs, eds. *World Missionary Atlas.* New York, Institute of Social and Religious Research, 1925.

Beaver, R. Pierce. "Pioneer Single Women Missionaries," *Missionary Research Library Occasional Bulletin* 4.12 (Sept. 30, 1953).

—— "The History of Mission Strategy," *Southwestern Journal of Theology* 12.2:7–28 (Spring 1970).

Beecher, Edward. "The Scriptural Philosophy of Congregationalism and of Councils," *Bibliotheca Sacra* 22.86:284–315 (April 1865).

Board of Missionary Preparation, Foreign Missions Conference of North America. *The Preparation of Missionaries Appointed to Educational Service.* New York, Board of Missionary Preparation, 1916.

Bremner, Robert H. *American Philanthropy.* Chicago, University of Chicago Press, 1960.

Brown, Arthur Judson. *Memoirs of a Centenarian,* ed. W. N. Wysham. New York, World Horizons, 1957.

Bryan, William J. and Mary Baird Bryan. *The Memoirs of William Jennings Bryan,* n.p., 1925.

Bryce, James. *The American Commonwealth.* 2 vols. London, Macmillan, 1891.

Bureau of the Census. *Religious Bodies 1916.* 2 vols. Washington, Government Printing Office, 1919.

Bushnell, Horace. "The Kingdom of Heaven as a Grain of Mustard Seed," *The New Englander* 2.8:600–619 (October 1844).

Cantril, Hadley. *The Psychology of Social Movements.* New York, John Wiley & Sons, 1941.

Capen, Edward W. *Sociological Progress in Mission Lands.* New York, Fleming H. Revell Co., 1914.

Capen, Samuel B. "The Supreme Opportunity," *The Missionary Herald* 96.1:1–20 (January 1899).

—— *A Million Dollars for Foreign Missions.* Boston, American

Board of Commissioners for Foreign Missions, 1901.

—— *Plan the Work and Work the Plan.* Boston, American Board of Commissioners for Foreign Missions, 1902.

—— *The King's Business Requires Haste.* Boston, American Board of Commissioners for Foreign Missions, 1903.

—— *Disloyalty and Its Remedy.* Boston, American Board of Commissioners for Foreign Missions, 1904.

—— *Save the World to Save America.* Boston, American Board of Commissioners for Foreign Missions, 1905.

—— *Facing the Facts.* Boston, American Board of Commissioners for Foreign Missions, 1909.

—— *The Uprising of Men for World Conquest.* New York, Laymen's Missionary Movement, 1909.

—— *The Next Ten Years.* Boston, American Board of Commissioners for Foreign Missions, 1910.

—— *Foreign Missions and World Peace.* World Peace Foundation, Pamphlet Series. Boston, World Peace Foundation, 1912.

Carroll, Henry K. *The Religious Forces of the United States.* New York, Christian Literature Co., 1893.

Carter, Paul A. *The Decline and Revival of the Social Gospel: Social and Political Liberalism in American Protestant Churches, 1920–1940.* Ithaca, New York, Cornell University Press, 1954.

Carver, William O. *Missions and the Kingdom of Heaven.* Louisville, Ky., John P. Morton & Co., 1898.

Christian Students and World Problems: Report of the Ninth International Convention of the Student Volunteer Movement for Foreign Missions, ed. Milton T. Stauffer. New York, Student Volunteer Movement for Foreign Missions, 1924.

Clark, C. M. "The Brethren: A Chapter in the History of the American Board." Typescript, 1893, American Board Papers.

Clark, Elmer T. *The Small Sects in America.* New York, Abingdon-Cokesbury Press, 1949.

Cole, Stewart C. *The History of Fundamentalism.* New York, Richard R. Smith, 1931.

Colton, Calvin (A Protestant, *pseud.*). *Protestant Jesuitism.* New York, Harper & Brothers, 1836.

The Continuation Committee Conferences in Asia, 1912–1913. New York, Chairman of the Continuation Committee, 1913.

Copley, Frank B. *Frederick W. Taylor: Father of Scientific Management.* 2 vols. New York, Taylor Society, 1923.

Cowman, Lettie B. *Charles E. Cowman: Missionary::Warrior.* 4th ed. Los Angeles, Oriental Missionary Society, 1928.

Daggett, Mrs. L. H., ed. *Historical Sketches of Woman's Missionary Societies in America and England.* Boston, Mrs. L. H. Daggett, 1883.

Dennis, James S. *Christian Missions and Social Progress: A Sociological Study of Foreign Missions.* 3 vols. New York, Fleming H. Revell, 1897–1906.

"Diminished Missionary Giving," *Literary Digest* 44.2:72 (Jan. 13, 1912).

"Discussing the 'Collapse' of the Interchurch Movement," *Current Opinion* 69.2:221–222 (August 1920).

Doherty, William T. "The Impact of Business on Protestantism, 1900–29," *The Business History Review* 28.2:141–153 (June 1954).

Dollar, Robert. *Private Diary of Robert Dollar on his Recent Visits to China.* San Francisco, printed by W. S. Van Cott & Co., 1912.

—— *Memoirs of Robert Dollar.* San Francisco, privately published, 1917.

The Duty of the Present Generation to Evangelize the World: An Appeal From the Missionaries At the Sandwich Islands To Their Friends in the United States. 2nd ed. Buffalo, Press of Charles Faxon, 1847.

Ecumenical Missionary Conference, New York, 1900. 2 vols. New York, American Tract Society, 1900.

Eddy, D. Brewer. "Raising Money for the American Board." Typescript, Dec. 6, 1942. American Board Papers.

Eddy, G. Sherwood. *The Kingdom of God and the American Dream.* New York, Harper & Brothers, 1941.

—— *Pathfinders of the World Missionary Crusade.* New York, Abingdon-Cokesbury Press, 1945.

—— *Eighty Adventurous Years: An Autobiography.* New York, Harper & Brothers, 1955.

Ellis, John Tracy, ed. *Documents of American Catholic History.*
Milwaukee, Bruce Publishing Co., 1956.
Ellis, William T. *Men and Missions.* Philadelphia, Sunday School
Times Co., 1909.
Elsbree, Oliver W. *The Rise of the Missionary Spirit in America,
1790–1815.* Williamsport, Pa., Williamsport Printing and Bind-
ing Co., 1928.

Fahs, Charles H. *Trends in Protestant Giving: A Study of Church
Finances in the United States.* New York, Institute of Social
and Religious Research, 1929.
Faunce, William H. P. *The Social Aspects of Foreign Missions.* New
York, Missionary Education Movement, 1914.
Fenn, Courtenay H. *Over Against the Treasury, or Companions of
the Present Christ.* New York, Laymen's Missionary Movement,
1910.
Ferm, Vergilius, ed. *An Encyclopedia of Religion.* New York,
Philosophical Library, 1945.
Federation of Woman's Boards. *Annual Report of the Federation
of Woman's Boards of Foreign Missions of North America.*
New York, Federation of Woman's Boards of Foreign Missions,
1926.
Findlay, James F., Jr. "Moody, 'Gapmen', and the Gospel: The
Early Days of the Moody Bible Institute," *Church History*
31.3:322–335 (September 1962).
—— *Dwight L. Moody, American Evangelist, 1837–1899.* Chicago,
University of Chicago Press, 1969.
*Foreign Mission Policies; A Report of the Special Conference of
the Boards of Managers and Delegates from the Ten Missions
of the American Baptist Foreign Mission Society and the
Woman's American Baptist Foreign Mission Society.* Boston,
American Baptist Foreign Mission Society, 1917.
Foreign Missions Conference of North America. *Interdenomina-
tional Conference of Foreign Missionary Boards and Societies
in the United States and Canada.* New York, E. O. Jenkins'
Son's, 1893.
—— *The Second Conference of the Officers and Representatives
of Foreign Mission Boards and Societies in the United States*

and Canada. New York, E. O. Jenkins' Son's, 1894. With the exception of 1900, when the New York Ecumenical Conference Report took its place, the title of subsequent annual volumes through 1910 differed only in numerical order and dates. After 1911, the title changed to the following form, with appropriate annual numerical and chronological adjustments:

Foreign Missions Conference of North America; Being the Report of the Eighteenth Conference of Foreign Missions Boards in the United States and Canada. New York, Foreign Missions Library, 1911.

—— *A Study of Foreign Missions Financing, 1919-1948.* Mimeographed). New York, Special Committee on Mission Financing, 1949.

Foreign Missions Year Book of North America, 1919, Burton St. John, ed. New York, Committee of Reference and Counsel of the Foreign Missions Conference of North America, 1919.

Fosdick, Harry Emerson. *The Challenge of the Present Crisis.* New York, Association Press, 1917.

Fosdick, Raymond B. *John D. Rockefeller, Jr.: A Portrait.* New York, Harper & Bros., 1956.

Gairdner, W. H. T. *Echoes From Edinburgh, 1910: An Account and Interpretation of the World Missionary Conference.* New York, Fleming H. Revell, 1910.

Garraty, John A. *Right-Hand Man: The Life of George W. Perkins.* New York, Harper & Bros., 1960.

Gates, Caleb F. *A Christian Business Man: Biography of Deacon C. F. Gates.* Boston, Congregational Sunday-School and Publishing Society, 1892.

Gates, Frederick T. "The Memoirs of Frederick T. Gates," *American Heritage* 6.3:71–86 (April 1955).

Gates, Isabel S. *The Life of George Augustus Gates.* Boston, Pilgrim Press, 1915.

Gladden, Washington. "Tainted Money," *The Outlook* 52.22:886–887 (Nov. 30, 1895).

—— "The Church and the Reward of Iniquity," *The Independent* 58.2942:867–870 (Apr. 20, 1905).

—— *Recollections.* Boston, Houghton Mifflin, 1909.

Goodsell, Fred Field. "Receipts and Expenditures, 1810–1956; Showing Increases and Decreases in Four Year Periods Together With Operating Surpluses and Deficits and Accumulated Surpluses and Deficits." Typescript, n.d. In Possession of Author.

—— *You Shall Be My Witnesses.* Boston, American Board of Commissioners for Foreign Missions, 1959.

Griffin, Clifford S. *Their Brothers' Keepers: Moral Stewardship in the United States, 1800–1865.* New Brunswick, N.J., Rutgers University Press, 1960.

Grose, George R. *James W. Bashford: Pastor, Educator, Bishop.* New York, Methodist Book Concern, 1922.

Grose, Howard B. and F. B. Haggard, eds. *The Judson Centennial, 1814–1914.* Philadelphia, American Baptist Publication Society, 1914.

Guinness, Geraldine. *See* Taylor, Mrs. Howard.

Haber, Samuel. *Efficiency and Uplift: Scientific Management in the Progressive Era, 1890–1920.* Chicago, University of Chicago Press, 1964.

Hall, J. M. W. *A Special Business Paper From the Prudential Committee.* Boston, American Board of Commissioners for Foreign Missions, 1897.

Handbook and Guide of the World in Boston: The First Great Exposition in America of Home and Foreign Missions Held in Mechanics Building, April 22–May 20, 1911. Boston, World in Boston, 1911.

Handbook of the Christian Movement in China Under Protestant Auspices, Charles L. Boynton and Charles D. Boynton, comps. Shanghai, National Christian Council of China, 1936.

A Handbook of the Northern Baptist Convention, And Its Cooperating and Affiliating Organizations, 1919–1920. Philadelphia, American Baptist Publishing Society, 1919.

Handy, Robert T. *The American Religious Depression, 1925–1935.* Philadelphia, Fortress Press, 1968.

Hawkins, Chauncy J. *Samuel Billings Capen: His Life and Work.* Boston, Pilgrim Press, 1914.

Headland, Isaac T. *Some By-Products of Missions.* Cincinnati,

Jennings and Graham, 1912.

Hiss, William. "Shiloh: Frank W. Sanford and the Kingdom, 1893–1948." Ph.D. dissertation, Tufts University, 1978.

The History and Program of the Laymen's Missionary Movement. New York, Laymen's Missionary Movement, 1912.

Hocking, William E. *Evangelism: An Address on Permanence and Change in Church and Mission.* Elgin, Ill., Department of Evangelism, General Brotherhood Board, Church of the Brethren, 1952.

Hofstadter, Richard. "Manifest Destiny and the Philippines," in *America in Crisis: Fourteen Crucial Episodes in American History,* ed. D. Aaron. New York, Alfred A. Knopf, 1952.

Hogg, William R. *Ecumenical Foundations: A History of the International Missionary Council and Its Nineteenth-Century Background.* New York, Harper & Bros., 1952.

Hogue, Wilson T. *History of the Free Methodist Church of North America.* 2 vols. Chicago, Free Methodist Publishing House, 1915.

Holcombe, Chester. *The Real Chinese Question.* New York, Young People's Missionary Movement, 1908.

Hopkins, Charles H. *The Rise of the Social Gospel in American Protestantism, 1865–1915.* New Haven, Yale University Press, 1940.

Howe, Frederic C. *The Confessions of A Reformer.* New York, Charles Scribner's Sons, 1925.

Hunt, William Remfry. *Heathenism under the Searchlight: The Call of the Far East.* London, Morgan and Son, 1908.

International Missionary Union, *The International Missionary Union; Nineteenth Annual Conference.* Clifton Springs, N.Y., The International Missionary Union, 1902.

—— *Twenty-Fifth Annual Conference of the International Missionary Union Held in Clifton Springs, New York, June 3–10, 1908.* Clifton Springs, N.Y., The International Missionary Union, 1908.

Jennings, Walter W. *20 Giants of American Business.* New York, Exposition Press, 1953.

Kamphausen, H. *Geschichte des Religiösen Lebens in der Deutschen*

Evangelischen Synode von Nord-Amerika. St. Louis, Mo., Eden Publishing House, 1924.

Keller, Morton B. *The Life Insurance Enterprise, 1885–1910: A Study in the Limits of Corporate Power.* Cambridge, Harvard University Press, 1963.

Kirkland, Edward C. *Dream and Thought in the Business Community, 1860–1900.* Ithaca, N.Y., Cornell University Press, 1956.

Kontinentale Missionskonferenz. *Verhandlungen der neunten Kontinentalen Missionskonferenz zu Bremen am 25., 26., und 28. Mai 1897.* Berlin, Martin Warneck, 1897.

Krebs, Dennis and Phillip Whitten. "Guilt-Edged Giving, The Shame of It All," *Psychology Today* 5.8:50–52, 76–77 (January 1972).

Lane, Ortha May. *Missions in Magazines: An Analysis of the Treatment of Protestant Foreign Missions in American Magazines Since 1810.* Tientsin, Tientsin Press, 1935.

Lankford, John E. "Protestant Stewardship and Benevolence, 1900–1941: A Study in Religious Philanthropy." Ph.D. dissertation, University of Wisconsin, 1962.

—— "Methodism 'Over the Top': The Joint Centenary Movement, 1917–1925," *Methodist History* 2.1:27–37 (October 1963).

—— "The Impact of the Religious Depression Upon Protestant Benevolence, 1925–1935," *Journal of Presbyterian History* 42.2:104–123 (June 1964).

Latourette, Kenneth S. *A History of Christian Missions in China.* New York, Macmillan, 1929.

—— *Missions Tomorrow.* New York, Harper & Bros., 1936.

—— *The Great Century, A.D. 1800–A.D. 1914: Europe and the United States of America,* vol. 4 of *A History of the Expansion of Christianity.* New York, Harper & Bros., 1941.

—— *Advance through Storm, A.D. 1914 and After, With Concluding Generalizations,* vol. 7 of *A History of the Expansion of Christianity.* New York, Harper & Bros., 1945.

—— *Missions and the American Mind.* Indianapolis, National Foundation Press, 1949.

—— *The Christian World Mission in Our Day.* New York, Harper & Bros., 1954.

—— *World Service: A History of the Foreign Work and World Service of the Young Men's Christian Associations of the United States and Canada.* New York, Association Press, 1957.

Lawrence, William. "The Relation of Wealth to Morals," *World's Work* 1.2:286–292 (December 1900).

Laymen's Foreign Missions Inquiry. *Home Base and Missionary Personnel.* Fact Finders' Reports, vol. 7 of Supplementary Series, Part Two. Orville A. Petty, ed. New York, Harper & Bros., 1933.

Laymen's Missionary Movement. *Annual Report of the Central Division of the Laymen's Missionary Movement.* N.p., 1912.

—— *The Laymen's Missionary Movement.* New York, Laymen's Missionary Movement, n.d.

Leete, Frederick D. *Christian Brotherhoods.* Cincinnati, Jennings & Graham, 1912.

Leiper, Henry S. "Reunion and the Ecumenical Movement," in Arnold S. Nash, ed., *Protestant Thought in the Twentieth Century: Whence and Whither?* New York, Macmillan, 1951.

Le Tourneau, Robert G. *Mover of Men and Mountains: The Autobiography of R. G. Le Tourneau.* Englewood Cliffs, N.J., Prentice Hall, 1960.

Light on Prophecy: A Coordinated, Constructive Teaching Being the Proceedings and Addresses of the Philadelphia Prophetic Conference, May 28–30, 1918. New York, The Christian Herald, 1918.

McConnell, Francis John. *Church Finance and Social Ethics.* New York, Macmillan Co., 1920.

McConaughy, David. *Money the Acid Test: Studies in Stewardship.* New York, Missionary Education Movement of the United States and Canada, 1918.

McLean, Archibald. *The History of the Foreign Christian Missionary Society.* New York, Fleming H. Revell, 1919.

Martin, W. A. P. *A Cycle of Cathay, or China, South and North with Personal Reminiscences.* New York, Fleming H. Revell, 1896.

Mathews, Basil. *John R. Mott: World Citizen.* New York, Harper & Bros., 1934.

Mead, Frank S. *Handbook of Denominations in the United States.* Rev. ed. New York, Abingdon Press, 1956.

Men and Missions. Official periodical of the Laymen's Missionary Movement, New York, monthly except July and August, 1909–1919.

Men and World Service: Addresses Delivered at the National Missionary Congress, Washington, D.C., April 26–30, 1916: A Survey of Achievement, A Council of War, A Summons to Advance. New York, Laymen's Missionary Movement, 1916.

Merriam, Charles E. *American Political Ideas: Studies in the Development of American Political Thought, 1865–1917.* New York, MacMillan, 1920. Reprinted: New York, Augustus M. Kelley, 1969.

Merriam, Edmund F. *A History of American Baptist Missions.* Philadelphia, American Baptist Publishing Society, 1900.

Methodist Episcopal Church. *Seventy-Ninth Annual Report of the Missionary Society of the Methodist Episcopal Church for the Year 1897.* New York, Printed for the Society, 1898.

Meyer, Lucy R. *Deaconesses, Biblical, Early Church, European, American.* 3rd ed. Cincinnati, Cranston & Stowe, 1889.

Millar, William B. *The Advance of a Decade.* New York, Laymen's Missionary Movement, 1916.

Miller, Perry. *Errand Into the Wilderness.* Cambridge, Belknap Press of Harvard University Press, 1956.

Missions of the American Baptist Missionary Union in East China and Minutes of the Eastern Baptist Mission Conference. Shanghai, n.p., 1907.

Moore, Edward C. "The Naturalization of Christianity in the Far East," *Harvard Theological Review* 1.3:249–303 (July 1908).

—— *The World Crisis and Missionary Work.* Boston, American Board of Commissioners for Foreign Missions, 1915.

—— "Bible Societies and Missions: Their Joint Contribution to Race Development," *Journal of Race Development* 7.1:47–73 (July 1916).

Mott, John R. *Liberating the Lay Forces of Christianity.* New York, Macmillan, 1932.

—— *Five Decades and a Forward View.* New York, Harper & Bros., 1939.

—— *The Student Volunteer Movement for Foreign Missions,* vol. 1 of *The Addresses and Papers of John R. Mott.* New York, Association Press, 1946.

Mowry, George E. *The California Progressives.* Berkeley, University of California Press, 1951.

Munger, Theodore T. *Essays for the Day.* Boston, Houghton Mifflin, 1904.

National Council of Congregational Churches. *Report of the Committee of Fifteen on Mission Work.* Boston, n.p., 1901.

Nevins, Allan. "Frederick T. Gates and John D. Rockefeller," *American Heritage* 6.3:66–70 (April 1955).

Newcomb, Harvey, ed. *A Cyclopedia of Missions: Containing a Comprehensive View of Missionary Operations Throughout the World.* 2nd rev. ed. New York, C. Scribner, 1860.

Niebuhr, H. Richard. *The Kingdom of God in America.* Hamden, Conn., The Shoe String Press, 1956.

"Nineteen Years of 'Shiloh'," *Literary Digest* 44.4:164–165 (Jan. 27, 1912).

North American Students and World Advance: Addresses Delivered at the Eighth International Convention of the Student Volunteer Movement for Foreign Missions, Des Moines, Iowa, December 31, 1919 to January 4, 1920. ed. Burton St. John. New York, Student Volunteer Movement for Foreign Missions, 1920.

Patton, Cornelius H. *The Business of Missions.* New York, Macmillan, 1924.

—— "Twenty-five Years After: An Appraisal of the Laymen's Missionary Movement," *The Congregationalist and Herald of Gospel Liberty* 116.41: 1360–1362 (Oct. 8, 1931).

Peabody, Francis G. *Jesus Christ and the Social Question.* New York, Macmillan, 1902.

—— *Jesus Christ and the Christian Character.* New York, Macmillan, 1905.

Pearson, Robert. "Report from Afghanistan," *Cranbrook Alumni News* 27.3:3 (February 1963).

Peck, Jesse T. *The History of the Great Republic Considered from a Christian Stand-Point.* Boston, A. W. Lovering, 1877.

Pentecost, George F. "The Enduement of Power and Foreign Missions," *The Independent* 50.2601:973–976 (Oct. 6, 1898).

Phillips, Clifton J. *Protestant America and the Pagan World: The First Half Century of the American Board of Commissioners for Foreign Missions, 1810–1860.* Cambridge, Mass. East Asian Research Center, Harvard University, 1969.

Pierce, Richard D. "A History of the Society of Inquiry in the Andover Theological Seminary 1811–1920, Together with Some Account of Missions in America Before 1810 and A Brief History of the Brethren, 1808–1873." B.D. thesis, Andover Newton Theological School, 1938.

Pierson, Arthur T. *The Crisis of Missions, or, The Voice Out of the Cloud.* New York, Robert Carter & Bros., 1886.

Powell, Luther P. "The Growth and Development of the Motives and Methods of Church Support with Special Emphasis Upon the American Churches." 2 vols. Ph.D. dissertation, Drew Theological Seminary of Drew University, 1951.

Presbyterian Church, USA. *Minutes of the General Assembly of the Presbyterian Church in the United States of America.* Philadelphia, Office of the General Assembly, 1902.

—— *The Sixty-Fifth Annual Report of the Board of Foreign Missions of the Presbyterian Church in the United States of America.* New York, Presbyterian Building, 1902.

Proceedings of the Men's National Missionary Congress of the United States of America; Chicago, Illinois, May 3–6, 1910. New York, Laymen's Missionary Movement, 1910.

Rabe, Valentin H. "The American Protestant Foreign Mission Movement, 1880–1920." Ph.D. dissertation, Harvard University, 1964.

Rauschenbusch, Walter. *Christianizing the Social Order.* New York, Macmillan, 1913.

Report of the Centenary Conference on the Protestant Missions of the World, Held in Exeter Hall (June 9th–19th), London, 1888. ed. James Johnston. 2 vols. New York, Fleming H. Revell, 1888.

Report of the Winding Up of the Interchurch World Movement of North America, Inc., Submitted by the Business Men's Committee. New York, n.p., 1923.

Re-Thinking Missions: A Laymen's Inquiry after One Hundred Years, Commission of Appraisal, William E. Hocking, Chairman. New York, Harper & Bros., 1932.

Riesman, David, with N. Glazer and R. Denney. *The Lonely Crowd: A Study of the Changing American Character.* New York, Doubleday Anchor Books, 1953.

Rockefeller, John D. *Random Reminiscences of Men and Events.* Garden City, N.Y., Doubleday, Doran, 1933.

Rockefeller, John D., Jr. "The Christian Church: What of its Future?" *The Saturday Evening Post* 190.32:16, 37 (Feb. 9, 1918).

Roosevelt, Theodore. *The Strenuous Life: Essays and Addresses.* New York, Century, 1911.

Schneider, Herbert W. *Religion in 20th Century America.* Cambridge, Mass., Harvard University Press, 1952.

Shenstone, Joseph N. *The Laymen's Missionary Movement: Its Responsibilities, Its Opportunities, Its Problems, Its Purposes, and Its Plans.* N.p., n.d.

Simpich, Frederick. "How Missionaries Help Foreign Trade," *The Saturday Evening Post* 196.10:6–7, 111, 114, 117–119 (Sept. 8, 1923).

Smith, Timothy L. *Revivalism and Social Reform in Mid-Nineteenth-Century America.* New York, Abingdon Press, 1957.

Soper, Edmund David. "The Study of Missions," Ohio Wesleyan University *Bulletin* 12.6:1–2, 4 (Nov. 1, 1913).

Speer, Robert E. *The World's Debt to the Missionary.* New York, Laymen's Missionary Movement, 1909.

—— "A Few Comparisons of Then and Now," *The Missionary Review of the World* 51.1:5–10 (January 1928).

Spring, Gardiner, ed. *Memoirs of the Rev. Samuel J. Mills, Late Missionary to the South Western Section of the United States, and Agent of the American Colonization Society, Deputed to Explore the Coast of Africa.* New York, New York Evangelical Missionary Society, 1820.

Stauffer, Milton T. "Shall We Send Fewer Missionaries to China?" *The Missionary Review of the World* 46.620–626 (August 1923).

Strachan, James. "Conversion," in *Encyclopedia of Religion and*

286

Ethics, James Hastings, ed. Edinburgh, T. & T. Clark, 1908–
1926.

Strachey, William. *The Historie of Travell Into Virginia Britania
(1612),* eds. Louis B. Wright and V. Freund. London, Hakluyt
Society, 1953.

Strong, William E. *The Story of the American Board: An Account
of the First Hundred Years of the American Board of Commissioners for Foreign Missions.* Boston, Pilgrim Press, 1910.

*The Student Missionary Appeal: Addresses at the International
Convention of the Student Volunteer Movement for Foreign
Missions, Held at Cleveland, Ohio, February 23–27, 1898.*
New York, Student Volunteer Movement for Foreign Missions,
1898.

*The Student Missionary Enterprise: Addresses and Discussions of
the Second International Convention of the Student Volunteer Movement for Foreign Missions, Held at Detroit, Mich.,
Feb. 28 to Mar. 4, 1894,* ed. Max W. Moorhead. New York,
Fleming H. Revell, 1894.

The Student Volunteer Movement Bulletin 8.8:270 (May 1928).

*Students and the Christian World Mission: Report of the Twelfth
Quadrennial Convention Of the Student Volunteer Movement
for Foreign Missions,* ed. Jesse R. Wilson. New York, Student
Volunteer Movement for Foreign Missions, 1936.

*Students and the Future of Christian Missions: Report of the Tenth
Quadrennial Convention of the Student Volunteer Movement
for Foreign Missions, Detroit, Michigan, December 28, 1927,
to January 1, 1928,* ed. Gordon Poteat. New York, Student
Volunteer Movement for Foreign Missions, 1928.

*Students and the Modern Missionary Crusade: Addresses Delivered
Before the Fifth International Convention of the Student
Volunteer Movement for Foreign Missions, Nashville, Tennes-
see, February 28–March 4, 1906.* New York, Student Volunteer Movement for Foreign Missions, 1906.

*Students and the Present Missionary Crisis: Addresses Delivered
Before the Sixth International Convention of the Student
Volunteer Movement for Foreign Missions, Rochester, New
York, December 29, 1909, to January 2, 1910.* New York,
Student Volunteer Movement for Foreign Missions, 1910.

Students and the World-Wide Expansion of Christianity: Addresses

Delivered Before the Seventh International Convention of the Student Volunteer Movement for Foreign Missions, Kansas City, Missouri, December 31, 1913, to January 4, 1914, ed. Fennell P. Turner. New York, Student Volunteer Movement for Foreign Missions, 1914.

Sweet, William W. *Religion in the Development of American Culture, 1765–1840.* New York, C. Scribner's Sons, 1952.

Swift, David E. "Conservative Versus Progressive Orthodoxy in Latter 19th Century Congregationalism," *Church History* 16.1:22–31 (March 1947).

Taylor, Alva W. *The Social Work of Christian Missions.* Cincinnati, Foreign Christian Missionary Society, 1911.

Taylor, Howard and Geraldine Taylor. *"By Faith . . .": Henry W. Frost and the China Inland Mission.* Philadelphia, China Inland Mission, 1938.

Taylor, Mrs. Howard. *Borden of Yale '09: "The Life that Counts."* Philadelphia, China Inland Mission, 1951.

Thoburn, James M. "The Gospel of 'Benevolences,' " *The Christian Advocate* 76.36:8–9 (New York, Sept. 5, 1901).

Thompson, A. E. *A. B. Simpson: His Life and Work.* Rev. ed. Harrisburg, Pa., Christian Publications, 1960.

Toynbee, Arnold. "Has America Neglected Her Creative Minority?" *The St. Olaf Alumnus* 10.1:4–8 (January 1962).

Trumbull, Charles G. *Foreign Missionary Betrayals of the Faith: A Crisis Confronting the Whole Church.* Philadelphia, Independent Board for Presbyterian Foreign Missions, n.d.

Tucker, William J. *My Generation.* Boston, Houghton Mifflin, 1919.

Turner, Fennell P. *The Missionary Uprising Among Students; Being an Account of the Origin, Work and Results of the Student Volunteer Movement.* New York, Student Volunteer Movement for Foreign Missions, n.d.

Twain, Mark. "To My Missionary Critics," *North American Review* 172.533:520–534 (April 1901).

Varg, Paul A. *Missionaries, Chinese and Diplomats: The American Protestant Missionary Movement in China, 1890–1952.* Princeton, N.J., Princeton University Press, 1958.

—— *The Making of a Myth: The United States and China, 1897–1912.* East Lansing, Mich., Michigan State University Press, 1968.

Wallace, Anthony F. C. "Revitalization Movements," *American Anthropologist* 58:264–281 (April 1936).

Warner, W. Lloyd, Marchia Meeker, and Kenneth Eels. *Social Class in America: A Manual of Procedure for the Measurement of Social Status.* Gloucester, Mass., Peter Smith, 1957.

Wayland, Francis. *The Moral Dignity of the Missionary Enterprise.* New York, American Tract Society, n.d.

Wentz, Abdel R. *A Basic History of Lutheranism in America.* Philadelphia, Muhlenberg Press, 1955.

Wheeler, W. Reginald. *A Man Sent From God: A Biography of Robert E. Speer.* Westwood, N.J., Fleming H. Revell, 1956.

White, J. Campbell. *The Genesis and Significance of the Laymen's Missionary Movement.* New York, Laymen's Missionary Movement, 1909.

—— *Methods of Enlisting Men in Missions.* New York, Laymen's Missionary Movement, n.d.

—— *The Origin and Work of the Laymen's Missionary Movement.* New York, Laymen's Missionary Movement, 1913.

—— *Our Share of the World: Or the Part Which the Churches of the United States and Canada Should Take in the Evangelization of the World in This Generation.* 2nd rev. ed. New York, Laymen's Missionary Movement, n.d.

Williams, Bascom W. *The Joke of Christianizing China.* New York, Peter Eckler, 1927.

Wilson, Jesse R. "Shall We Change Our Declaration Card?" *The Student Volunteer Movement Bulletin* 8.2:55–56 (November 1927).

World Missionary Conference, 1910. 9 vols. Edinburgh and London, Oliphant, Anderson & Ferrier, 1910.

World-Wide Evangelization, The Urgent Business of the Church: Addresses Delivered Before the Fourth International Convention of the Student Volunteer Movement for Foreign Missions, Toronto, Canada, February 26–March 2, 1902. New York, Student Volunteer Movement for Foreign Missions, 1902.

Worman, E. Clark. *The Silver Bay Story, 1902–1952.* Silver Bay, N.Y., Silver Bay Association, 1952.

Yearbook of the Churches, various eds. New York & Washington, Federal Council of Churches, 1918–1925.

INDEX

HARVARD EAST ASIAN MONOGRAPHS

83.   Sang-Chul Suh, *Growth and Structural Changes in the Korean Economy, 1910–1940*